M000311737

Calais

For DM

Calais

A History of England's First Colony

Julian Whitehead

PEN & SWORD
HISTORY

First published in Great Britain in 2022 by
Pen & Sword History
An imprint of
Pen & Sword Books Ltd
Yorkshire – Philadelphia

Copyright © Julian Whitehead 2022

ISBN 978 1 39901 071 9

The right of Julian Whitehead to be identified as Author of this work
has been asserted by him in accordance with the Copyright, Designs
and Patents Act 1988.

A CIP catalogue record for this book is
available from the British Library.

All rights reserved. No part of this book may be reproduced or
transmitted in any form or by any means, electronic or mechanical
including photocopying, recording or by any information storage and
retrieval system, without permission from the Publisher in writing.

Typeset by Mac Style
Printed in the UK by CPI Group (UK) Ltd, Croydon, CR0 4YY.

Pen & Sword Books Limited incorporates the imprints of Atlas,
Archaeology, Aviation, Discovery, Family History, Fiction, History,
Maritime, Military, Military Classics, Politics, Select, Transport,
True Crime, Air World, Frontline Publishing, Leo Cooper, Remember
When, Seaforth Publishing, The Praetorian Press, Wharncliffe
Local History, Wharncliffe Transport, Wharncliffe True Crime
and White Owl.

For a complete list of Pen & Sword titles please contact

PEN & SWORD BOOKS LIMITED
47 Church Street, Barnsley, South Yorkshire, S70 2AS, England
E-mail: enquiries@pen-and-sword.co.uk
Website: www.pen-and-sword.co.uk

Or

PEN AND SWORD BOOKS
1950 Lawrence Rd, Havertown, PA 19083, USA
E-mail: Uspen-and-sword@casematepublishers.com
Website: www.penandswordbooks.com

Contents

List of Illustrations

English Possessions in France in 1154. (*Macmillan & Co 1903*)

English Possessions in France in 1361. (*Macmillan & Co 1903*)

North-west France in 1477 showing the Calais Pale and neighbouring counties. (*Wikimedia Commons*)

King Henry V, unknown artist. (*National Portrait Gallery*)

Sir Richard Whittington, engraving by Renold Elstrack from unknown artist. (*National Portrait Gallery*)

King Edward IV, unknown artist. (*National Portrait Gallery*)

Queen Mary I, by Hands Eworth 1554. (*National Portrait Gallery*)

Map of Calais 1557 by Florimi. (*Copy in possession of author*)

Queen Elizabeth I, unknown artist 1588. (*National Portrait Gallery*)

George (Beau) Brummell, unknown artist. (*National Portrait Gallery*)

Lady Hamilton, by George Romney. (*National Portrait Gallery*)

1802 French plan for a Channel tunnel. (*Wikimedia Commons*)

Soldiers evacuated from Dunkirk arrive at Dover 1940. (*Wikimedia Commons by War Office Photographer, image H1623 of Imperial War Museum Collection*)

German soldier in Calais after British surrender in 1940. (*Wikimedia Commons by Bundesarchiv, Bild 1011-383-0337-11/Böcker*)

V-1 Flying bomb from Calais. (*Wikimedia Commons by Bundesarchiv, Bild 146-1975-117-26 / Lysiak / CC-BY-SA 3.0*)

Front cover: The Field of the Cloth of Gold, unknown Flemish artist (*Royal Collection, Hampton Court Palace*) and The Burgers of Calais by Auguste Rodin. (*GNU Free Document License*)

Back cover: The coat of arms of Henry VIII and Edward VI. (*Inkscape*)

Acknowledgements

Like most people, I knew that Calais had featured in English history, but it is only in recent years that I decided to look into it in more detail. Delving into the subject I was surprised to discover just how important a part Calais has played over the last 675 years. I became so struck by the fascinating events surrounding Calais' entwining with England's past that I decided to share what I had discovered by writing this book, in the hope that others would find it equally interesting.

There are many I would like to thank for enabling me to turn what I think is an enthralling subject into a book. I am indebted to all the authors of the books and periodicals listed in the Bibliography and to the Bodleian Library for making them available to me. I would also like to thank the Royal Collection and National Portrait Gallery for their assistance and permission for me to use their images for illustrations. Mention must also be made of the help I have obtained through the Internet, particularly information available on Wikipedia and imagery from Wikimedia Commons. As always, I have received advice and encouragement from the staff of Pen and Sword, particularly Claire Hopkins, the Senior Commissioning Editor, and Laura Hirst the Production Manager. Finally, I want to thank my wife for her help and support.

Introduction

To most British people Calais is a town to pass through swiftly when crossing the Channel by sea or rail. They will be aware that it is a major trade route between the United Kingdom and the Continent and that in times of disruption long queues of lorries can be found along the A20. They will also know that it has been a base for illegal immigrants attempting to cross the Channel. However, there may be little awareness that Calais was England's first colony and that for over two hundred years the town and its twenty-one square mile territory was an integral part of England, with its own MPs sitting in the Westminster Parliament.

Few will think, even after England lost Calais in 1558, that it played an important part in British history, not least as the site for planned invasions by Louis XIV, Napoleon and Hitler. Also, that the loss spurred England into exploration and trade outside Europe, resulting in other colonies that evolved into the British Empire. Indeed, this history is by no means obvious. The massive destruction inflicted on Calais during the Second World War has left virtually no trace of the town's long association with England. This book seeks to reveal this vanished past and help Calais take its rightful place as an important thread running through British history.

Geography is the key to the historical importance of Calais. The ancient settlement which was to become Calais had a sandy beach and a creek providing a potential harbour at the west edge of the estuary of the River Aa. There are several natural harbours along the Northern French coast, but the Calais harbour is closest to England and just twenty-four miles from the English port of Dover. The proximity of Calais to England enabled it to offer a short crossing for traders, visitors or invading armies. Over the years the geography changed as the estuary silted up and surrounded the town with inaccessible marsh land. This was to give the town a strong watery defence which in later years would be turned into canals to provide commercial links with other towns in the region.

Julius Caesar was the first person in English History to take advantage of the geography of Calais and to use its creek to embark two legions for his expedition to Britain in 55 BC. Caesar made another short expedition to Britain the next year, with five legions, but it was not until AD 43 that the major Roman invasion of England occurred. Aulus Plautius landed with 40,000 troops which eventually conquered the country. This great force was not embarked at Calais but at the more suitable natural harbour of Gesoriacum (present-day Boulogne), and landed in Richborough in Kent. Little use was made of Calais during the Roman occupation and apart from being the embarkation area for Julius Caesar's expeditions, it did not really feature again in English history for one thousand and one hundred years, until the reign of Edward III. Nevertheless, it is worth spending a few moments to see how the relationship between England and France developed during that long passage of time.

The departure of the last Roman legions from Britain led to attacks, followed by colonisation, from Angles, Saxons, Jutes and finally Vikings. The north mainland of Europe was invaded, principally, by the Franks, who eventually established the great empire of Charlemagne. After the death of Charlemagne's successor, his empire was divided in three, in the year 843. West Francia eventually became France, East Francia was to become Germany, and the short lived Middle Francia became Burgundy and the Low Countries. Calais was on the borders of Middle Francia and it was this region of former Middle Francia which was destined to be a battle ground for European powers right up until 1945, with Britain often dragged into the conflict.

By the time of the reign of Edward the Confessor, 1042–1066, Britain's overseas settlers had coalesced into an Anglo-Saxon kingdom, but one with a French connection. Edward's mother was Emma of Normandy, and he spent twenty-five years of exile in Normandy while England was under Danish rule, and then returned as king after the death of Cnut's son. Edward brought several Norman friends with him to England and may well have wanted his cousin, William of Normandy, as his heir. Whether or not that was the case, when Edward died William invaded, in 1066, and Britain became a conquered land under Norman rule, with a king and his barons having domains on either side of the Channel.

Through inheritance, marriage and warfare, William the Conqueror's grandson, Henry II, came to rule territory stretching from the Scottish border to the Pyrenees, in what became known as the Anjevin Empire. Philip II was King of West Francia at that time and was the first to style himself 'King of France'. This was a slightly empty title as Philip was notionally feudal overlord of all the largely autonomous dukes and counts ruling all the regions of France, but retained actual control only over Paris and the east of the country. Henry II was as French as Philip II. His mother was a granddaughter of the Franco-Norman, William the Conqueror, and Henry was born in Le Mans and brought up in the court of his father, the Count of Anjou. Henry, like Philip, was also a king and no doubt regarded himself as having as much right to his territories in France as Philip.

Henry II's eldest son, Richard I, further increased the Anjevin Empire, but Richard's brother and successor, King John, lost all his French possessions except for Aquitaine. John's son, Henry III, made attempts to win back the Anjevin lands but with very little success and ended up losing all except for Gascony. When Henry's son, Edward I, inherited the crown he was largely taken up with rebellion in Wales and war with Scotland, but found himself at war with France when King Philip IV of France invaded Gascony. This ended in a peace treaty in 1299, partially sealed by agreement that Edward, the son of Edward I, would marry Philip's daughter, Princess Isabella.

By this time all English monarchs had been at war with French kings, on and off, for a period of about 150 years, but the marriage of Edward and Isabella was not to bring hostilities to an end, and Edward's bisexuality did not engender marital harmony. After Edward II became king and gave to his favourites many positions of power, his English barons rebelled. King Philip's son, Charles IV, took advantage of the rebellion to invade Gascony. Opposition to Edward increased, not least from his wife Isabella. She travelled to France to negotiate a peace in Gascony with her brother Charles IV. There she was joined by her lover, the leading rebel, Roger Mortimer, Earl of March. Isabella and Mortimer enlisted the support of Count William of Hainault for an invasion of England. The bargain for this support was that William's daughter, Philippa, should marry Isabella's son, Edward Prince of Wales. The invasion was successful. The regime of Edward II crumbled, he was captured, imprisoned and forced to abdicate in favour of his 14-year-old son, Edward. Finally, Edward II was murdered.

So it was that a teenager from a dysfunctional family became King Edward III. However, the power in the land lay with his mother and Mortimer, who had made themselves co-regents. Edward was a young man of some character and within a couple of years had organised a coup against Mortimer, had him hanged, and his mother removed to Castle Rising. With the regency overthrown, Edward was at last king in reality as well as name. It was now up to him to establish his authority over his unruly nobility, protect England from Scottish attack, and defend the coastal strip of Gascony, which was all that remained of the Anjevin Empire. These were daunting enough challenges for any 18-year-old, but Edward's ambitions exceeded the mere protection of his inheritance.

We now move to the main body of this book, to see that while the great Anjevin Empire might have gone, it had not been forgotten; certainly not in the youthful mind of Edward III.

Chapter 1

Claim to the French Throne, 1327–47

E dward III married Philippa of Hainault two years before he seized control of his kingdom from Queen Isabella and Roger Mortimer. The wedding fulfilled the marriage bargain struck by Count William of Hainault, in exchange for supporting Isabella's rebellion against her husband, Edward II. Philippa's father died and her brother William II became Count of Hainault as well as Count of Holland and Zealand. William was therefore a valuable military ally and useful for enhancing England's commercial relations with the Low Countries. These had steadily increased while English monarchs had been more occupied with protecting their possessions in Western France. The reason for this commercial expansion was wool.

Flemish sheep were not producing enough wool for the growing manufacture of cloth in Ypres, Ghent and Bruges. Also, it was not long, fine wool of the type provided by English sheep in the Cotswolds, Lincolnshire and Leicestershire, which was essential for high quality cloth. Flemish towns exported most of their cloth to the annual Champagne Fair. Most of the cloth bought at the fair was sent to Italy for dyeing and then sold to other countries via export centres such as Genoa. English long, fine wool became a vital part of the increasingly prosperous European cloth trade, to the enrichment of all concerned. By the time Edward III had ascended the throne in 1327, English wool production had been flourishing for about a hundred years and was exporting about 25,000 sacks per year.[1] Not only was wool a major part of the country's economy, but it had become an important part of crown revenue after Edward I imposed a permanent tax on wool merchants in 1275. English trade in Flanders also brought the bonus of contact with Flemish bankers, such as the Jews in Ghent, who became an important source of loans to the crown.

Edward III was well aware of the need to foster economic ties with Flanders, but, being young and ambitious, was more interested in seeking fame and fortune through military conquest. He wanted to control Scotland and make the Scottish king his vassal (a person granted the use of land by a superior, in return for their homage, fealty, and military service). King Robert the Bruce had died and been succeeded by his 5-year-old son, King David II. Earlier, Edward's grandfather, Edward I, had tried to install John Balliol on the Scottish throne as an English puppet. Edward decided to do the same with Balliol's son, Edward. This went well at first but then fell apart. King Edward encouraged some of his nobles to invade Scotland, which they did, and managed to have Edward Balliol crowned king, but he was soon forced out by the Scottish nobility.

By invading Scotland Edward had immediately put himself into potential conflict with France. Since 1295 Scotland and France had operated in terms of an agreement that came to be called the *Auld Alliance*. The Auld Alliance ensured that if one of the parties was attacked by England, the other would provide assistance, forcing England to fight on two fronts. France sent men and money to support King David. Edward himself led a further expedition to Scotland but despite achieving a major victory and restoring Balliol, the Scots forced out the unwanted king as soon as Edward returned to England.

While this struggle was being waged in Scotland the young King David was offered refuge in France by King Philip IV. Philip, as Count of Valois, had grabbed the French throne when his uncle Charles IV had died, leaving an only child, Blanche, who had been born two months after his death. Philip's support for young King David was a slight to Edward, who retaliated by providing refuge for Philip's hated brother-in-law, Robert of Artois, sentenced to death by Philp for treason. The tension between England and France began to escalate. Robert of Artois became a close advisor and friend of Edward and pressed for war with France.

In May 1337 Philip's Grand Council of Paris ruled that Edward was in breach of his duty as a vassal, for having sheltered Robert of Artois, a mortal enemy of the king of France. Accordingly, Edward's fiefdom of Gascony should be confiscated by the French crown. To Edward, as king of England, this was an insult and a virtual declaration of war. And indeed, it became a war, the war which historians later would name the 'Hundred Years' War'. Philip prepared to attack Gascony and began to carry out raids on Rye, Hasting, Portsmouth, Southampton and Plymouth, burning the towns and capturing some English merchant ships. Edward retaliated by attacking the coast of Normandy and Brittany and began toying with the idea of claiming the French crown.

However, Edward's claim was a bit tenuous. (See family tree at Appendix 1.) As we have heard, Charles IV had died leaving just a baby daughter, but under the French *Salic Law* the crown could not pass to a woman, nor could any claim to kingship pass through a female line. It had been on this basis that Philip, then Count of Valois, had seized the throne when his uncle Charles had died. However, Edward III's mother, Isabella, was the daughter of King Philip IV and sister to his three sons, who had reigned one after another (Louis X, Philip V and Charles IV), so it could be said that Isabella had a better claim to the throne. But Edward held no inhibitions about *Salic Law* or the fact that both his mother and Charles IV's daughter, Blanche were still alive. He was a man of action with little interest in foreign legal niceties.

Edward convinced himself that as he was the nearest male descendant of Philip IV, he was the true heir to the French throne. In 1339 he decided to launch a major attack on Philip IV, but first needed to confirm military alliances with the rulers on the boundaries of north east France. Setting sail from the River Orwell in Suffolk with 15,000 men, he landed in Antwerp; and then everything began to go wrong. His allies got cold feet. Brabant virtually pulled out of the alliance, the German states said they could not take part without the consent of the emperor, and the counts of Flanders, Namur, and Edward's brother-in-law, William II of Hainault, were threatened with a papal interdiction if they rebelled against the king of France. To overcome this obstacle Edward then proclaimed himself King of France, thus enabling French vassals to give him their support. To display his claim, he quartered the fleur-de-lis of France with the three lions *passant guardant* of England on the royal coat of arms.

Although Edward's formal claim to the throne of France provided a good reason for rebellion against King Charles, it did little to increase the number of Flemish troops in his army. Undaunted, Edward entered French territory and burned a few villages, but failed to bring King Philip IV to battle. Having run out of money he returned to Ghent, and then to England. His continental allies had given him little or no help but nevertheless pocketed his subsidies. The whole enterprise had left him frustrated and in considerable debt.

On returning to England Edward began raising money and men for another expedition to France. In early 1340, in retaliation for earlier French attacks, England carried out successful raids against French ports and destroyed much of the French fleet in Boulogne. This prompted King Philip to create a new major fleet to carry out more raids on the English coast. By the summer this had become more than 230 ships, mainly Genoese galleys, carrying a 40,000-strong army. In the meantime, Flanders had rebelled against France and was being supported by elements of the Holy Roman Empire. King Philip despatched a large army to put down the rebellion and the Flemish asked Edward urgently to come to their aid. Edward agreed and assembled an invasion fleet in the River Orwell, intending to land at Sluys (now Sluis), the main port in Flanders. His objective was to join the Flemings and their allies in pushing back the French army, and then to invade north east France. The French naval commander knew that Sluys was the only friendly harbour where Edward could land his troops, so he moved his 230 ships to block the port.

Edward had no option but to transport his invasion army in just 130 ships and attempt to defeat the vastly superior French fleet barring the entrance to Sluys. When the English fleet was sighted the French bound their Genoese galleys together with chains to stop the attackers breaking through and into the port. But this plan backfired and the French fleet became un-manoeuvrable while the English used groups of three ships, (two with archers and one with men-at-arms), to attack and overcome individual galleys. When the archers won the firefight with the Genoese crossbowmen, the men-at-arms boarded and killed everyone on board. As a result, the French suffered a major defeat, losing 16,000 to 20,000 men, while the English lost only a few hundred.[2] Edward was able not only to land his force, but the extent of his victory encouraged his Flemish allies to join him. Morale in Edward's army was high and a joke went round that the fish at Sluys now spoke French, having feasted on so many dead Frenchmen. All seemed to be going well and Edward began a major effort to project himself as the rightful king of France. He issued a proclamation declaring his rights to the crown which he aimed to have affixed to all church doors in France. The following is an extract from the English translation:

Since, therefore, the kingdom of France has by divine disposition devolved upon us by the clearest right owing to the death of Charles of noted memory, brother german of our lady mother, and since the Lord Philip of Valois, son of the king's uncle and thus further removed from the royal blood ... has intruded himself by force into the kingdom while we were of tender years, and holds the kingdom by force against God and Justice ... we have recognized our right to the kingdom ... and to cast out the usurper when the opportunity shall seem most propitious.[3]

Edward was by then in deadly earnest about his claim. Indeed, subsequent English monarchs kept the title of King of France and retained the fleur-de-lis on their royal coat of arms, until 1802 when George III gave up the title and removed the fleur-de-lis. Although Edward's title 'King of France' was helpful in providing a legal excuse for those who wished to rebel against King Philip, it was not accepted by the great majority of the French nobility. When Edward and his army arrived at Tournai its citizens remained loyal to Philip and refused to open the city gates. Edward then began the siege of Tournai which he was forced to abandon after two months, to return to England, having once again run out of money. Equally depressing was that within a month of his victory at Sluys, a French fleet captured thirty English merchantmen from a wool convoy and threw all the crew members overboard. A couple of months later France was again carrying out raids on south coast towns.

Edward was discovering that things are never so bad that they cannot get a great deal worse. He was deeply in debt, French raids were harassing the south coast and, if that was not enough, Scotland rose up against him. The Scottish nobles who wanted independence from England gained control of the country and restored David II as their king. This meant that if Edward launched another attack on France, he could expect a Scottish invasion. However, just when it seemed Edward's hopes of taking the French crown had evaporated, an unexpected opportunity appeared in the next year.

Duke John III of Brittany had died, without children, and his dukedom was coveted by two rival claimants: John de Montfort and Charles of Blois, nephew of King Philip IV. De Montfort knew he could expect no help from King Philip, so he went to England to pay homage to Edward, in his assumed role of King of France, for Brittany. This did not go down well with either Charles of Blois or King Philip. Brittany was invaded, de Montfort captured and the whole minor incident appeared to be over. However, no one had taken account of de Montfort's wife, Countess Joanna, who bravely rallied much of Brittany to her husband's cause. When Charles of Blois led a large army against Joanna, she took refuge in the fortified port of Hennebont and called for Edward's support. Charles of Blois then began to besiege Hennebont but an English fleet under Sir Walter Manny relieved the town and a truce was eventually arranged, and lasted until May the next year (1343).

Edward sent Robert of Artois with a force from England to help the countess, but Robert was defeated and died soon after. Edward wanted to avenge his friend's death so he took an army of 12,000 men across the Channel and landed in Brittany. Soon after landing Edward discovered that his small army was about to be confronted by the 40,000-strong army of Charles of Blois. For once Edward felt discretion was the better part of valour and agreed to a truce brokered by the new pope, Clement VI, the Truce of Malestroit, which lasted three years and eight months. Edward returned to England, once more having achieved nothing further than to increase his debts. But Philip IV was not a man to be deterred by a papal truce, so as soon as Edward and his army had left, he resumed operations against Countess Joanna in Brittany.

The English barons and Parliament were incensed at Philip's contempt for the truce and agreed with Edward that warfare should resume. Edward decided to attack France on three fronts. A small force would land in Brittany under the Earl of Northampton, a larger force would be sent to protect Gascony, and the main assault would be led by Edward on northern France. Edward's cousin, Henry, Earl of Derby, set sail from Southampton with a 2,000-strong contingent to help defend Gascony and landed in Bordeaux in August 1345. Having assembled an Anglo-Gascon force, Derby took the offensive, captured Bergerac then won a major battle against the French at Aube Roche, giving him at least temporary control of Gascony. In July 1346 Edward sailed from Portsmouth with 30,000 men and landed at La Hogue in Normandy. Edward had taken with him his eldest son, the 15-year-old Edward of Woodstock, Prince of Wales, who later became known as the 'Black Prince'.

As soon as King Charles realized Edward was about to invade, he used the Auld Alliance and called upon David of Scotland to invade England. David obliged and crossed the border with a small army but was beaten back and agreed a truce, to last until September. This enabled Edward to concentrate on his French campaign. When Edward landed in Normandy, he found it undefended and advanced with pent up fury, destroying all he encountered. He swiftly took the town of Caen and killed all its 3,000 inhabitants, regardless of their age, sex or rank. He then marched towards Paris, laying waste everything in his path. The main French army, under Philip's eldest son John, Duke of Normandy, which had been deployed against the English in Gascony, was ordered to race north to join Philip and block the English. When John arrived, Philip had assembled an army of about 70,000 men including large contingents from his allies, comprising the King of Bohemia, Charles Duke of Luxembourg, the King of Majorca, the Count of Savoy and 6,000 Genoese mercenary crossbowmen.

This was too great a force to be engaged by Edward and his 14,000 English, Welsh and Breton soldiers, so he withdrew and headed for the Low Countries. Louis followed in pursuit, hoping to stop Edward's escape at the barrier of the River Seine, but Edward found a crossing and went on to the River Somme, where he again managed to find a crossing. At this point Edward decided not to retreat further through the hazardous open plains of Picardy, but to prepare a strong defensive position at the top of a small hill near the village of Crécy, about eleven miles south-east of Abbeville. Despite the prospect of almost guaranteed defeat, Edward remained in excellent spirits and managed to inspire an equally high morale among his men.

While Edward's army was able to rest, having prepared its defences, the French had become strung out and tired by their pursuit. On 26 August 1346 French scouts reported they had located the English position and Philip ordered his force to halt, so that it could rest and reform before the coming battle. Whether unaware of the king's orders or choosing to disregard them, the Genoese crossbowmen and other forward troops saw certain victory, and plunder, within their grasp, and pushed forward into the attack. In pouring rain Philip was swept along with them and a chaotic stampede occurred. The Genoese advanced over muddy terrain, taking too long to reload their crossbows, and were unable to compete with the devastating rate of fire of the English archers. They tried to turn back but the mounted knights behind them charged onwards.

While the confused French attack had started badly it soon became a great deal worse. The English position was protected by a river on one side and a wood on the other. The French had to advance uphill, through mud and hidden horse traps, while at the same time facing rapid fire from the English and Welsh longbowmen. These archers had been issued with seventy-two arrows per man, some of which had been fitted with bodkin point tips which could penetrate armour at 225 metres. Once the breathless and muddy French eventually arrived at the English position they were met by battle-hardened, dismounted men-at-arms. During the afternoon the French knights and infantry charged again and again, each time through a storm of arrows which killed or wounded their unarmoured horses.

Despite heavy casualties, some of the French cavalry reached the English men-at-arms and engaged in furious hand-to-hand fighting but failed to break the English line. Each charge worsened their situation – the mud was becoming deeper and deeper, and their ascent was obstructed by mounds of dead and dying men and horses. Between these attacks the English would run forward to retrieve their arrows and stab and loot the enemy wounded. On one occasion the French knights broke through the English line but were eventually beaten back in fierce fighting. King Edward's teenage son, Edward the Black Prince, nearly lost his life, fighting bravely in the thick of the combat. The bloody battle raged on and on and gradually ceased only at midnight. By that time King Philip had left the field, having been wounded by an arrow in the jaw and most of his army had melted away. The English army slept where they had fought, exhausted.

Next morning Philip's rearguard arrived at the battlefield, at last, but was charged by mounted English men-at-arms. The late arrivals were routed and pursued and more than a thousand were killed, including their leader, the Duke of Lorraine. It was then time to strip and loot the French dead and finish off the French wounded, other than those of rank who could be taken as prisoners for ransom. Casualties on either side are hard to calculate but it seems that Edward's army lost about three to four hundred dead. According to English heralds the bodies of 1,542 French knights were found. The total number of dead among the

French and their allies has been estimated as 20,000, including two kings (Bohemia and Majorca), nine princes, ten counts, a duke, an archbishop and a bishop.[4] The extent of the victory was breath-taking. The Battle of Crécy had been won by English and Welsh soldiers without help from allies or mercenaries and so earned them a fearsome reputation. On 13 September news of the victory reached Parliament in Westminster and was immediately recognized for what it was: (the victory was) a clear sign of God's favour and divine justification for the king's claim to the French throne, and the enormous cost of the war.

It took a few days to bury the dead and then Edward marched his army north from Crécy to find supplies and reinforcements. As they marched, he continued his policy of looting and burning everything in his way. It could be said that this behaviour was unlikely to win him the affection and support of those he regarded as his French subjects. However, Edward was not intending to hold any territory or use fear to instil obedience. He was following a recognized mediaeval military tactic called *chevauchée* (an armed raid by cavalry) to achieve the destruction of enemy territory to weaken resistance. Having razed a few small towns, he took the little port of Wissant in north east France. He then rested his army outside the burning town and held a council of war. The meeting agreed that the army should neither withdraw to England nor continue with the *chevauchée*, but attempt to capture Calais, farther up the coast.

Over the centuries Calais had grown from a small Flemish fishing village into a harbour large enough for King Richard the Lionheart to have stopped there, with his great Crusader fleet on the way to the Holy Land, in 1191. Calais had since gained its own town charter and was controlled by the counts of Boulogne, who were vassals of the counts of Flanders, who in turn were vassals of the kings of France. In 1224 Count Philip I of Boulogne recognized the defensive potential of Calais, given its location close to the Flemish border, and built fortifications for its protection. It was given strong town walls forming a rectangle 1,200 yards in length and 400 yards in breadth, with a moated castle in the north-west corner. These defences included the Tour de Guet watch tower, which still stands 128 ft tall today. In short, although the majority of the population spoke Flemish, Calais had become a well defended French port with a population of about 4,500.[5]

There were a number of reasons why Edward decided to capture Calais. The battle of Sluys had shown that possession of Calais would help England to establish naval supremacy in the Channel. Also, it was felt that possession of the town would provide an ideal secure base for future expeditions to France at a location conveniently close to Edward's Flemish allies. Perhaps the most important reason was the hope that attacking Calais would encourage King Philip to bring his army to battle and result in a final devastating encounter. On 4 September Edward's army arrived outside Calais which, much like Tournai, was not impressed by Edward's claim to the French throne and refused to open its gates. There was nothing for it but to begin a siege and prepare to take the town by storm.

This was no easy task. Successive counts of Boulogne had increased the fortifications at Calais, having recognized its growing importance as both a frontier fort and a port, while other harbours, such as Wissant, had begun to silt up. To the north the harbour was separated from the town by a line of walls, a single moat and a long, fortified dyke. The other sides had a double moat and thick city walls, with a well-fortified citadel in the north west corner, which was itself surrounded by a moat and curtain walls. Such defences would make any town difficult to storm although, under normal circumstances and given enough time, the walls could be undermined or breached by artillery fire. Also, the will of the defenders could be sapped by the use of trébuchets (gravity-powered catapults) to throw stones, incendiaries and diseased carcasses into the town. Unfortunately, these options were not easily achievable. The town was surrounded by marshes, some parts of which were tidal, making it difficult to create stable platforms for mounting trébuchets or artillery. For most fortified towns there was always the long-term expedient of a siege which would eventually starve the defenders into surrender. But even this possibility was not a strong option for Edward, as Calais could be re-supplied by sea. Under these circumstances taking the town would not be easy, unless for some reason the garrison lost its will to resist.

Calais was well stocked with provisions and had a strong garrison commanded by Jean de Vienne. He was a son of the Lord of Pagny in north east France, an experienced soldier and a previous commander of the garrison at Montagnein. Buoyed by formidable fortifications and a well manned garrison, de Vienne was not likely to consider surrender.

Indeed, de Vienne was of the knightly class and so brought up to chivalric ideals that courage and personal honour overruled personal safety. It had been this ingrained duty that had resulted in so many men of the French aristocracy being killed at Crècy, rather than withdrawing to fight another day.

It soon became clear to Edward that forcing Calais to succumb would take some time. The day after the siege began, English ships arrived offshore to deliver much needed supplies for Edward's army. These enabled Edward to begin the siege in earnest and soon a semi-permanent wooden hutted camp was established to the west of Calais, called Nouville or New Town. As well as providing shelter for the army, it became the warehouse for weapons, equipment and rations off loaded from what became regular supply ships. Nouville also received overland supplies from nearby Flanders and was to become so established as a commercial settlement that it held two market days a week.

Edward had expected that King Philip would not tolerate the English force settling in to besiege Calais and would bring the French army forward to engage him in battle. But this was not to be. The truth is that Philip had miscalculated, having assumed that Edward would head for the friendly territory of Flanders and then sail home. The war had rendered Philip as indebted as Edward, so he decided to save money by disbanding the majority of his army. His son, Duke John of Normandy, had thought the same way and disbanded most of his army. No sooner had the constituents of these armies been allowed to drift away when Philip realized his mistake. On 9 September he ordered that the army should re-assemble at Compiègne by 1 October, to be ready to march to the relief of Calais.

The dispersal of Duke John's army had created an opportunity for the Earl of Derby who was striving to hold on to Gascony. In the absence of a French opposition, Derby had launched a series of raids from Gascony and advanced 160 miles north, capturing a number of towns including the rich city of Poitiers. Philip heard the news of Derby's advance and feared he was heading for Paris, so sent orders that the army's assembly point should be changed to Orléans and it should be ready to block the English. At this point Derby decided to return to the defence of Gascony. Once this became apparent, the French troops that had been ordered to assemble for Orléans were instructed to gather at Compiègne. Given the means of communication at the time, it is no surprise that these orders and counter orders resulted in complete confusion, giving Edward the opportunity to consolidate his siege preparations without interference.

While Edward had been absent in France, Queen Philippa had remained in England as regent, but had not had an easy time. The 17-year-old King David II of Scotland had gathered enough forces to fulfil his commitments under the Auld Alliance and had invaded England on 7 October, with an army of 12,000 men. Queen Philippa raised a force of Northern nobles and caught up with David's army outside Durham. She had given command to Lord Ralph Neville, but it is said that she did her bit by riding up and down the English lines, giving encouragement to the troops. The battle took place on 17 October 1346 and resulted in a major English victory; King David was captured, about fifty Scottish barons were killed or captured, and at least 1,000 Scots soldiers were eliminated.

When Edward heard of the victory at what became called the 'Battle of Neville's Cross', he did not give the customary agreement to release senior captives on receipt of ransom but instead decided to keep them confined. As a result, Scotland was deprived of most of its leadership including the king, who would be held captive for the next eleven years. Just to ensure there would be no further attacks on England, a force entered Scotland and ravaged the south of the country. The threat from Scotland was removed and Edward no longer had to be concerned about having to fight a war on two fronts.

The defeat of the Scots had an important impact on the Calais situation. Had King David succeeded in continuing to harry the north of England, Edward would have had to raise the siege and return to his country's defence. As it was the siege continued despite the fact that, with winter approaching, it was the end of the traditional campaigning season.

Meanwhile King Philip had eventually managed to gather 3,000 men-at-arms at Compiègne. The only problem was that his treasury had no money to pay them. Philip had to accept that he was unable to undertake any more offensive operations. On 27 October he acknowledged an end to the French campaign season by disbanding his army. The year 1346 had not been a good year for French prestige and the autumn was spent in recriminations and accusations of blame. Charles de Montmorency, the Marshall of France, was dismissed, along with most members of the French treasury. Philip's son, the Duke of Normandy, blamed his father and refused to attend court. Queen Joan of Navarre ceased being neutral and negotiated a peace with the Earl of Derby which denied the French army access to her lands or fortifications. To cap it all, the Countess de Montford's forces had gained the upper hand in Brittany and captured Charles de Blois. He was sent to the Tower of London where he remained for the next nine years.

While King Philip was having an uncongenial autumn, King Edward was becoming increasingly frustrated outside Calais. Some matters were going well, in particular the resupply of his force at Nouville. But this was a major effort which was becoming more difficult, with winter storms making crossings by ships more sporadic and hazardous. Parliament reluctantly voted increases in taxation to cover the cost but its goodwill could not be expected indefinitely. It began reviewing the funding for Edward's besieging force which gradually shrank to about 5,000 men, as soldiers were paid off to save money. Another factor contributed to the reduction in the size of the force – serious attacks of dysentery and malaria in the camp resulted in many deaths and desertions.

Morale was slipping away among the soldiers in their hastily erected buildings which gave only limited relief from the cold and wet of winter, and no relief at all from the rats and diseases that were the usual companions of any static force with its attendant increasing waste and excrement. Edward decided to distract his soldiers from their woes by keeping them busy. Between November and late February the next year (1347), Edward made a number of attempts to breach the walls at Calais with cannon, but got nowhere. He had trébuchets made but these too appeared to have no effect. He also carried out several attempts to storm the town, attacking it sometimes from the land and sometimes from the sea, but all to no avail. To make matters worse, although the Calais garrison and citizens were living on reduced rations, they appeared not to have run out of food and were not being starved into surrender.

While Edward spent month after month in a winter siege, Philip was borrowing money to strengthen his navy. He not only built new warships but converted some merchant vessels into fighting ships, by the addition of wooden castles, and also obtained some Italian mercenary galleys. Once the winter weather was over and the ships assembled, Philip began using them to deliver supplies to Calais which by then had become seriously short of food. Between March and April 1347 about 1,000 tons of supplies were conveyed by sea to Calais, much to the relief of its citizens and garrison. In late April Philip began a new campaign season but his attempts to assemble a substantial army had limited success. The old problem of funding reared its head. Nine years of war had left most of the nobility in debt and the economy in tatters, which made it difficult to collect taxes.

There was a war weariness among both the French and the besieging English, but this did not stop the resumption of fighting in April. Edward had called for the recruitment of 7,200 archers as reinforcements and they began arriving in April. Some inconclusive fighting took place; the French tried to cut the English supply route to Flanders, and the English attempted to capture Saint-Omer and Lille. Neither country's operations succeeded. A positive action for the English, at the end of April, was to begin building a fortification on the narrow spit of sand called the Rybank to the north of Calais. Once finished this would enable the English to command the entrance to the Calais harbour and so prevent any further supply of provisions. The French remained concerned about Flanders supplying the English besiegers and threatening the French flank, so John I, Duke of Normandy, conducted a major offensive against Flanders, only to be beaten back at Cassel.

In May the English fortification at the mouth of the Calais harbour was basically complete, with cannon in place. The structure became known as Fort Risban. Almost at once the newly completed fort was able to prevent the passage of a French supply fleet. Over the next two months the French made several unsuccessful attempts to get their supply ships into the harbour. By June 1347 the food shortage had become desperate and serious famine had set in. Jean de Vienne, the commander, managed to get a letter delivered to King Philip, saying that their food was exhausted and they were begging for relief.

While Calais was starving Edward had been reinforcing. He had increased his force to 26,000 soldiers, which was an amazingly large number, given the financial constraints of his government. In fact, it was the largest English force ever to be deployed abroad, at that time. Edward also had his best generals with him. The Earl of Derby had joined him in Calais after his successes in Gascony, and Sir Walter Manny had arrived from Brittany. Everything was coming together for Edward, who had moved his household to a more comfortable site at Bergues, outside Dunkirk, where he was able to live in reasonable royal splendour with much feasting. During these months Edward had made an alliance with Louis de Mâle who had succeeded his father as Count of Flanders. Previously the Flemish had not been official English allies but they had taken advantage of the French defeat at Crécy to plunge into Artois and lay siege to Saint-Omer. A formal alliance with Flanders, England's principal trading partner, was both natural and strategically important.

In late spring of that year (1347) things started to go wrong. Within weeks of being entertained by Edward, Count Louis I of Flanders decided to change horses and transferred his support to King Philip. Worse was to come. Duke John III of Brabant, (Edward's first cousin and the most powerful of the Low Countries princes), like Flanders, had enjoyed strong connections with the English wool trade. England and Brabant had been natural allies and John's second daughter, Margaret, had been betrothed to Edward the Black Prince. Since 1337 King Edward had paid Brabant to provide men-at-arms to fight against France but the relationship soured when Edward ran out of money and John had begun to drift back to the French camp.

In June that year Duke John of Brabant reached a formal agreement with King Philip and returned to being his vassal. More than that, John also allied with the Count of Flanders and agreed that his daughter, Margaret, would marry Louis de Mâle, the Count's son. The only other important power in the region was Hainault. King Edward's ally, William II, Count of Hainault had died and Hainault was by then nominally ruled by Countess Margaret, Queen Philippa's elder sister, who was married to the Holy Roman Emperor, Louis IV, the Bavarian. However, complex disputes within the family of the emperor meant that Hainault was unable to provide support to England. By the late summer of 1347 individual Flemish towns, only, in the whole region of the Low Countries, were supporting Edward.

It was a blow to England to have lost its alliances with the rulers of its two main trading partners, Flanders and Brabant, but fortunately the Count of Flanders had little control over the Flemish municipalities of Ghent and Ypres. They continued with their English wool trade and were prepared to provide Edward with military support against France. The English fleet had ensured that most merchantmen carrying wool had been able safely to reach the Flemish towns. The fleet was of course also protecting the supply line from England to Calais and an efficient ferry service had been established. One of these ships had brought Queen Philippa to Bergues, not long after she had given birth to her tenth child, Princess Margaret, at Windsor in July 1346.

Unusually for a royal arranged marriage, there was genuine affection between Philippa and Edward. Philippa was then aged about 36 and had shown herself to be lady of some courage. She had previously joined her husband on his military expeditions to Scotland and his early campaigns in France, as well as being present at the battle of Sluys, close enough to the fighting for one of her ladies to be killed by an arrow. As regent in Edward's absence, she had accompanied the army which defeated the Scots at Neville's Cross, so it was no surprise that soon after Margaret's birth she endured a rough Channel crossing to be at Edward's side for the Calais siege.

In the town of Calais famine had made life intolerable for the citizens and the garrison. De Vienne decided that he could hold out with the remaining very small amount of food only if he removed some of the hungry mouths. He decided to expel 1,700 non-combatants, mainly women, children, the old and the sick. Somewhat surprisingly for Edward, he showed compassion for these refugees when they were pushed out of the town's gates. He gave orders that they should receive some food and drink before they continued their journey and their forlorn quest for food and shelter. Sometime later the scarcity of food in Calais reached crisis point, with citizens having to eat horses, dogs and rats. De Vienne felt he had to expel a further 500 citizens and a second tranche of non-combatants was driven out of the town gates, but they were given a very different reception.

At that time sieges normally lasted for a couple of months, but the Siege of Calais seemed to endure forever. Edward had become increasingly angry about the duration and cost of the siege and was in no mood to make life easier for the defenders. The displaced persons in the second group were barred from entering the English lines and so had to stay in no man's land, between the besieging force and the town walls, where they starved to death. Even this failed to break de Vienne's resolve to fight on. He had sent urgent messages to King Philip begging him to rescue the town which had no more food, of any sort, and the inhabitants were having to consider cannibalism.

By 17 July 1347 King Philip had gathered an army of between 15,000 to 20,000 men which marched north to relieve Calais. On 27 July he arrived at the Sangatte escarpment, six miles from town, from where his banners were seen, leading to general rejoicing. Although seriously weak from starvation, some of the citizens summoned the strength to light celebratory bonfires, unfurl banners and try to make martial music with whatever instruments they could find. However, once Philip could see for himself the English position around Calais, he realized that an attack was not feasible. Although his force was outnumbered it might have been possible to defeat the English on an open battlefield, but the land around Calais and the English position was surrounded by marsh and there were only two approaches. One was along the coast road which was vulnerable to attack from archers on the beach and the Earl of Warwick's fleet, moored off the coast. The other route was across the only bridge over the River Hammes at Nieulay, and along a causeway road through the marsh, but this was protected by extensive earthworks, palisades, towers and drawbridges. These defences had been built by Edward during the winter in preparation for an expected attack by Philip in the spring. This southern approach was placed under the command of the formidable English generals Sir Walter Manny and the Earl of Derby.

King Philip soon recognized that the strength of the English besieging force and its defences would make any attack upon them extremely hazardous. His options were narrowing. It would be no use to besiege the besiegers, as the English had a good supply line back to England from their camp at Nouville. Even if a siege was successful, the time it would take would undoubtedly ensure the death by starvation of all the inhabitants of Calais and the capture of the town by the English. Philip had two options left: lure the English out from their defences and into open battle, or negotiate a settlement in exchange for Edward's withdrawal. The lives of the citizens of Calais rested on one of these choices being successful.

Chapter 2

Becoming an English Colony, 1347–57

The starving citizens of Calais were anxiously awaiting King Philip's next move. Would he launch an attack, or would Edward abandon the siege in the face of a large French army? Philip decided to negotiate. He offered Edward the whole of Aquitaine if he would hold it as a vassal to the French crown. This received a frosty reply. Philip then sent a challenge to Edward to come out from behind his defensive lines and meet him in single combat. Edward declined the offer. Philip realized there was now no hope of breaking the siege, and no purpose for keeping his army in the area; with the utmost sadness he issued the order to withdraw. The people of Calais were thrown into the depths of despair when they saw the French army packing up to leave. They had been convinced that they were about to be relieved and their starvation would soon end. Instead, the retreating French army proved that all hope was now extinguished. Two days later they lowered the French banner as a token that they were prepared to surrender. Edward sent Sir Walter Manny to the foot of the town walls to discuss surrender terms with Jean de Vienne, above on the battlements.

De Vienne said that the inhabitants were dying from hunger and that his sole condition for surrender was to ask for their lives and liberties. Although this might seem a reasonable request by today's standards, it was not a rational plea in 1347. Under the conventions of war at the time, the surrender of a town after a long resistance meant that the victor could take the homes, possessions and even the lives of all the inhabitants. Manny explained that he did not think de Vienne's request would be granted as King Edward was angry about the length of the siege and wanted to punish the town for its resistance. De Vienne said that he knew the English king to be a gallant prince and expected him to respect and honour the bravery of the Calais garrison, in the same way that he would an English garrison that had done likewise. Manny was a tough soldier and used to the savagery of war, having fought with distinction in

Scotland, Sluys and northern France. But he could not help being moved by De Vienne's plea. He returned to Edward, reported his discussion with De Vienne and recommended that some mercy be shown.

A number of barons also felt that in exchange for surrender the town should not be put to the sword, and Edward eventually agreed to show clemency. The king's mitigated demands were that six of the principal citizens of Calais should be sacrificed instead of the whole population. These citizens were required to come to the king's camp in their shirts, bare-headed and bare-footed, carrying the keys of the town and the fortress. As an additional humiliation they were to arrive with halters about their necks as a sign of utter submission, and as preparation for being hanged. When Manny returned to Calais to make known the king's decision, the ultimatum was received with horror by De Vienne. The church bells were rung to summon citizens to the marketplace where he informed them of Edward's demands. When the crowd had gathered and the demands had been explained there was much weeping and many cries of anguish. But no one volunteered to sacrifice themselves for their fellow citizens. At length, Eustage de St Pierre, one of the most eminent citizens, stepped forward to offer himself as a sacrifice. His offer was followed by other leading burgesses, Jehan d'Aire, Jacque de Wissant and his brother Peter, and two others, bringing the number of sacrificial victims to six, as required. These six men took off their clothes and prepared themselves in the manner dictated by Edward. They were then led to the gates of Calais by De Vienne who was riding on a small palfrey, hunger and wounds having made him too weak to walk. The six were then admitted into the English lines and conducted to the king. Arriving before Edward they knelt down and presented the keys, then implored his mercy. Edward was in no mood to be merciful and ordered their immediate execution. At this point many of the barons and knights, including Edward the Prince of Wales, began to entreat Edward to show mercy. Sir Walter Manny even went so far as to say that the execution would be a stain on the king's reputation for chivalry. Edward was not moved by this and insisted that the executioner was summoned. It is said that Queen Philippa intervened at this critical moment and begged her husband to show mercy. She may have reminded Edward of her love for him, or of her recent success in defeating the Scots, we cannot be certain. But the result was that Edward responded to her pleas for mercy and said that the queen could take the six captives and dispose of them as she thought fit.

According to the chronicler. Froissart,[1] Queen Philippa thanked her husband and arranged for the six captives to be taken to her tent where they were given clothing suitable to their rank and provided with a good meal. The six were then safely escorted back to the town gates. The surrender of Calais was completed on 4 August 1347, its brave citizens having endured for almost a year since the start of the siege on 3 September 1346.

The day after the surrender, Edward and Philippa rode into the town followed by all the great lords, knights and men-at-arms. The inhabitants of Calais no doubt regarded this glittering spectacle with mounting apprehension. Their lives had been spared, but they were still starving and the surrender agreement had made no mention of protecting their property. They had every reason to be anxious.

Soon after Edward and Philippa had assumed residence, the order was given that all the inhabitants of Calais should leave the town, except for a few knights such as De Vienne, who would be held prisoner until ransomed. All premises in the town were systematically searched and anything of value was confiscated for later distribution among the victors. Over the next few days, the unfortunate starving citizens and their children were forced out of the town, and prevented from taking anything with them. They received no help from the French king. Some were able to muster the energy to reach friends or relations in Saint Omer and other neighbouring towns. Those who were too weak or unable to find help died on the roads. King Edward's clemency to the citizens of Calais went only so far.

Inside Calais the English army made itself at home, having appropriated most of the property of the French defenders. Edward prepared to return to England but first took action to ensure that Calais and its immediate surroundings should become an English colony within what he regarded as his kingdom of France. Sieges in this period seldom lasted more than a few months, but the exhaustingly long siege of Calais had been worth the wait. By holding Calais, Edward could secure the Straits of Dover and have a permanent entry point to France. It had been necessary to fight the Battle of Sluys in order to secure a safe landing place in the Low Countries. Now England could land an army unopposed in France itself. That said, how long could this isolated outpost be expected to remain in English hands? After all, English kings at different times had held towns in most of the western half of France, but these had all been lost to England, except for those in Gascony.

Edward was determined to make Calais a strong English colony both militarily and economically. He decided to allow some French citizens to stay in Calais as long as they acknowledged him as King of France, and even encouraged the wealthier French merchants to remain by confirming the town charter which had been granted in 1317. Then, having expelled all other French occupants of the town, he began replacing them with English settlers from London. Settlers were able to take over the vacated houses and were given tax breaks to help them establish their own businesses. About 200 initial colonists arrived, providing a full range of skills ranging from barbers to leather workers to clerks and goldsmiths. However, getting the colony established would take time, and Calais needed constantly to be on its guard against a new French attack. The capture of Calais had brought a significant amount of booty but even this could not cover the cost of maintaining the largest English army ever to be deployed overseas. Almost immediately after the surrender the lack of funding obliged Edward to disband most of his army, which made his newly acquired colony even more vulnerable.

Fortunately, Philip was in financial difficulties equal to those of Edward; in fact, France was probably in a worse state. The English wool trade had fluctuated during the period but had always provided sufficient revenue for the crown to contribute to the cost of the war, or to be used as collateral, or for the payment of interest for war loans from Flemish or Italian bankers. France had its taxes but could not provide a similar level of funding. The result was that Philip ordered the French army to stand down. Edward seized the opportunity and carried out a series of raids about thirty miles deep into French territory, which secured some of the area immediately surrounding Calais. Philip felt he had to respond and immediately recalled his army, expecting it to be assembled by 1 September. This was not practicable. The French treasury was exhausted and despite resorting to collecting taxes at sword point, the money was not forthcoming. There was also war weariness among the French nobility, and many sent excuses for failing to muster, despite Philip's threats to confiscate their estates for disobedience. Philip was obliged to defer the assembling of the army.

Edward was also chronically short of funding and had to use similar draconian measures in England, to scrape together enough money to maintain his position in Calais. Even after sending the bulk of the army back to England, maintenance of the greatly reduced garrison of 1,200 men cost £8,000 to £10,000 per year.[2] Concurrently, local hostilities continued around Calais. The garrison at Saint-Omer completely routed one of Edward's raiding parties, and the forces of Countess Joan of Boulogne captured an English supply convoy en route to Calais. As both kings were suffering setbacks, they decided to engage with papal emissaries who had been trying to broker peace between the two monarchs. The Truce of Calais was signed in September 1347 and stipulated that it should remain in force until 7 July 1348. It also confirmed that England should retain all its recent conquests in France and that the Count of Flanders should cease to be a vassal of the French crown.

The positive terms of the truce allowed Edward to leave Calais and return to England. Prior to leaving he made preparations for the government of the town and set up a formal administration under the control of the Captain of Calais. This included a marshal, seneschal and constable, as well as a captain of the Calais fortress. He also ordered that some farm labourers from Kent should be settled in the mainly marshy land around Calais. The area amounted to about twenty-one square miles and was named the Pale of Calais. The responsible position of Captain of Calais was given to Sir Walter Manny. Edward was able to leave Calais with strong defences extending well beyond the city walls, garrisoned by English troops under an experienced commander.

Edward landed at Sandwich in October and spent the rest of the year catching up with royal administration, much of which had been on hold while he had spent the best part of two years away in France. By the beginning of 1348 Edward was sufficiently in control of his kingdom to be able to relax and celebrate his great victory – the capture of Calais. He launched into a number of extravagant tournaments accompanied by feasting and merriment, first in Reading then on to Bury-St-Edmunds, Litchfield, Eltham, Windsor and, finally, Canterbury. Most of the nobility of the country had taken part in the war against France, so it gave them a time of well-earned partying, with feasting, dances and the wearing of fantastic costumes. On one of these occasions Edward appeared dressed as a pheasant in a costume with flapping wings made of copper and covered with real feathers.

While these glittering social and chivalric occasions were taking place Edward developed the idea of creating the Order of the Garter. It would take another year before the Order's first formal meeting, but the concept was a combination of King Arthur's knights of the round table and Edward's victory and its tangible result, the capture of Calais. The king decided that the garter should be blue, in recognition of the French coat of arms, and the motto should be *Honi soit qui mal y pense* meaning 'Shame on him who thinks ill of it'. The 'it' is now thought to refer to Edward's right to the French throne. However, the euphoria of victory celebrations did not last long. The nobles and knights who had so bravely risked their lives on the field of battle now had to prepare to face a death that had no glory or chivalry about it.

The Truce of Calais had come just in time for both England and France, as both countries were about to face a danger far greater than the long lasting and costly war. In 1348 a pandemic known as the Black Death arrived in France. It had started in central Asia about two years earlier, then spread along the Silk Road to reach the Crimea, and continued on to Sicily, probably carried by fleas living on the backs of black rats that invaded and occupied merchant ships. It then spread northwards to France. The symptoms of this plague usually began with large boils which erupted in the groin and armpits, followed by acute fever, breathlessness, vomiting of blood and finally an agonising death within two to five days of infection. It was no respecter of rank and its severity was brought home to the English court when word arrived in July that Edward's 14-year-old daughter, Joan, had succumbed to the plague in Bordeaux, while journeying to marry the heir of the throne of Castile. This news brought the merriment at court to an end, and a month later the plague arrived in England. In September Edward lost another child to the Black Death; this time it was William, Philippa's twelfth baby, just three months old. The plague travelled the length of England and arrived in Scotland and Ireland in 1349.

The death toll over the next three to six years was enormous, but it varied in different areas. It is estimated that in the South of France, including English Gascony, it killed about 50 per cent to 70 per cent of the population, whereas in Northern France the fatality rate was 45 per cent to 59 per cent. The death rate was also generally higher in crowded towns, with open sewers, than in the less populated countryside. It is thought that 60 per cent of the population of London died, equivalent to about 62,000 people. We may assume that deaths in Calais were probably 60 per cent of the population. The impact of the Black Death was immense – France lost about 50 per cent of its population of 17 million, and although England lost a smaller number of people, total deaths were between 20 and 30 percent.[3]

Mediaeval people had no idea how such a disease had occurred, how it was spread or how it might be cured. The general explanation was that it was God's punishment on a sinful world. In Germany it was believed that the Jews were responsible, which resulted in several thousand Jewish people being massacred.

The Black Death meant that nearly the whole population had the heartbreak of losing at least one member of their family and lived in constant fear of who next would be struck down. The horrifying trauma of the plague meant that the economy fell apart. There were too few people to plough the fields, reap the harvest, or to produce, transport and market goods. Certainly, there was very little profit from which to draw any taxes. Under these circumstances neither Edward nor Philip could seriously contemplate continuing the war, so when the truce expired in 1348, they agreed to extend it to May 1349. When that date drew close, and the pandemic was still raging, subsequent extensions were agreed, right up to 1355.

Despite there being no full-scale resumption of war, there was sporadic local fighting between English and French forces in Gascony and Brittany, as well as a number of naval clashes. Calais also saw some military action. Immediately after the first truce had expired, Philip had sent a force to cut off Calais from its Flemish city allies, but threat of invasion by Edward and the chaos of the Black Death meant this was soon called off and the truce was extended. After the next extension of the truce, Edward crossed over to Calais to negotiate an alliance with Count Louis II of Flanders, against Philip. The condition of the agreement was that Edward would give up his separate alliances with the towns of Ghent and Ypres, who had been refusing to accept subservience to Flanders. This would have been a useful strengthening of Edward's hand had not Count Louis reneged on the agreement as soon as he had Ghent and Ypres under his control, and then made an alliance with King Philip against England. This turn of events placed Calais at risk. Fortunately, the alliance between Count Louis and France was of short duration. The next year Count Louis refused to pay homage and assumed a position of neutrality and independence in the Hundred Years' War. However, a grave threat to Calais was soon to manifest itself.

On 24 December 1349 while preparations were under way for Christmas Day celebrations at Queen Philippa's manor of Havering, in Essex, urgent intelligence arrived at the royal court. Edward was informed of a plot by Geoffrey de Charny to capture Calais. De Charny was a Burgundian knight, in French service, and an experienced soldier who had become a member of King Philip's council. He had been placed in command of such French forces as there were in north east France and had managed to suborn one of the Calais sub-captains to betray the town. The officer in question was Aimeric of Pavia, an Italian mercenary who had previously fought for France. Aimeric had later moved into the service of the English and in April 1348 was appointed Galley Master of Calais. In that post he was responsible for commanding a tower overlooking Calais harbour, which contained an entrance into the town citadel. The truce had enabled some contact between the Calais garrison and the French, and de Charny used this to bribe Aimeric to betray the town. After some negotiations, Aimeric agreed to a bribe of 20,000 écus (£3,400)[4] in exchange for which he would arrange for the gate of his tower to be opened at night to allow de Charny's force to enter the town and catch the garrison by surprise.

Records of this event differ. One version is that on hearing of the plot Edward sent for Aimeric and offered to spare him his life for his act of treason, if he acted as a double agent against de Charny. A more likely version is that Aimeric travelled to England to inform Edward of the plot, in hope of a reward. Whatever the truth, Aimeric definitely promised to fully support the king in countering de Charny's plot. However, just to be on the safe side, the king took Aimeric's son as a hostage. Edward then gathered 300 of his household men-at-arms and 600 archers and sailed to Calais with his 19-year-old son Edward, the Prince of Wales – and Aimeric. The sailing was carried out in the utmost secrecy, as was their entry into Calais which was made to look like a routine troop change led not by the king but Sir Walter Manny. The deception was made easier because de Charny was twenty-five miles away at Saint-Omer, making final preparations with his army. During the few days before the expected attack, Edward kept himself hidden and his additional troops stowed out of sight, as much as was possible.

De Charny had gathered an army of 5,500 men-at-arms and 4,000 infantry, led by most of the militarily experienced lords and knights of north east France. On the face of it this should have been more than enough to overcome what de Charny thought was the 1,200-strong English garrison, particularly if they were surprised while in their beds at night. However, de Charny had a particular problem – Aimeric's tower could be approached only at low tide, along a narrow beach that ran beside the town walls; such a route would be unsuitable for so large a force. So, de Charny decided that he would launch the attack on New Year's Eve, just before dawn, when the tide was low and the English garrison would either be sleeping or celebrating. He would send just 112 men-at-arms through the gate in Aimeric's tower and they would then make their way to the Boulogne Gate of the town. This was one of the main gates and de Charny's men would seize the gate house and open the gates. The majority of de Charny's force would be waiting out of sight, not far from the Boulogne Gate, and would then charge into the town and overwhelm the English garrison.

The man chosen to lead the Aimeric Tower group was a French knight named Oudart de Renti who had been banished and who had subsequently served with the English during the siege of Calais. He had later been pardoned by King Philip and joined de Charny's army to redeem his honour. De Renti therefore had both military experience and detailed knowledge of the town of Calais, which made him ideal for leading the vital task of opening the Boulogne Gate. The French plan was a good one and we must assume that de Charny somehow sent word to Aimeric about the timing of the attack. Having received confirmation that the gate would be opened, he began to put his plan into operation. On the evening of 31 December de Charny started to advance towards Calais and by night-time his force was assembled close to Calais, having managed to circumvent the English outer defences. De Charny was now fully prepared to launch his bold scheme to recapture Calais for France. Edward was also fully prepared to prevent this from happening.

As planned, de Renti led his men quietly beside the town walls and then crossed the drawbridge over the moat and found the gate to the tower open. Aimeric was waiting to receive them and exchanged his son as the first instalment of the bribe. Aimeric then led a few of the de Renti soldiers into the tower and they unfurled the French standard. When the rest of de Renti's group had crossed the moat, the drawbridge was suddenly raised, preventing their retreat, while a portcullis was lowered in front of them, to prevent any escape. De Renti's group found themselves surrounded by English men-at-arms who set upon them shouting 'To the death! To the death!' As it happened, only a few of the Frenchmen were killed and the rest surrendered. The first phase of Edward's counter plan had gone rather well.

For the second phase Edward had arranged for a trumpet to be blown as a prearranged signal to de Charny and his main force that the Boulogne Gate was being opened. The gate did indeed open, but through it came Edward, leading his household troops supported by archers. The king was in plain armour and under the banner of Sir Walter Manny. The initial attack caught de Charny's army so much by surprise that many soldiers fled, but de Charny rallied his force, took up a defensive position, and began to repulse Edward's attacks. Amazingly, so tight had been the security about Edward's plan that the Calais garrison was completely unaware of his presence in the town, or the French stratagem for capturing the town. Hearing the fighting, the garrison took up arms and groups of them joined the battle. However, de Charny's army, despite being reduced, still easily outnumbered Edward's troops and was fighting with brave determination. Meanwhile, Edward, Prince of Wales, had exited through the town's Water Gate in the north, with his own household knights, and advanced along the beach to attack de Charny's exposed left flank. The shock of the attack turned the tide and eventually the whole of de Charny's force had fled or been killed or taken prisoner.

The number of casualties on either side is not known, but it is clear that the English probably lost about a hundred men and no leaders of note. The French certainly lost 200 men-at-arms and possibly at least the same number of ordinary soldiers, some of whom drowned as they fled at night through the marshes. Thirty French knights were captured, including Eustace de Ribemont, who had been the French standard bearer at Crécy, and de Charny, who had received a serious head wound. That evening Edward displayed his famous chivalric spirit by hosting his senior French captives to dinner. During the feast he revealed that he had led the English force incognito, and that he had been knocked down by de Ribemont in hand-to-hand combat, prior to de Ribemont's capture. He then made courteous conversation with them all – with one exception. Edward denounced de Charny for his dishonourable conduct; not only had he broken the Truce of Calais, but he had tried to capture Calais by subterfuge rather than open military action. De Charny found this more painful than his head wound – he had always had a reputation for maintaining the highest chivalric standards and had even written a book on chivalry.

It has to be said that if de Charny's plan had succeeded, he would have been regarded as a hero who had restored French honour by the recapture of Calais. As it was, de Charny took Edward's remarks as a major stain on his honour and put the blame for this squarely on Aimeric for having betrayed him. De Charny had to wait eighteen months in confinement until the ransom was paid for his release, after which he was restored to a position of trust by the king of France and even made custodian of the *Oriflamme*, the sacred French royal battle standard. However, none of this reduced de Charny's hatred for Aimeric, and as we shall see, he eventually exacted revenge. In contrast to de Charny, Edward immediately released de Ribemont on parole, so that he could return to King Philip and report the failure of this dishonourable attempt to capture Calais. Such was de Ribemont's knightly honour that after visiting King Philip he voluntarily travelled to England to surrender himself, until his ransom was paid.

With Calais saved Edward returned to England, having appointed Sir John Beauchamp as Captain of Calais. Beauchamp was a son of the Earl of Warwick and an experienced commander who had fought at Sluys and carried the royal banner at Crécy. He held the appointment of Captain for a little over a year before he was promoted to the post of Admiral of the Southern Fleet, responsible for patrolling the Channel and the North Sea. This was a suitable appointment because it meant protecting not only the English Channel ports but also Calais from French naval attack. He was replaced as Captain of Calais by Baron Thomas Holland who was another highly experienced soldier, having fought in Flanders, Gascony and been a commander of the vanguard at Crécy. Calais was in safe hands and King Philip was distracted from the colony by the problems of high inflation and economic turmoil, caused by the Black Death. Any attempts to expand his territory were directed to the South of France where he was engaged in acquiring Montpellier and Languedoc.

In 1350 King Philip VI died and was succeeded by his soldier son, John, Duke of Normandy, who became King John II. A few months before his father's death John had remarried, following the loss of his first wife during the Black Death. John's new wife was Joan of Auvergne whose husband, the Duke of Burgundy, also had recently died. As well as being Countess of Auvergne in her own right she was also Countess of Boulogne, of which Calais was technically a part. John had become responsible for his wife's lands which is the likely cause of his increased desire to retake Calais. However, John was distracted from immediate military action as his reign had got off to a bad start. He had managed to alienate many of the aristocracy over his treatment of Raoul II of Brienne, Count of Eu and Guînes, the Constable of France.

Raoul had been captured in 1343 when the English took Caen and held him prisoner in England, awaiting the raising of a ransom. After four years in which Raoul had been unable to raise the huge sum of 80,000 (£14,000) *écus* that was required, he was given permission to return to France on parole, personally to raise the ransom money. Once back in France it seems Raoul was considering either mortgaging his town of Guînes, to raise the money, or handing it over to Edward in lieu of payment. Guînes was five miles south of Calais and had a castle which was one of the most important strongholds of the French defensive ring around Calais. When King John heard about the possibility of Guînes falling into Edward's hands he invited Raoul to have dinner with him, and then had him arrested. Quite whether Raoul was going to hand over the town to the English we shall never know; he was immediately executed without trial. This summary execution of a leading nobleman had made most other members of the French nobility disenchanted with their new king.

Unpopularity was just one of King John's problems. The Black Death was coming to an end but had left the country's economy in a depression, and therefore the royal coffers were empty. On top of this was the chaos caused by the excesses of the Hundred Years' War. Although there had been a period of extended truces, a new military threat had developed –the so called *routiers*. These were bands of freelancing soldiers who decided to carry out their own form of *chevauchee*, for personal gain. The *chevauchée* led by Edward and his generals had been pretty merciless, but it had also shown some element of discipline and restraint. The *routiers* had no such inhibitions. These were mainly English, Gascon and Breton discharged soldiers, led by adventurers. They roamed much of France, raping, pillaging and practising extortion in return for not burning villages or crops.

In January 1352 a band of English *routiers* under John Doncaster entered Guînes at night, scaled the walls of the castle and captured it. The commander of Guînes escaped and succeeded in informing de Charny, who was by then back in command of French forces in the region. It is seldom beneficial to be the bearer of bad news; the commander was hanged, drawn and quartered for dereliction of duty. King John made a strong protest to Edward about this dishonourable flagrant breach of the truce and demanded that Guînes be returned to French hands. Edward considered himself the epitome of chivalry, so this highly advantageous but dishonourable breach of the truce placed him in a difficult position.

Parliament was sitting at this time and scorned King John's protest as he had allowed intermittent attacks against English Gascony during the truce. Parliament was so incensed that it voted three continuous years of taxes for the defence of the realm. This prospect of good financial backing for starting a new war overcame Edward's concerns about his honour and he ordered the Captain of Calais to take over the garrisoning of Guînes, in the king's name. John of Doncaster acknowledged that as a subject of King Edward he had to accept the order, and no doubt received a reward for having captured the castle and delivered it to the English crown. The breach of the truce by the formal English occupation of Guînes resulted in the resumption of the Hundred Years' War.

In the first part of this phase of the war, both England and France concentrated their initial military efforts on the Calais region. In the case of England, this was a further strengthening of the outer perimeter of Calais and included the construction of a tower at Fretun, about three miles south-west of Calais. Meanwhile Geoffrey de Charny had assembled an army of 4,500 in preparation for an assault to recapture Guînes. The English garrison was only 150 strong and de Charny managed to take the town but failed to take the castle. In July the Calais garrison carried out a surprise night attack on de Charny's besieging army, resulting in a large number of French casualties and the destruction of their siege works. De Charny abandoned the siege and decided to attack the far less fortified English outpost at Fretun. Aimeric was back in English service and had been given command of Fretun's small garrison. On the night of 24–25 July de Charny and his entire army made a surprise night attack on Fretun, at which the English night watch fled. The French occupation of the fortress was so swift that Aimeric was captured while still in bed with his mistress.

We now have an interesting example of a mediaeval knight's concept of both revenge and honour. De Charny had Aimeric taken back to Saint-Omer. There de Charny organized a public spectacle of his revenge against Aimeric for having betrayed the plan to capture Calais. The whole army was summoned, together with the populace from miles around, to witness Aimeric's punishment for having made de Charney appear dishonourable. Red hot irons were used to torture Aimeric, slowly, until he eventually died. His body was then quartered with an axe and his body parts displayed above the town gates. De Charny's honour was satisfied but to reinforce his chivalric reputation he made it clear that he would not garrison Fretun as he had taken it only because of his personal reasons for wanting to capture Aimeric. Fretun thus returned to English hands and Calais' outer defences were restored. De Charny disbanded his army and an uneasy peace returned to the area.

Such peace as existed was disturbed by the revolt of Charles II, 'Charles the Bad', the King of Navarre, against his father-in-law, King John II. Charles was a good looking, intelligent, charming and charismatic man, who was utterly unprincipled. As well as being King of Navarre, Charles held considerable estates in Normandy. In 1353 he became involved in a dispute with the Constable of France, Charles de la Cerda, and had him assassinated. As Cerda had been a royal favourite, King John prepared to invade Charles' territories in Normandy. Charles then made an alliance with Edward, with a plan for Edward to invade France, but this resulted in John making a hurried peace with Charles by granting him extra lands. The next two years saw fruitless Anglo-French peace negotiations during which Charles conspired with the English and encouraged John's eldest son, Prince Charles (the heir apparent and first royal to be given the title of Dauphin) to plot a coup against his father. In April 1356 Charles the Bad was staying with the dauphin at his castle in Rouen when King John and his guards burst in and arrested Charles, then took him as a prisoner to Paris. This was not to be the end of the matter.

While John was being distracted by the conspiracies of Charles of Navarre, King Edward III had appointed his eldest son, Edward Prince of Wales, as his lieutenant in Gascony. Prince Edward was charged with leading a *chevauchée* into Aquitaine, which he did without mercy, pillaging and destroying 500 towns and villages in his path, as well as sacking Carcassonne and plundering Narbonne. It is about this time that he became known as the 'Black Prince'. This may have been because of his ceremonial black armour or, more likely, because of what the French rightly regarded as his black deeds. At the same time as the Black Prince was mercilessly plundering the South of France, King Edward landed in Normandy to join the supporters of Charles of Navarre who were protesting against his arrest. King John responded by sending a force to Normandy but would not be enticed into open battle with Edward, who then marched to Calais. There he heard the news that the Scots had invaded England. He quickly left Calais and travelled north, capturing Berwick and burning Edenborough. Unable to goad the Scots forces into a major engagement he then left for England and returned his attention to France.

Later that year the Black Prince renewed his *chevauchée*, turning northwards and capturing Auvergne and Limousin. By this time John had managed to assemble an 11,000-strong army near Poitiers, which included contingents from Scotland and Germany. The Black Prince realized his force of 6,000 was heavily outnumbered and offered terms which John refused. A battle took place which followed much the same pattern as at Crécy. The English prepared a defensive position on a hill that could be approached only by a narrow road flanked with hedges. The French knights were ordered to dismount and as they attacked up the road they were mown down by English archers in the hedges. At this moment of French disarray, the English made a mounted charge at the French centre which crumbled. King John and his 14-year-old son, Prince Philip, were surrounded. The king and his son fought on bravely, but eventually surrendered and were taken prisoner. With their king captured the French army broke and fled. The Battle of Poitiers was a glorious victory for the English. A large number of the French nobility were killed or captured. Among the dead was de Charny, demonstrating his chivalry to the last, having fallen with the sacred *Oriflamme* standard still clutched in his hand.

Such were the strange ways of chivalry that the Black Prince, who thought nothing of carrying out what would be regarded as serial war crimes, received King John with the utmost courtesy and respect. A banquet was given in King John's honour, the Black Prince waited upon him at table, and declared him the hero of the battle for his bravery on the field. The Black Prince then returned to Boulogne with King John and Prince Philip. The following April (1357) Prince Edward sailed to England with his royal captives. King John arrived in London and was received by King Edward not as a prisoner, but as a neighbouring monarch arriving on a state visit. The hospitality flourished: King John and the other captive monarch, King David of Scotland, attended banquets and tournaments, sitting on either side of Edward. Protracted negotiations ensued, with each party proposing how much each country should pay for the release of their respective sovereigns.

The sums demanded by Edward for ransom were enormous and so negotiations were difficult. Indeed, King David by this time had been a prisoner for eleven years, during which his kinsman, Robert Stewart, nephew of Robert the Bruce, had been running Scotland. Robert Stewart had tired of the negotiations, invaded England and sent troops to France to fight for King John against the English. But Edward's destruction of the Lowlands and the victory of Poitiers had brought the Scots to the negotiating table, and by the end of the year, 1357, King David was released on the promise of a ransom of 100,000 marks. David's years as a privileged prisoner in the English court had resulted in him becoming an anglophile, so Edward now had a compliant northern neighbour unlikely to seek an alliance with France.

Across the Channel, in France, King John's captivity had resulted in his 18-year-old-son, the dauphin, becoming regent. Much of the French nobility had been killed at Poitiers or were being held prisoner for ransom. The country began to fall into anarchy; *routiers* were still roaming the countryside and Charles of Navarre's supporters in the Estates General were clamouring for his release. Charles' brother, Philip, had joined with the English Army under the Duke of Lancaster (formerly the Earl of Derby) to wage war on the dauphin's forces in Normandy. In November (1357) Charles of Navarre was sprung from gaol and entered Paris in triumph, where he demanded the dauphin give him the duchy of

Normandy and the county of Champagne. The dauphin fled Paris, and as if this was not enough, a separate uprising erupted.

This was an uprising of the peasantry north of Paris, against the gentry and aristocracy who had been exacting crippling taxes, while failing to protect their tenants' villages from marauding armies. For over a year, enraged peasantry burned down chateaux and slaughtered men, women and children of the aristocracy, resulting in equally brutal reprisals. With the dauphin so hard-pressed, and general chaos in the French kingdom, Calais was a haven of stability and safe from any French attack. In some ways this period marked King Edward III as having achieved his most powerful position so far during his reign. Scotland was under a friendly monarch, the king of France was his captive, and France itself was in such chaos that it would be obliged to accede to any of his demands. The question was, would this run of luck continue?

Chapter 3

A Commercial Centre, 1357–1400

While the hard-pressed dauphin was struggling with his many problems, he received news that his captive father, King John, and King Edward had reached a peace agreement at Windsor. The most important part of the agreement was that Edward was to be given all Henry II's former vast possessions in France. Far from bringing peace, it renewed the hostilities.

Charles of Navarre thought he could use the war to his advantage. He created chaos in Paris by releasing all prisoners from the gaols, then set off to Normandy to build up his army. The dauphin rejected the peace and also began raising an army to fight against Charles, or Edward, or both. With the peace rejected by the dauphin, Edward lost patience and decided to resume his attempt to take the French crown. By 1359 Edward had raised a 100,000-strong army which he transported from Sandwich to Calais. With so strong a force there seemed a very good prospect that Edward at last would take the crown he believed was rightfully his.

Edward marched confidently out of Calais to claim his crown. Such a large force must have been an amazing sight. The 100,000 troops, if they were knights, men at-arms or mounted archers, would each have had at least two horses. Then there was the baggage train, consisting of 12,000 carts each pulled by three horses.[1] Then there were the courtiers, members of the royal household, packs of hounds, teams of falconers, musicians and camp followers. With their garments as yet unstained by campaigning, this great body of people, carriages and horses, with their heraldic banners, surcoats and horse coverings, made a glittering and colourful spectacle. It was after all almost a coronation procession. Edward's objective was Rheims, whose cathedral was the traditional holy place for the coronation of French kings.

Things did not go according to plan. Rheims refused to open its gates to Edward, so he marched off to try to destroy the dauphin's army, but the dauphin kept eluding battle. So Edward consoled himself by laying waste to Picardy, but time was passing. Winter was approaching and his men and horses were dying from disease. As Edward and his army drew near to Chartres they were caught in a ferocious thunderstorm. The rain and the hail were so fierce and caused so much damage, that Edward perceived it as a sign from God that he should make peace with France. He entered Chartres and within its cathedral made a promise to seek peace. So it was that a weather event brought about the Treaty of Brétigny, the following year. Brétigny is a village outside Chartres where Edward and the dauphin began agreeing the terms both for King John's ransom and for a lasting peace. The negotiations began in May 1360 and were not concluded until the October, during which time Edward had returned to England and was finalising matters with King John. The negotiations had taken a long time, but they were worth the wait. King John's ransom was agreed at three million écus (£500,000)[2] and the treaty stated that Edward should hold Aquitaine, Calais and some of north east France, with full sovereignty, but would renounce his claim to the French throne. The treaty was comprehensive in that England and France agreed to terminate their respective alliances with Flanders and Scotland.

With a few final details still to be agreed, King John was moved to Calais, attended by the Black Prince. King Edward joined them in October where the full Treaty of Calais was signed, amid much banqueting. The Treaty covered the earlier agreements made in Brétigny, but also stipulated that Edward's undertaking to renounce the French crown would be contained in a separate document, to be ratified on condition of France transferring the lands it had ceded. In other words, it included a potential escape clause. The Treaty also included additional provisions: that Edward would remove his troops from Normandy, and that John would restore to Charles of Navarrre all his lands and pardon him and his followers. In return, Charles agreed to renew his homage to the French crown and use his forces to put down the marauding *routiers*. It seemed, following these sensible concessions on all sides, that the Treaty of Calais would bring a lasting peace.

King John was released from Calais to begin the difficult task of raising his ransom. As a token of good faith, French hostages were provided to take John's place in England. The hostages were John's second and third sons, the Dukes of Anjou and Berry, together with his brother, the Duke of Orléans, and some forty nobles. All these princes and nobles made their way to England, accompanied by their attendants.

England and France could at last start to enjoy peace and, in the case of France, begin to recover from continual destruction by armies, rebels and *routiers*. England would still bear the expense of garrisoning greater Calais and its Aquitaine territories, but would not have to find the huge sums necessary for keeping armies in the field. France too would save money by disbanding most of its army but faced the added difficulty of trying to raise the funds for a huge ransom, from a country that had been ravaged by war and had not yet recovered from the economic chaos of the Black Death. Indeed, while the Black Death pandemic was over, local outbreaks still occurred in both France and England.

The peace treaty had stipulated that the ransom for King John should be paid within six months, but the economy of France was in such desperate straits that this was impossible. The Duke of Anjou and the other hostages had gone to England in October 1360, expecting to be released six months later and felt it would be no great hardship to remain in England for that period, where they were treated as honoured guests. However, time passed, the ransom still was not paid, and the hostages remained captive. They all wanted to get on with their lives. For example, Anjou was 31 years old when he started his captivity; he had been active in the Hundred Years' War, was also the Count of Maine, and, as the adopted heir of the Queen of Naples, he was heir to the kingdoms of Naples and Jerusalem. In short, he was an important man in his own right and could not be expected to waste his time kicking his heels in England.

Six months of captivity turned into two years, with still no sign of the ransom being paid. Anjou applied to Edward for the hostages to be released and although Edward refused release, he granted bail for the hostages and in May 1363 they were transferred to Calais, on parole. Once in Calais they had considerable freedom and were better able to manage their French affairs. But this arrangement was still not enough for Anjou who had suffered almost three years in captivity. Two months after arriving in Calais, Anjou broke his parole and escaped to France. When Anjou visited his father, King John, he received anything but a warm paternal welcome. John was angry and distraught that his son could be so unchivalrous as to break his parole and took a step that would amaze Christendom – and also earn him widespread acclaim for his devotion to the highest standards of chivalry. He declared that his honour obliged him to redeem his son's bad faith by returning to England as a hostage, and to remain there until the full ransom was paid. Consequently, the Dukes of Berry and Orléans also felt honour bound to give up their lives of relative freedom in Calais, for captivity in England.

John duly returned to England in January 1364 accompanied by roughly 200 courtiers. On arriving in London, he was received by Edward with parades and feasts, but his stay was to be short. John's health had never been strong, and he fell ill and died, three months later, at the Savoy Palace in London, aged only 44 years old. His son, the dauphin, became King Charles V of France. While King John had demonstrated firm intentions to honour the terms of the Treaty of Calais, his son felt no such obligation. Charles regarded the treaty as a national humiliation which he planned to reverse when he was strong enough to do so. Edward was also having doubts about the Treaty, despite it having been so much to England's advantage. He wondered whether he should have given up his claim to the French throne in exchange for full sovereignty over Aquitaine, Calais and his other French possessions. Many English nobles felt that Edward having surrendered his claim to the French throne was a stain on the nation's honour, and this view was not confined to sections of the nobility, only. A minor cleric called William Langland wrote a poem called 'Piers Ploughman' in which he said that the king had sold his birth right for silver. Circumstances seemed to be conspiring towards a return to hostilities.

Ever since the Treaty, Edward had been trying to exploit the situation by attempting to widen its scope. He had made the Black Prince 'Prince of Aquitaine' and had sent an army to help him rid Aquitaine of *routiers* and remaining French garrisons. Then he went further. He managed to get the new King Charles V to recognize Countess Jeanne de Montfort's son as Duke of Brittany, but Charles was infuriated when the new Duke of Brittany said he would pay homage only to the king of England. Discord was growing between Edward and Charles and there were potential flash points from Aquitaine in the south to Brittany and Normandy in the north. An area of France which remained relatively peaceful was the Pale of Calais, comprising Calais, Guînes and Marck. Peace had brought prosperity to this newly established English colony which had already become The Staple for exports of cloth, wool, tin and lead. So much so that it was decided to move the important wool Staple from Antwerp to Calais in 1363. The twists and turns of warfare meant that The Staple would later temporarily move to Middelburg but in 1393 it returned to Calais where it remained for the rest of English rule.

The concept of The Staple had been established in 1314 when the crown required all wool, tin, lead and leather exports to be traded at a designated market called 'The Staple'. This allowed the crown to monitor the trade and levy taxes on exports. The Staple had moved to different locations, depending on circumstances, but had always provided an important income for the crown. In 1363 all raw wool sold overseas had first to be taken to Calais where a group of twenty-six traders had been incorporated as the Company of the Staple of Calais, with exclusive rights to sell English wool. In exchange for this privilege the company managed the collection of a wool export tax per sack of wool sold. The tax was 26s 8d. per sack and exports peaked in 1310, when 39,000 sacks were sold. The accompanying tax represented a substantial revenue for the crown.[3] The reduction in the export of wool arose from an intervention by Edward. Earlier in his reign he had had used his wife's Hainault connections to bring Flemish weavers from Belgium to England. These weavers settled in Norwich, Ipswich and Colchester and began producing broad cloth for home consumption. This industry became so successful that Edward wore English broad cloth only and insisted that his courtiers did likewise. By 1363, 14,500 yards of English broad cloth was being exported to the continent annually, via Yarmouth and the River Orwell. This would gradually increase over time, but the fact remained that raw wool export via Calais produced a vital source of income for Edward. Unfortunately, no sooner had The Staple been established in Calais than the security of the colony as a whole came under potential threat.

The threat to Calais arose through the coincidence of a number of marriages which resulted in a young woman becoming heiress to a potentially greatly expanded Flemish empire. The lady in question was Margaret, the 13-year-old daughter and heir of Louis de Mâle, Count of Flanders. Louis himself had inherited Nevers, Bethel, Brambant, Linberg, Artois and the county of Burgundy (or Franche-Comté). Margaret's husband, the Duke of Burgundy, had died in 1361, without an heir, and the duchy of Burgundy escheated (was transferred to the crown), to King John of France. Two years later, John gave the dukedom of Burgundy to his son Philip, who had fought so bravely beside him at Poitiers and who had joined him in captivity in England. By 1364 Margaret was not only a substantial heiress but free to be married and have her future husband assume control of her lands.

Bearing in mind that Flanders was the primary export for English wool, it was a matter of some importance to ensure that it remained in friendly hands. Louis de Mâle had tried to remain independent by playing France and England against the other, sometimes supporting one country and sometimes the other. Edward thought that a good way to ensure that Flanders became permanently allied to England was to arrange a marriage between Mâle's heiress daughter and one of his sons. The Black Prince was married, as was his second son, Lionel, the Duke of Clarence and Lieutenant of Ireland. The third son was John of Gaunt, so named because he had been born in Ghent, which the English pronounced as 'Gaunt'. John of Gaunt was married to Blanche of Lancaster and had inherited her father's huge Lancastrian estate. That left the fourth surviving son, Edmund of Langley, the Earl of Cambridge, who was a 22-year-old bachelor. In the spring of 1364 Edward despatched John of Gaunt to Calais, to begin negotiations with Mâle for Edmund to marry Margaret.

This courtship by proxy did not result in a romantic happy ending. Another suitor was also in play – Duke Philip of Burgundy, the younger brother of King Charles V of France. Mâle proceeded to play each one against the other, and after a five-year negotiation he agreed that Margaret should marry Duke Philip. This was a blow for King Edward, but although Mâle had decided in favour of the French, he remained content for his Flemish towns to continue trading with the Calais Staple. The marriage was not the only successful strategy employed by Charles V, who was later to become known as 'Charles the Wise'. Instead of leading armies himself, Charles appointed experienced soldiers as his generals, and employed talented servants to manage the royal finances. As a result, the crown was able to overcome its debts and Charles' general, Bertrand du Guesclin, defeated Charles of Navarre in battle in 1364. Having eliminated one major adversary, Charles turned his attention to the marauding bands of *routiers*. He managed to persuade them to leave France and fight under du Guesclin in the civil war raging in Castile, between King Peter the Cruel and the rebels supporting his illegitimate brother, Henry.

In 1367 the Black Prince, as Prince of Aquitaine, joined the war in Castile on the side of King Peter, while the French supported Henry. France and England were thus at war again, albeit indirectly. After initial success for the English and Peter being restored to the throne, Peter reneged on his promise to provide provisions and pay for Edward's army. The Black Prince withdrew his support from Peter and led his army back to Aquitaine. Dysentery hit both the Black Prince and much of his army and four out of five warriors died during the Castilian campaign. King Peter had lost the support of the English and du Guesclin took advantage of the situation. He defeated and captured King Peter who was stabbed to death by his brother, Henry, in du Guesclin's tent. Consequently, Henry became King of Castile and an ally of France. Meanwhile the Castilian campaign had generated enormous debt for the Black Prince which he attempted to clear by imposing new taxes in Gascony. This was so unpopular that in 1369 Gascon nobles petitioned King Charles V for his aid and Charles summoned the Black Prince to Paris to answer the charges. When his heralds informed the Black Prince of the summons he fell into a fury and said that he would be delighted to visit his fair cousin in Paris, but it would be at the head of an army. Having received this response, Charles felt that he was at last strong enough to accuse the Black Prince of disloyalty and declare war on England.

So it was that the Treaty of Calais was abandoned and the Hundred Years' War was resumed. Edward began styling himself 'King of France' once again, but the title was to become increasingly hollow. This phase of the war was disastrous for the English. It proved impossible to provoke the French army to battle and the English forces constantly were being eroded by attrition. In 1371 the Black Prince was forced to return to England, his health broken. In the same year the anglophile King David of Scotland died and was succeeded by Robert Stewart, who became King Robert II and renewed the alliance with France. The following year Edward, 50 years old and in failing health, tried to lead an army to invade France, but contrary winds meant the expedition had to be aborted. This was Edward's last attempt to lead his forces. With the Black Prince out of action through illness, and most of the great warriors of Poitiers dead, or too old for combat, England lost its military leadership.

The English situation in France went from bad to worse. Du Guesclin pushed back an English offensive in northern France and went on to achieve a decisive victory at the Battle of Pontvallain. Things were little better in the south where some of the Black Prince's Aquitaine territories switched their allegiance to France. In 1373 Edward sent John of Gaunt with an army to Calais, from where he carried out a *chevauchée* through France to Bordeaux. Gaunt caused considerable destruction but was unable to tempt the French to a pitched battle. Continual small attacks by the French on the rearguard of Gaunt's force meant that his army arrived in Bordeaux in a much depleted and sorry state. Gaunt's expedition achieved nothing to England's advantage but resulted in increasing French hatred for his marauding tactics. This gave the French confidence to nibble away at English possessions. Soon the nibbles became bites and English castles and whole provinces were being taken over by the forces of King Charles. At the same time France began taking the war to England. A combined French and Castilian fleet destroyed the English forty-strong resupply fleet off La Rochelle and gave France sea supremacy in the Channel. This was exploited by du Guesclin who launched a series of destructive raids on thirteen English ports including Folkestone, Southampton, Plymouth and Gravesend. By 1375 English territory in France had been reduced to Calais and the territories skirting Bordeaux to Bayonne.

For some time, the pope had been sending envoys to the two belligerent kings, in attempts to bring about a peace. In early 1375 England's major setbacks induced Edward to agree to peace talks in Bruges. When the talks started it soon became clear that there was little or no room for agreement and a peace agreement was impossible. However, there was a truce, and so an uneasy accord was established. Although Edward refused to give up his claim to the French throne, the fact of the matter was that Charles V was firmly established as King of France and England's once great possessions were reduced to the shore of Gascony, Calais and the Calais Pale.

But what of Calais during this disastrous phase of the war? The renewal of hostilities in 1370 had led King Philip to advance into the province of Ponthieu to the south of Calais. Philip was received with enthusiasm and the citizens of Abbeville opened their gates to him. Soon other towns followed, and most of the province fell to Philip. In response to this the strength of the Calais garrison was increased to 500 men, and the outlying fortresses of the Pale swelled to 1,000 men. The extent of the reinforcement and other defensive measures is shown by the increase in their costs, from £12,000 in 1350 to £20,000 in 1370.[4] The military situation at Calais was greatly improved by the arrival of Gaunt and his army, and his *chevauchée* to Bordeaux cleared some of the French who had been occupying Ponthieu. In fact, after Gaunt had returned to England, Calais had a military success in August 1374, one year before the peace negotiations. The Count of Saint-Pol led an attack on the Calais Pale and this resulted in a skirmish in which the English were victorious. Saint-Pol was captured together with his senior captains, emphasizing that the removal of the English from Calais would be no easy task.

During this phase of the war Calais managed surprisingly well commercially. It had been a disappointment to King Edward that none of his traditional Flemish allies – Flanders, Brabant, Hainault and the independent cities of Ghent and Bruges – had come to his aid against France. There is no doubt that this contributed to England's failures during the war. However, the Flemish rulers, like Mâle, had remained neutral and there had been no disruption in commerce between the Calais Staple and its main customers for wool. In fact, in 1372, Mâle, despite being neutral, had signed a new trade agreement with England. The average quantity of wool sold during this period of the war was only slightly down, at 25,868 sacks a year.[5] As the English Parliament had authorized an increase on the wool tax to £2 per sack, Calais was able to make an important contribution to the royal coffers at a time when they were being overstretched by the unsuccessful war. The population of Calais had risen to about 12,000 people, of whom 5,400 were engaged in the wool trade. In 1372 the importance of Calais was recognized, and it became a parliamentary borough. Calais was thus regarded as part of England with its own two Members of Parliament to represent it at Westminster.

The partial success of Calais was perhaps the only positive news for Edward in his declining years. The Bruges truce held, which meant that Philip was able to consolidate his position in his recently gained English territories. Edward had become frail and after his wife Philippa died, he came under the influence of his grasping mistress, Alice Perrers. The year after the Treaty of Bruges was signed (1376), the Black Prince died aged 46, following a long illness. Edward's second son, Lionel of Antwerp, had already died, which meant that Gaunt was his next oldest son, and he began to take the reins of government from his enfeebled father. In June the following year, 1377, King Edward III died, aged 65, having reigned for fifty years. In his final hours his courtiers deserted him; there was no profit to be had from attending a king whose power had almost gone. Even his mistress, Alice Perrers, abandoned the dying king, having first removed the rings from his fingers. Such was the end of the great warrior monarch who, in his day, had humbled the kings of France and Scotland, and captured Calais and the Calais Pale.

The crown passed to the Black Prince's surviving son, Richard of Bordeaux, who became King Richard II. The new king was just 10 years old so the kingdom was governed by a regency council dominated by his uncles: John of Gaunt, Duke of Lancaster and Thomas of Woodstock, Earl of Buckingham. Almost at once after Richard's coronation, the Council decided to renew the war with France.

Unfortunately, this was just at the time that the famous French admiral, Jean de Vienne, (nephew of the Jean de Vienne who surrendered Calais),[6] had decided to bring the war to English shores. He attacked the ports and harbours of the south coast and made an agreement with Duke Philip II ('Philip the Bold') to assault Calais. De Vienne blockaded the port at Calais about a year after the young King Richard II had inherited the throne. At the same time Duke Philip attacked on land and in September 1378 he captured Ardres, the south-eastern fort in the Calais Pale; a week later the fort of Audruicq surrendered. The town of Calais was now wide open for Burgundy to attack, or it would have been had there not been a period of heavy rain. The marshy land surrounding Calais became impassable, and Duke Philip was obliged to withdraw his force. The Captain of Calais was a seasoned soldier, Sir Hugh Calveley. Once Burgundy had pulled back, Calveley sallied forth and raided the town of Étaples, held its merchants to ransom and carried off all the town's wine. This was a minor military success in a period which would see the loss of further English possessions in France.

English military expeditions were sent to Brittany and Gascony during the period 1377 to 1381 but achieved nothing other than considerable debt, which resulted in the imposition of the hated Poll Tax. This burdensome tax caused the peasantry of Kent and Essex to rise up against their landowners in 1381, in what was called the Peasants Revolt. Soon the revolt spread to other parts of the country. In the summer of that year the rebels attacked London, burning Gaunt's Savoy Palace and killing the

Archbishop of Canterbury and the Lord Chancellor. King Richard II, by then 14 years old, bravely left the safety of the Tower to negotiate with the rebels at Smithfield. A fracas took place and the rebel leader, Wat Tyler, was killed by the Mayor of London. Richard saved the situation by riding into the peasant force and promising to accept their demands and grant them pardon for rebellion. Once the rebels had dispersed, Richard revoked the pardon and had the rebels hunted down. By 28 June the last peasant force was destroyed at a skirmish at Billericay. The Peasants Revolt had ended, but it had been a serious threat to the monarchy. With such a threat at home, it is hardly surprising that England's affairs in France did not prosper.

King Charles V of France died in 1380 and was succeeded by his 11-year-old son, who became Charles VI. France's great general, du Guesclin, died in the same year and this reduced the momentum of the war. France by then was experiencing a new bout of plague, and economic recession which, coupled with the burden of high taxation to support the war, resulted in a peasant uprising. Fighting between France and England was reduced to occasional expeditions and acts of piracy on both sides of the Channel.

Two years later the situation changed once again. For several years the powerful guilds of Ghent had wanted commercial independence from their count, Louis de Mâle of Flanders. In 1382 they rose up against him and defeated an army from the town of Bruges which remained loyal to Mâle. Soon much of Flanders had joined the revolt, so Count Louis decided to enlist the support of his son-in-law, Duke Philip II of Burgundy. Philip II had been the de facto regent of France while his nephew, the young King Charles VI, had been underage. The Duke of Burgundy took a 10,000-strong French army and routed the Flemish rebels. Burgundy entered Bruges and confiscated the goods of the English merchants and then ordered the cessation of commercial relations with England. This edict had even wider commercial ramifications, as Bruges controlled the road to Ghent and the rest of England's trading partners in Flanders. It was a major blow to English merchants, especially those in Calais, and meant a significant drop in income for the crown, caused by diminished taxes.

This came at a time when the crown was already heavily in debt and when England's economy was at a low ebb. The obvious answer was to send an expedition to drive the Duke of Burgundy and his French forces out of Bruges. The problem was that Parliament had no wish to risk further unrest by imposing the extra taxation required to pay for an army. It is at this point that Henry le Despencer, the Bishop of Norwich, offered a solution. Norwich had made a name for himself by donning armour and leading a force which had savagely hunted down those who had supported Wat Tyler's rebellion. After every engagement he sat in judgement on his prisoners and having granted them absolution for their sins, had their heads struck off. Norwich's solution was to exploit the division that had taken place in the church.

A papal schism had occurred in 1378 which had given rise to two popes. A French pope (Clement VII in Avignon), supported by France, Scotland, Spain and Sicily; and an Italian pope (Urban VI in Rome), supported by England, Flanders, Poland and Denmark. Norwich was in contact with Pope Urban who agreed that he, Norwich, should raise a force to attack France on his behalf, and that he would sanction the military intervention as a crusade against the supporters of the false pope, Clement VII. This allowed papal indulgences to be granted to all those who agreed to serve for a year, in exchange for forgiveness of their sins. Indulgences could also be sold in the name of the crusade to raise money to cover the costs of the expedition. The good bishop put his proposal to Parliament, which was happy to agree to this private venture method of military funding. On 21 December 1382 Norwich took his crusading vows at St Paul's Cathedral and set up a cross as a rallying point for crusader volunteers and financial backers. By February 1383 there were between 4,000 and 5,000 volunteers for the crusade, and Parliament gave its final approval for the campaign. On 16 May the expedition set sail from Sandwich under the command of several captains but with Norwich in charge overall.

The bishop and his small army arrived in Calais and soon moved out to capture Gravelines and slaughter its inhabitants, according to the best crusader traditions. They then took Dunkirk and Nieuport in an equally bloody fashion. Then they decided to attack Ypres. This was an unfortunate choice. The citizens of Ypres were mainly Urbanist supporters, the very pope for whom Norwich was supposedly fighting. However, this contradiction did not deter Norwich from investing (surrounding and cutting off) the town in June. There followed four months of failing to breach the walls, during which time Norwich lost much of his army to disease. At this point word arrived that a large French army was being raised to oppose him. Norwich sent a message to England requesting reinforcements, but none were forthcoming. In fact, John of Gaunt blocked the provision of help, even from the Calais garrison, because he resented Norwich having been given command of the expeditionary force rather than himself. Norwich had no option but to give up the towns he had taken and return to Calais and then England. The Norwich crusade had been doomed from the start; it was far too small a force to be able to take on the French army. Further, the fact that Parliament had supported the inadequately resourced crusade did not mean that it was prepared to take any responsibility for its failure. The blame was laid on Norwich who was impeached and fined, having to pay for the full public cost of the crusade. Although he had his lands confiscated, Norwich retained his bishopric and was able to busy himself with the persecution of Lollards (followers of John Wyclif, the English religious reformer) in his diocese.

Soon after the disastrous Norwich expedition, Gaunt agreed an armistice with France and Burgundy which resulted in the resumption of trade with Flanders, much to the relief of the merchants of the Calais Staple. Norwich's operations around Gravelines had been the nearest Calais had come to military action in this phase of the war; such military operations as there were took place far away. The French sent Admiral Jean de Vienne, with an expedition, to support the King of Scots against England. This resulted in Richard II ravaging Scotland, and the Scots and French ravaging Westmorland, but then matters fizzled out and both the French and English armies returned home.

The chronicler Froissart records that de Vienne pulled out of Scotland because he and his men 'had never met worse people than the Scots, and nowhere had they found such false and treacherous savages'.[7] Richard had left Scotland because he had heard a rumour that his powerful uncle, John of Gaunt, was considering taking the crown. This was not the case, then, but in 1385 Gaunt decided to pursue another crown, that of Castile. This he claimed on behalf of his wife, Constance, daughter of the murdered King Peter the Cruel of Castile. Gaunt was invited by the King of Portugal to defend his Portuguese crown, which was being claimed by King Henry of Castile, supported by the French. The next year Gaunt set sail with 12,000 men, landed in Portugal, then advanced into Spain.

It would have been a relief for King Richard to have his overbearing uncle out of England, but no sooner was he rid of one threatening uncle than he was confronted by another. Thomas of Woodstock, the Earl of Buckingham, had been made Duke of Gloucester and had begun encouraging other peers to support him in wresting power from Richard.

Gloucester and his adherents were known as the Lords Appellant and they successfully rebelled against King Richard in 1388, forcing the king to dismiss his advisers and relinquish much of his power. The failure of the Appellants to build an anti-French coalition, together with a Scots incursion in the north of England, undermined their position, and they suffered a further setback when Gaunt returned to England having struck a deal with the King of Castile. Gaunt had agreed that his daughter, Catherine, would marry Prince Henry, heir to the Castile throne, and Gaunt was to receive a large annual payment. Gaunt had renounced his own claim to the throne of Castile but was well satisfied that his future grandchild would be king. Gaunt was so pleased with his achievement that he was content to be reconciled with Richard who, by then, was over twenty-one years of age. Gaunt considered him mature enough to assume the reins of government and offered Richard his support.

By May 1389 Richard felt sufficiently secure of his throne to decide to change government policy, by seeking peace with France and ending the high taxation which had been necessary to support the long war. Peace negotiations lasted several years during which there was a lull in hostilities. A major obstruction arose when Richard II was offered the expanded Aquitaine territory, but only on condition that he paid homage for it, to Charles VI. This was unacceptable to England, and so instead, a truce was agreed. It was also agreed that, in pursuit of a lasting peace, the 29-year-old Richard would marry Isabella of Valois, the 6-year-old daughter of King Charles VI of France.

It was decided that King Charles would give his daughter away to Richard at a ceremony at Ardres, where the Calais Pale met French territory. Royal weddings take a lot of organising, but this was in a special league, being an alliance between two rival mediaeval kings determined to make it a demonstration of their power and wealth. Richard travelled to Calais in August 1396 to oversee the wedding arrangements and meet with the Duke of Gloucester, who was liaising with the French court. Richard returned to England while arrangements for what was to be one of the spectacles of the age took another two months. There was a great deal to achieve in a short amount of time: there was food to be ordered, transport to be arranged, accommodation to be found, and 240 gaily painted pavilions to be erected. The number of people attending on both sides was huge. Richard returned to Calais in September, escorted by 400 knights and esquires and accompanied by most of his court, soldiers, servants and the large retinues of the Dukes of Lancaster, Gloucester, and the Earls of Nottingham and Northumberland. King Charles was escorted by 400 knights and esquires and accompanied by his courtiers, soldiers, servants and the retinues of the Dukes of Berry, Bourbon and Orléans and others, such as the Count of Harcourt.

At 3 pm on 26 October 1396, the two kings met for the first time. They shook hands, kissed and then took turns to entertain each other in their respective pavilions. The next day they held a four-hour conference on how to organize a lasting peace and bring an end to the schism in the papacy. There were no meetings on Sunday, but on Monday Princess Isabella was formally delivered by Charles to Richard and placed in the care of the English duchesses who took her to Calais. Charles and his vast retinue withdrew, having spent more than four days in lavish banqueting, entertainment and the exchange of expensive gifts. The English contingent continued partying in Calais until a little after Richard and Isabella were married at the Church of St Nicholas on 4 November 1396. It is estimated that the whole event cost 40,000 marks (£26,000).[8] This was at a time when the exchequer was already in annual arrears of nearly £2,000.

The meeting between Richard and Charles was not merely a frivolous opportunity to display princely power. It resulted in the Truce of Calais which was to last for twenty-eight years, during which Calais could prosper without warfare disrupting trade. Although quietly concentrating on peaceful trade, Calais still featured in English affairs of state. The year after the truce, Richard felt strong enough to take revenge against his uncle Gloucester and the Lords Appellant and ordered the arrest of Gloucester and several others. A series of trials took place resulting in executions, imprisonments and fines. Gloucester was taken to Calais under open arrest to await his trial for treason.

Richard had made Thomas Mowbray, the Earl of Nottingham, both Earl Marshall and Captain of Calais, so it was he who was responsible for Gloucester's imprisonment. As the date for the trial drew closer Nottingham delivered the news that Gloucester had died. Most people assumed that Richard had arranged his murder, and they were absolutely right. Richard had ordered Nottingham discreetly to organize Gloucester's death and after some misgivings, he had made the necessary arrangements. Nottingham and other conspirators including the Duke of York's son, the Earl of Cork, used their servants to lure Gloucester to an inn where they smothered him to death under a feather bed. There were no marks on Gloucester's body but few people believed he had died of natural causes. Gloucester's death meant that Richard had removed one of his main opponents without the embarrassment of his uncle being tried and executed for treason. There was an outcry among the nobility about Gloucester's murder, and the fact that Richard had elevated Nottingham to become Duke of Norfolk left little doubt about who was responsible. Animosity towards Richard increased after he confiscated the lands of the many of the Lords Appellant and distributed them among his own supporters.

The powerful Gaunt had backed Richard in this action and he and his family in particular had gained from the redistribution of property. Gaunt was endowed with the Duchy of Aquitaine, and his son Henry Bolingbroke, Earl of Derby, despite having been a former Lord Appellant, was made Duke of Hereford. Richard had tried to strengthen his position by giving confiscated lands and titles to those of doubtful loyalty, to gain their support. This became a problem when Bolingbroke, now Duke of Herford, openly accused Mowbray, now Duke of Norfolk, of murdering Gloucester in Calais. The last thing Richard wanted was allegations flying about concerning the murder of Gloucester, so it was agreed that Bolingbroke and Mowbray should settle the dispute by single combat. But just when the two rode into the lists with lances at the ready, the king intervened to stop the fight and banished both of them for ten years. The following year Gaunt died and Richard disinherited Bolingbroke and seized the vast Lancastrian estates for the crown. Opposition mounted against Richard's autocratic ways, and at this time of discontent he left England, unwisely, to put down rebellions in Ireland. With Richard out of the country, Bolingbroke and a small force arrived in Yorkshire in June 1399, to demand the restitution of the Lancastrian lands.

Bolingbroke was warmly welcomed by the northern lords and advanced south gaining support as he went. Richard returned to England to negotiate with Bolingbroke, but when they met Richard was arrested and taken to the Tower. Richard abdicated in exchange for his life, and Parliament proclaimed Bolingbroke as King Henry IV. A few months later some of Richard's supporters rose up against the new king but their rebellion was soon crushed. Henry's government realized that the deposed king was too dangerous to live and Richard was killed at Pontefract Castel, probably by being starved to death. The only person who now had a stronger claim to the throne than Henry, was Edmund Mortimer, Earl of March, a direct descendant of Lionel, the Duke of Clarence, Gaunt's elder brother. But Edmund was just 6 years old and Henry rapidly arranged for him to be confined at Windsor Castle. Henry's usurpation had established the Lancastrian dynasty, but as he would discover, usurpation was not a sound basis for a secure throne.

It was as well for England that it was not at war with France in this unsettled period. Likewise, the truce had come at a welcome time for France, which had its own problems. In 1392 King Charles VI suddenly descended into madness. His psychosis would come and go but became more severe over the years, until he was sometimes unable to recognize his wife and children and became delusional – he sometimes thought he was Saint George, sometimes that he was made of glass. While this was a personal tragedy for King Charles and his close family, it also left a serious vacuum in the government of France. As had been the case when Charles was underage, the vacuum was filled by his uncles, the most powerful of whom was Philip II, the Duke of Burgundy. However, the regency council was presided over by Isabeau of Bavaria, queen to King Charles VI, and included Charles' brother Louis, the Duke of Orléans. There had been a continuing power struggle between Philip II and Queen Isabeau, complicated by perceptions that the Duke of Orléans was the queen's lover.

The fourteenth century drew to a close with the government of France arguing among itself, and the new Lancastrian dynasty focused on establishing itself in England. With the rulers of France and England otherwise occupied it seemed that the Truce of Calais would continue for some time, which would enable Calais to build up its commercial position without the disruption of war.

Chapter 4

The Burgundian Factor, 1400–26

Parliament expected, now that Henry was king, that he would rectify their grievances against Richard II. Prominent among these grievances was that no one had been brought to justice for the murder of Gloucester in Calais. The Duke of Norfolk had died in exile by this time, but there were other close supporters of Richard who were thought to have been accomplices to the murder, and they were put on trial. These included three dukes, a marquis and two earls. One of these was Henry's cousin, the Earl of Cork, the son of the Duke of York, who had joined Henry against Richard. This was difficult for Henry as he was more interested in winning the backing of these powerful men than turning them into enemies. Fortunately, a scapegoat was found in the form of John Hall, a servant of the now dead Duke of Norfolk, who confessed to having been forced by him to join the group to murder Gloucester.

Hall said he had witnessed the murder being carried out by a servant of the Earl of Cork but had taken no part in it himself. This was enough for Hall to be taken to Tyburn, partially hanged, his entrails removed and burnt before his eyes, then beheaded and quartered. Hall's limbs were put on public display and his head was sent to Calais, the scene of the murder. The execution showed that revenge had been taken for Gloucester's death and made it possible for the accused peers to be sentenced merely to the loss of any estates recently bestowed on them by Richard. Life could now move on from the Gloucester murder, except in the case of poor John Hall.

King Henry IV had attained the throne by force, having been placed there by barons who had lost patience with the autocratic Richard. Henry would spend most of his reign looking over his shoulder wondering whether these barons would turn against him and arrange for his own removal. From the start of his reign Henry faced difficulties. He made an unsuccessful expedition to Scotland and then, two years later, in 1402, the Scots invaded England but were utterly defeated by Henry Percy, the Earl of Northumberland. Unflattering comparisons could be made between the military prowess of the king and that of Northumberland. To make matters worse, a bitter dispute arose between Northumberland and King Henry, over who should receive the ransom money for captured Scots noblemen.

In 1400 Wales rose up under Owen Glendower who was declared Prince of Wales and eventually took control of most of that country. The Earl of Northumberland and his son Henry Percy, nicknamed 'Harry Hotspur', rebelled in 1403 in an alliance with the Scots and Welsh to replace King Henry with the young Edmund Mortimer, Earl of March. Hotspur and the Scots had a 14,000-strong army and intended to link up with Glendower but were intercepted by Henry and his army at Shrewsbury. Hotspur was killed in the hard-fought battle and Edward won a decisive victory. He then travelled north and received the surrender of the Earl of Northumberland.

Henry already had quite enough on his hands, holding on to his English throne, just when the truce with France was approaching breaking point. The French court were not happy that their king's son-in-law, King Richard II, had been deposed. What was the position of Queen Isabella? Henry wanted to maintain the truce and proposed that Isabella should marry his own son, Henry, Prince of Wales, but Isabella refused and went into mourning for her husband. Considerable wrangling went on between England and France and in 1402 Isabella was allowed to return to France, but Henry kept her dowry. A few years later she married her cousin, Charles Duke of Orléans, but sadly died in childbirth at the age of nineteen.

However, English–French relations had not been improved by allowing Isabella to return to France. France was making attacks on English shipping in the Channel and carrying out raids on some of the ports in southern England. In 1405 the French launched an operation against England's remaining possessions in Gascony and made an alliance with Glendower against England. At the same time, the Count of Saint-Pol led a 3,000-strong force against the Calais Pale and captured the fort of Marck, but then retreated after being defeated by a sortie from Calais town. That year galleys belonging to France's ally, Castile, made destructive raids on England, from Cornwall to Southampton. Simultaneously, the French landed in Milford Haven, linked up with

Glendower and marched through Herefordshire and on to Worcester where they were met by a large army under Henry. Glendower wanted to avoid a pitched battle, so he and his French allies pulled back into the Welsh hills. Although appalling weather prevented Henry pursuing the Franco-Welsh force, the French commander decided to withdraw his men back to France, as winter was approaching and there was now no prospect of a successful invasion of England.

The next year King Henry deployed a force from Ireland which landed in Anglesey and began to push back the Welsh rebels. Although Glendower's forces managed to advance as far as Birmingham, the tide turned when the king's son, Prince Henry, took the lead in retaking Wales. Aberystwyth Castle surrendered to Prince Henry while Glendower was fighting elsewhere, and in 1409 Harlech Castle fell to the young prince. In the final battle Glendower's wife and two daughters were captured and taken to the Tower, where they were to end their days as prisoners. Glendower remained free but a fugitive. He managed to carry out occasional minor raids on English garrisons with his few remaining supporters until 1412, after which no more was heard of him.

The pacification of Wales was an eventual success for Henry IV, but while it was under way, he still had to face rebellions elsewhere in his kingdom. In 1405 the Earl of Northumberland again revolted, supported by Richard Scrope, the Archbishop of York, and the Earl of Nottingham, the Earl Marshal. Their force of 8,000 men was met by the Earl of Westmoreland. During a parley they were tricked into believing that their demands would be accepted, so they disbanded their army. That done, they were arrested. Scrope, Norfolk and others were beheaded under the walls of York, but Northumberland fled to Scotland. Three years later Northumberland invaded England with some Lowland Scots but was defeated and killed at Bramham Moor, near Leeds.

It was only after 1408 that Henry's tenure as king became reasonably secure. It had taken the first nine years of his reign to achieve this, which had given him little opportunity to consider renewing war with France. During the time there had been a French invasion of Wales and Gascony, as well as French and Castilian attacks on Channel ports and shipping. Despite this, the truce officially held, because their own internal problems made it too difficult for each side to return to all-out war.

As we have heard, at that time France was ruled by a regency council, as a result of Charles VI's madness. The regency was dominated by Philip II Duke of Burgundy, uncle to King Charles, and the king's younger brother, Louis, Duke of Orléans. Louis was favoured by Queen Isabeau and was thus in a strong position as Charles VI had become a mere cypher to his wife. On the other hand, Philip of Burgundy was a powerful man in his own right. He had been made Duke of Burgundy by his father, King John II, and had married the great heiress, Margaret, the daughter of Count Louis Mâle. When Mâle died in 1384 Duke Philip increased his dominions to include Flanders, the duchy of Brabant and the counties of Artois and Burgundy (Franche Comté).

Philip Duke of Burgundy died in 1404 and was succeeded by his son, John, who was married to the daughter of Albert I, the Duke of Bavaria, who also ruled Holland, Hainaut, and Zeeland. The death of Duke Philip did nothing to reduce the struggle for power with Louis of Orléans. Both Louis and Duke John were ambitious and energetic young men in their early twenties, but John was merely a cousin to the king, while Louis was his brother. The rivalry between the two men included each of them trying to kidnap the young Dauphin Louis, so as to have him under their respective control. Eventually it was agreed that the dauphin should be put under the guardianship of John of Burgundy, much to the annoyance of Louis of Orléans.

In 1406 these two contestants tried to burnish their credentials by attempting to gain victories over the English. Orléans led a force against the English garrisons of Aquitaine, and Burgundy decided to attack Calais and the Calais Pale. Burgundy had developed a particular interest in Calais because his mother, Margaret of Flanders, had died the previous year and he had been on a tour of his new estates. His visit to Flanders would have brought home to him that Calais fell within the County of Artois, which he had inherited from his mother. Burgundy's presence in Flanders came at a time when the Count of Saint-Pol had been defeated while attacking the English fortress of Marck in the Calais Pale, and the English had retaliated by sending a fleet to attack the Flemish port of Sluys (modern Sluis). The duke immediately sent a force to defend his town of Sluys, at which the English fleet retired to Calais. Having saved Sluys from attack, Burgundy decided it was time to deal with Calais and achieve the honour of returning it to French rule, under his own dominion. He moved his force to occupy Gravelines and began to make preparations for an assault on Calais itself.

Capturing Calais would be no easy operation, so Burgundy began to use his considerable resources to prepare for a siege and assault. He arranged for 200 cannons to be gathered from his dispersed territories and brought to Calais. This was a formidable amount of artillery, but Burgundy also needed additional manpower to be able to mount an assault, once any of the defences had been breached. Burgundy turned to the Council of France in Paris to authorize the money to finance the necessary reinforcements. The king was having one of his bouts of insanity and Orléans persuaded the Council to reject the request because there was insufficient money in the treasury. This might have been a reasonable decision were it not that Orléans and the Queen together had appropriated virtually all the proceeds from recent taxes for themselves. As a result, Burgundy suffered the humiliation of having to abandon the siege and his hopes of military glory. The conflict over Calais turned Burgundy's dislike of Orléans into hatred. The feeling was mutual. The young dauphin's uncle, the Duke of Berry, tried his best to achieve a reconciliation between the two men and it appeared to work – Orléans and Burgundy became publicly reconciled and took communion together.

Nonetheless, it seems that neither of the antagonists was entirely honest in their professions of friendship, as each of them was planning to murder the other. Burgundy achieved this first. In November 1407 he arranged for Orléans to be attacked by seventeen of his men in a Paris street and Orléans was stabbed to death. King Charles happened to be in one of his more lucid periods and denounced Burgundy for having killed his brother, so Burgundy removed himself from Paris. However, as Orléans had made himself unpopular in Paris, the Parisians sided with Burgundy, who returned to the city leading an army of 6,000 men.

This might have been the end of the contest, but Orléans had a young son, Charles, who inherited the duchy. Soon after his father's murder, his mother also died and on her death bed she made Charles swear a solemn oath of vengeance against John of Burgundy. As Charles was only 14 years old, he was not in much of a position to take any action, but his cause was taken up by Bernard VII, Count of Armagnac. The importance of Armagnac's support was recognized by the Orléans' faction, who became known as the 'Armagnacs'. This was strengthened when Charles married

Bernard's daughter a couple of years later. The French nobility took sides: the Dukes of Berry and Brittany supported Orléans and the Armagnacs, against Duke John of Burgundy. The feud between the Armagnacs and Burgundians soon developed into a civil war which was to last for 28 years.

While the Burgundian-Armagnac feud bedevilled France, Calais had continued as normal, apart from the short period in 1406 when the Duke of Burgundy had been preparing to besiege it. Despite considerable piracy in the Channel the average sale of wool had increased to 15,968 a year.[1] The Merchants of The Staple were very well established and included some gifted businessmen. One of these was Richard 'Dick' Whittington who already had been elected twice as Lord Mayor of London, before being elected Mayor of the Calais Staple in 1407, which position he held for seven years. Dick Whittington was an extreme case of success: he was to be re-elected Lord Mayor of London again in 1419, was a Member of Parliament for the City of London and received a knighthood. Whittington was an exemplar of the rise of the merchant classes. He had made a considerable fortune from the import of silks and velvet and the export of wool and broadcloth. Such was his fortune that he provided large loans to the crown and became a trusted royal servant. Few merchants rose to the heights of Whittington, but it was the increasingly prosperous traders, such as members of the Calais Merchants of The Staple, who provided the loans to enable the crown to continue the Hundred Years' War.

The way the Hundred Years' War developed was very much shaped by the Burgundian-Armagnac civil war. Neither the Burgundians nor the Armagnacs were strong enough to achieve a decisive victory over the other. In 1411, Duke John of Burgundy drove the Armagnacs from Paris, and in so doing secured the persons of King Charles and the dauphin. With this semblance of being a royalist, Burgundy then marched against the Armagnacs and besieged the Duke of Orléans in Bourges. With the Armagnac position in peril, Orléans sought aid from King Henry IV. The English king was pleased to give his consent as the terms of the agreement stated that Orléans would acknowledge Henry as Duke of Aquitaine, and his feudal lord, and would assist him in recovering his lost territories. In return Henry would provide 3,000 archers and 1,000 men-at-arms for three months, with Orléans covering their pay (men-at-arms received 1s 6d. per day and archers received 9d. per day).[2]

This all looked very promising for England, but soon after the agreement, the Duke of Berry brought about a reconciliation between Orléans and Burgundy, in which Burgundy agreed to give one of his daughters in marriage to a younger brother of Orléans. The widespread French rejoicing at the reconciliation was dampened by the news that Henry IV's younger son, the fiery Thomas, Duke of Clarence, had landed in Normandy with 4,000 men and had been joined by the counts of Alencon and Richemont. A deputation was rapidly sent to Clarence to say that he was no longer required, as a peace had been agreed. Clarence demanded payment for the expenses of his expedition, and when this was not forthcoming, he advanced into Maine, laying waste all before him. At the same time another body of English troops landed in Calais and occupied the greater part of Artois. While negotiations continued, English troops overran Maine and prepared to invade the duchy of Orléans. This brought the Duke of Orléans to Clarence's camp where he agreed to pay for the whole expedition (209,000 crowns or £35,000). He left his brother, the Duke of Angoulême, as hostage for the payment.

Clarence returned to England satisfied that he had caused massive destruction to Northern France and so avenged the recent French attacks on the English coast. It was even more gratifying to know that the French would cover the cost of this good work. As satisfying as this was, the expedition had done little to change the actual English situation in France. This was to be the last attack on France during Henry IV's reign. For some years the king's health had been deteriorating. He had contracted epilepsy and was becoming increasingly disfigured by leprosy. When the epileptic fits began occurring with greater frequency, he became a semi-recluse in his palace of Eltham but appeared to recover slightly and moved to Westminster. Soon after his arrival he was seized by a prolonged fit, in March 1413 and subsequently died. Henry IV had not been popular and was little mourned. Despite fourteen years of rule, many could not forgive him for having usurped the throne. The stigma of usurpation was lifted for his heir, the popular Henry, Prince of Wales, who became King Henry V at the age of 27 years.

Henry V came to the throne greatly respected as a soldier who had more than proved himself in battle at Shrewsbury and against Glendower. He had also won affection by his informal, friendly manner, which contrasted with his father's reserve. In those times virtually everyone had a deep religious conviction. In the case of Henry these were particularly strong, and he felt he had been given a divine mission – to take the throne of France. He was convinced that the throne was his by right and it was his divine destiny to save France from the present chaos and misery caused by its squabbling rulers. Once he had chastised the inadequate rulers of France and taken the crown, he would be God's instrument and lead a united army from both realms to capture Jerusalem from the infidel.

While Henry was considering these laudable and high-minded objectives, events in France served to confirm his low opinion of its rulers. The peace between the Armagnacs and Burgundians had lasted no more than three months. The situation had become even more complicated as the dissolute dauphin, Louis, quarrelled with Burgundy and Paris began successively to change hands between Armagnac and Burgundian forces. With the government of France in even greater chaos than normal, in July 1414 Henry V sent a formal message to King Charles demanding the French crown. He did not receive a reply. So Henry sent a second message with a new proposal, including that he should marry Catherine, the daughter of King Charles, and receive an enormous dowry of 850,000 crowns (£161,000).

Some desultory negotiations took place but it was clear to all concerned that any demand made by Henry would be completely unacceptable to France. Henry had used the period of the negotiations to raise money from Parliament in the form of loans to support the military preparations necessary for an invasion. Dick Whittington was one of the main providers of loans and through this became close to the king. He was later rewarded with several favourable appointments, such as Commissioner for import duties and financial overseer for the completion of Westminster Abbey. Once Henry had his war funding and manpower in place, he needed to finalise his plans for the invasion. Instead of landing in the safe harbour of Calais, Henry decided to launch his attack on Normandy, having received the Duke of Burgundy's assurance that it would be unopposed. In August 1415 he set sail from Southampton with about 2,000 men-at-arms, and 6,000 archers, in some 1,500 ships, mostly hired or commandeered for royal use.

Henry landed at the mouth of the River Seine and his first action was to besiege Harfleur, the chief port on the north bank of the estuary. It took five weeks before the town surrendered on 22 September. Henry displayed his annoyance at the length of the siege by demanding that the deputies of the town hand him the keys while dressed in hair shirts and with nooses around their necks. Five days later, about 60 French knights and 200 other persons of quality were allowed to leave the town, having promised to return to Calais, as prisoners, by 11 November and remain there until their ransoms were paid. Henry made his uncle, the Earl of Dorset, governor of Harfleur and decided to turn the town into an English colony like Calais. English families were invited to settle there and move into the houses which local citizens had been forced to abandon. The newly acquired town was given an English garrison comprising 300 men-at-arms and 900 archers.

On the face of it this was all very positive; however, Henry's position daily was becoming more precarious. Dysentery was rife among his troops as well as other diseases that accompanied the unhygienic lives of besieging armies. Two thousand of his men died of the epidemic and a further 5,000 had to be sent back to England, being too ill to fight. Henry could have returned to England at this point but decided to keep to his original plan of marching to Calais in a show of strength. When he departed Harfleur on 8 October for the 300 miles march to Calais, Henry's army had been reduced to just 900 men-at-arms and 5,000 archers.

The march went badly. Many of his army were still suffering from dysentery and the lack of provisions meant that men went without food for days on end. The journey was made even longer because the French had destroyed the bridges over the River Somme, forcing Henry to march south to find a ford. By this time a large French army had assembled under the Constable, Charles d'Albert, and was shadowing Henry's movements on the opposite side of the river.

Henry's force was weakening through sickness, malnourishment and exhaustion from their long march. At last, they found a crossing for the Somme just south of Péronne and reached the other bank unopposed. They marched north with new hope as they were only about thirty-five miles from the safety of Calais, and even less from the fortresses of the Calais Pale. On 24 October Henry learnt that d'Albert had deployed his army near the village of Agincourt which effectively blocked the route to Calais. There was no way of avoiding battle against the fresh, well equipped, 20,000-strong French army. Later that day d'Albert sent a herald to Henry offering to allow him to pass freely to Calais, on condition that he relinquished Harfleur and abandoned his claim to the French throne. The offer was refused. Henry remained confident of God's guiding hand and his soldiers remained confident in him as their commander. In both cases the confidence was well placed. The next day Henry deployed his force in a narrow stretch of land between two woods with his archers protected from cavalry by metal tipped stakes. The French began a series of charges, bunched together and through slippery mud, while receiving a storm of arrows. The battle lasted three hours and followed much the same pattern as Crécy. The French suffered massive casualties and eventually fled the field.

The only French success had been an attack on Henry's baggage train but that was mistaken by Henry for French reinforcements attacking from the rear. In order to respond to this new onslaught, Henry gave the order to kill all prisoners. Hundreds were slaughtered before it was realized that it was a false alarm and the order cancelled. By the end of the battle 6,000 French lay dead, not counting the slaughtered prisoners. The English had lost less than 500. Among the French dead were roughly 100 great lords, including three dukes, and 3,060 knights and esquires. Over 1,000 prisoners were taken, including the Duke of Orléans, who was found alive under a pile of bodies.[3]

After the battle Henry made his army sing the *Te Deum* and thank God for the miraculous victory, and then it was off to Calais with prisoners and booty. Henry realized that with the campaigning season over there was no point in further operations in France, so he returned to England on 16 November. On arriving in England, he was received as a conquering hero, seen as blessed by God in the eyes of his own subjects and the rulers of Christendom. In France there had been a fragile truce between Burgundians and Armagnacs while Henry laid siege to Harfleur, but after Agincourt that broke down. The Armagnacs had been the principal participants in the battle and so had suffered the most serious casualties, and their nominal leader, Orléans, had been captured. The Burgundians seized the opportunity, marched on Paris and assumed control of the city.

The continued Armagnac-Burgundian fighting had allowed Henry some eighteen months in which to plan and organize a major expedition to finally secure the French crown. It was a mark of Henry's new status, after Agincourt, that Sigismund, King of Hungary and emperor elect of Germany, asked to visit him in England. Sigismund wanted talks on two subjects. The first was how to resolve the schism in the papacy, as by then there were three elected popes (Benedict XIII in Avignon, Gregory XII in Rome and John XXIII in Pisa). The second equally intractable problem was to resolve the dispute over the crown of France. Sigismund arrived in Calais in 1416 with a retinue of 1,000 horsemen, together with other followers, servants and baggage. Henry was intent on making this a spectacular state visit and after a short stay in Calais, Sigismund and his retinue boarded 300 ships to take them to Dover. The administration and logistics required to host and despatch such a large number of guests must have stretched Calais to the limits. An even greater effort was required to receive and host Sigismund and his entourage when they arrived in England, in a manner that would display the wealth and splendour of the English crown.

Amid lavish entertainment, discussions took place between Sigismund and Henry, together with French envoys who joined them for peace negotiations. In France the Dauphin Louis died and was succeeded by his brother, John. As d'Albert had been among the many dead at Agincourt, John had replaced him as Constable of France. Having become the dauphin, he felt he needed to win military popularity by wresting from England its recent conquest of Harfleur. Dauphin John raised an army, began to besiege the town and hired Genoese galleys to blockade the harbour. Henry was furious that the dauphin should take this action while peace negotiations were in progress. The king's first instinct was personally to lead an army to relieve Harfleur, but he was persuaded by Sigismund to send his brother, John, Duke of Bedford, instead.

Bedford mustered at Rye such vessels as he could gather and arrived off Harfleur on 14 August, to find that he was seriously outnumbered by enemy ships. The French fleet were eager for battle and went to meet him the next day, leaving the Genoese galleys in their secure moorings. Bedford managed to defeat the French fleet, then went on to attack the galleys and boarded them. At the same time the Harfleur garrison attacked the dauphin's besieging army which began to flee. By the end of the day all French and Genoese ships had been destroyed, captured or had fled, and the French army had withdrawn. The duke landed in Harfleur and once he had satisfied himself that it was sufficiently well defended, returned to England with his fleet. Not only had Dauphin John's expedition been a failure, having mounted an attack during the peace negotiations had demonstrated that he had been unchivalrous.

The talks in England had been unable to come up with a solution to the embarrassing number of popes or indeed a formula for peace between England and France. A positive outcome was that Sigismund had concluded an alliance with Henry, in August 1416, and was enrolled as a Knight of the Garter. In September Henry accompanied his imperial guest on his return to Calais, from where, with continued pomp, Sigismund set off with his huge retinue to Constance (modern Konstanz), for further discussions about the papacy. Henry returned to England to prepare to invade France. The preparations included the use of agents to gather intelligence on the Continent's shifting political alliances, and the strengths and vulnerabilities of the forces and fortresses that he would have to overcome in France. Responsibility for a significant part of this intelligence gathering was given to the Earl of Warwick, the Captain of Calais, who was provided with £100 for the purpose. From then on, Calais would continue to be used for intelligence gathering in the surrounding areas, and it became standard for Captains to receive an annual £100 grant for a secret intelligence fund.

At about this time Dauphin John decided to end his alliance with the Armagnacs and come to an agreement with the Duke of Burgundy. They agreed that the dauphin would ally with Burgundy to overcome the Armagnacs, and Burgundy would support the dauphin in driving the English out of France. The Armagnacs were furious about this new coalition and summoned the dauphin to Paris, in the name of the king. The dauphin replied that he would go to Paris only if it was accepted that he could bring the Duke of Burgundy and his followers with him. However, no such visit took place. The situation was resolved when Dauphin John died in agony, in April 1417, exhibiting all the symptoms of poisoning.

Consequently, the 16-year-old Charles, Queen Isabeau's youngest son, became the new dauphin. Charles heartily disliked his mother and had her arrested and placed in close confinement at Tours. At the same time the Count of Armagnac seized all her property. Isabeau was furious and wanted revenge on her son and Armagnac. She managed to escape from Tours on the pretext of attending mass on the outskirts of the town, and then did the unthinkable. She joined her oldest and most detested enemy, the Duke of Burgundy, who had assassinated her beloved Duke of Orléans. Burgundy and his men had been party to the plan and rescued her from her guards. Once safe, Isabeau proclaimed herself regent of France for the period of King Charles' illness, and appointed Burgundy as her lieutenant.

Such was the chaotic situation in France when Henry landed at Harfleur in August 1417. He was accompanied by 16,000 men-at-arms, the same number of archers and a long train of artillery and siege engines which had been transported to Normandy in a fleet of 1,500 ships. This was a well-planned and determined invasion. While Henry was landing at Harfleur, the Duke of Burgundy and Queen Isabeau led an army to march on Armagnac-held Paris. The king and dauphin were both in Paris, as was their court, but Queen Isabeau established her own royal court on the grounds that the king was being held prisoner by the traitorous Armagnacs. During the advance to Paris more and more of the aristocracy joined them and in May they captured Paris. A few days later the Paris mob rose up to kill about 2,500 Armagnac supporters, including the Count of Armagnac himself. The dauphin managed to escape with some followers, but Burgundy and the queen were able to take control of the king and the seat of government. Meanwhile, Henry had been besieging towns in Normandy and had captured Caen, Bayeux and Falais, before moving into winter quarters.

The new campaign season of 1418 began with Henry receiving 15,000 reinforcements and beginning to besiege Rouen in July. Rouen was one of the major cities in France with a strong garrison that had received a reinforcement of 4,000 men. The town walls were well fortified with sixty towers and six gates protected by barbicans. Henry's siege of Rouen was very similar to the siege of Calais by his great-grandfather, Edward III. Like Calais it lasted a long time and caused appalling suffering to its citizens. The food shortage became so severe that the governor decided to expel 12,000 'useless mouths' as they were called. In other words, those who could not fight, such as the elderly, women and children. As with Calais, Henry would not allow the useless mouths to pass through his lines, so they had to settle in the ditch outside the city walls and the majority starved to death. It was not until January the next year, 1419, after 30,000 of the population had died from disease or starvation, that Rouen finally surrendered. Henry was more magnanimous in success than Edward III had been and allowed the remaining citizens to keep their property on payment of 300,000 crowns (£50,000).

Once Rouen had been occupied, finally, it became Henry's base for the remainder of his campaign. Calais remained a vital commercial centre and source of crown revenue, but Harfleur had become Henry's chosen bridgehead into France, and Rouen his headquarters. Having established a firm base in Rouen, Henry soon captured the remainder of Normandy and began to advance on Paris. After escaping from Paris, Dauphin Charles had gathered together numbers of Armagnac supporters and in 1419 he formed a court in Bourges and a Parliament in Poitiers. In July he held a preliminary peace meeting with the Duke of Burgundy and arranged for a further meeting in September, on the bridge at Montereau. When Duke John of Burgundy arrived at the bridge on the appointed day, he was murdered by some of the dauphin's men. This guaranteed that the Burgundian-Armagnac war would continue with fresh vigour.

Duke John was succeeded by his 23-year-old son, Philip, who understandably swore vengeance against the dauphin and decided to make an alliance with King Henry. Prior to this, Burgundy had been relatively neutral in the war between Henry and the dauphin; for example, Duke John had made no attempt to relieve Rouen and had been more than content with the mutual commercial benefit of Calais functioning as the English wool staple. The new alliance bound England and Burgundy firmly together. It was agreed that Henry would support Duke Philip against the dauphin, and Philip would recognize Henry's right to the French crown. King Charles was suffering from his mental problems in Paris and was very much under the influence of Queen Isabeau, who continued to detest their son, the dauphin. These strange circumstances led to the Treaty of Troyes in 1420, allowing King Charles VI to disinherit his son, the dauphin, and making Henry his heir to the crown of France. It was agreed that the English and French royal houses should be united by a marriage between Henry and Catherine, the daughter of King Charles.

Henry and Catherine were married in June 1420, in Troyes Cathedral. In November they entered Paris with the mentally ailing king and his queen, amid rejoicing from the citizens. The three estates were summoned and confirmed the Treaty of Troyes and pronounced the assassins of Duke John of Burgundy to be traitors. Queen Isabeau was declared regent of France until Henry's succession, and the young Charles ceased to be regarded as dauphin. Henry and his bride spent a festive Christmas in Paris before making their way to Calais, being welcomed by all the towns on their route. They sailed to Dover, then travelled to London, where Catherine was crowned queen.

It seemed that Henry had miraculously achieved both the French crown and a lasting peace, but – soon after the coronation celebrations news arrived indicating that neither the crown nor the peace was a forgone conclusion. The dauphin had made an alliance with the Scots who had sent 6,500 troops to support the Armagnac cause. Henry had left his brother, the Duke of Clarence, as commander of Normandy and Clarence had attacked what he thought was a smaller combined Scottish-Armagnac force at Beaugé. It turned out the enemy army was far larger than expected and the English lost 1,200 killed, including Clarence, and 300 men had been taken prisoner. The defeat was not serious militarily, but it was a major boost to the morale of the dauphin and the Armagnacs and showed that English troops were not invincible.

This relatively minor engagement in which the Scots and French combined had lost 1,000 dead, heralded the unwinding of Henry's great achievements. Various French aristocrats in Picardy began harassing the English, both on land and at sea, causing some disruption to merchant ships bound for Calais. In Paris there were anti-English riots which had to be put down by the Duke of Exeter. Henry responded to this by gathering 4,000 men-at-arms and 24,000 archers and landing with them at Calais in June 1421. He then made for Paris where he called on the king, his father-in-law, after which he re-joined his army to march to Chartres which was being besieged by the dauphin. The dauphin pulled back from Chartres and then retreated farther, as Henry advanced. By then the whole of northern France to the Loire was in the hands of the English or their Burgundian allies. Henry spent the remainder of the year besieging the city of Meaux on the Marne, which did not surrender until May. Queen Catherine travelled to join him, having recently given birth to a son at Windsor and the two of them spent Whitsuntide in Paris.

While relaxing in Paris, messengers arrived from the Duke of Burgundy requesting Henry's urgent assistance to relieve Cosne which was being attacked by 20,000 Armagnac–Scottish troops. Henry led his army to save Cosne at which the dauphin's force abandoned the siege, but Henry was struck down by illness at the castle of Vincennes. The cause of his illness is not known; it might have been dysentery or, more probably, heat stroke from riding all day at mid-summer in full armour. Whatever it was, it proved fatal. Before dying he appointed his brother, the Duke of Gloucester, protector of England, and his other brother, the Duke of Bedford, regent of France. Also on the regency council was Henry Beaufort, bishop of Winchester, a son of John of Gaunt and a former Chancellor. These three men would spend the next twenty-five years competing for power. And so, Henry V died in August 1422 at the age of just 36, with his great work nearly, but not totally, completed. The new king of England, and heir to the French throne was now Henry VI, a 9-month-old baby.

Two months after the death of Henry V, his mentally unbalanced father-in-law, King Charles VI, also died. This meant that an 11-month-old baby, King Henry VI, was officially King of England and France. Just as France had been stricken by an incapacitated king and the clashing ambitions of his blood relations, it was now the turn of England. Henry V had been popular, inspirational and had achieved great things in his short life. He had also left his country in considerable debt when he died. He had nearly succeeded at uniting England with France, but that would only have been possible if there had been no French claimants to the French throne. The Dauphin Charles still had supporters in the South of France and would have to be removed if the promised union was to become a reality. Fortunately, despite Henry V's death, the vital alliance with the Duke of Burgundy did not waver. Indeed, it was further cemented the next year by the marriage of Duke Philip's sister, Anne, to John, Duke of Bedford. The close alliance with Burgundy could only help to improve trade between the Calais Staple and its Flemish customers.

Bedford began his time as the regent in France for King Henry VI with some success. He won the battles of Cravant in 1423 and Verneuil in 1424. He was a good soldier and statesman but had the difficult mission of holding down the occupied territories in Northern France, while trying to defeat the dauphin in the south. Lack of funds made a difficult task virtually impossible. The Dauphin Charles claimed the French throne but was ensconced in Bourges, south of the Loire. Charles had established a court but it was wracked by a conflict between his chamberlain and his constable, which became so bitter that fighting broke out between their adherents. Bedford was already busy with risings in Maine but decided to mount a major attack on the dauphin. He requested reinforcements from his brother, Humphrey, Duke of Gloucester, the Protector in England. Rather than providing help, Duke Humphrey took action which completely undermined Bedford's campaign in France. He got married.

Duke Humphrey's bride was Jacqueline of Bavaria, a former wife of the short-lived Dauphin John. After her father had died Jacqueline had inherited Hainault, Holland, Zeeland and Friesland. There were two problems about this marriage: the first was that Jacqueline was already married to Duke John IV of Brabant; the second was that Duke John was a near relative of England's vital ally, the Duke of Burgundy, who also had a claim to Jacqueline's lands through his mother, Margaret of Bavaria. Jacqueline had broken with her husband, the Duke of Brabant, fled to England, where she had met Duke Humphry, and the two had fallen in love.

Duke Humphrey had persuaded one of the popes (Martin V) to agree that Jacqueline's marriage to Duke John should be annulled because of consanguinity. This done, they married, and in late 1424 Duke Humphrey and his wife Jacqueline arrived at Calais with a 6,000-man force. At first the Duke of Burgundy thought they were bringing reinforcements to support his and Bedford's campaign against the Armagnacs. He was horrified to discover that Duke Humphrey had marched into Hainault and taken possession of the county on Jacqueline's behalf. The Duke of Burgundy responded by taking the troops that had been fighting with Bedford against the dauphin and the Armagnacs and using them to support the Duke of Brabant to drive Duke Humphrey and Jacqueline from Hainault.

With the Duke of Burgundy at war with the Protector of England, in Hainault, the English-Burgundian alliance in France was brought to near breaking point. Fortunately, Burgundy did not blame his brother-in-law, Bedford, for Duke Humphrey's actions, and the alliance held. It took about three tense years before Duke Humphrey and Jacqueline ceased to be an issue. Duke Humphrey returned to England to re-establish his authority after a power grab by Henry Beaufort, Bishop of Winchester. In the meantime, Duke Humphrey's force was driven from Hainault, Jacqueline was captured and her marriage to Duke Humphrey was dissolved by the pope. Jacqueline was bullied into a treaty with Duke Philip, which required that she handed all her lands and titles to him, in exchange for a pension. Jacqueline's pension was never paid, and she moved to native Zeeland and married a local nobleman, but died of tuberculosis two years later, aged 35.

However, there were major consequences arising from Duke Humphrey's marriage. It meant that Burgundian troops had been deployed away from supporting the Duke of Bedford against the dauphin and Armagnacs, and also that reinforcements and supplies that should have gone to Bedford were siphoned off by Duke Humphrey to bolster his campaign in Hainault. In addition, Bedford had to return to England for eight months to prevent the rift between Gloucester and Beaufort from turning into a civil war. These Gloucester-related setbacks meant that Bedford had been unable to follow up his victory at Verneuil by striking a decisive blow against the greatly weakened dauphin and the Armagnacs. It also meant that the Duke of Burgundy had become even more powerful, having taken over Jacqueline's extensive lands in the Low Countries. His total possessions now covered a huge area that almost mirrored the short-lived ninth-century Frankish kingdom of Middle Francia.

From 1416 to 1424 Calais had been well out of danger from the war in France, as the dauphin and his supporters were far away, south of the Loire. When the dukes of Burgundy and Brabant took up arms against Duke Humphrey in Hainault, the war drew much closer. Indeed, Calais was very fortunate that the armies of Burgundy and Brabant had stopped short of pursuing Duke Humphrey's force to Calais. Luckily Duke Humphrey's adventure in Hainault did not significantly disrupt Calais commerce with its key trading partners, who had virtually all become subjects of the Duke of Burgundy. In fact, Calais had continued to prosper in the 1420s: wool sales were slightly up at an annual average of 14,425 sacks[4] and the economic activity that accompanied being a major logistic port for the English armies in France had increased. The continued prosperity of Calais and the future of the new Anglo-French kingdom depended on the English-Burgundian alliance. That alliance had had been severely strained by the actions of Duke Humphrey. It was vital that the Duke of Burgundy continued to believe that his interests lay in a continuing alliance with England, rather than his own French countrymen.

Chapter 5

The Loss of France, 1426–64

Once the ill-fated Hainault adventure was out of the way, England scraped together an army of 2,700 to support Bedford, the English regent in France. These reinforcements landed in France in 1428 under the command of the Earl of Salisbury, and was soon enlarged by levies from Normandy, Paris and Burgundy, to increase their strength to 10,000. At a council of war in May, Bedford decided that the English army should advance westwards to Maine.

Salisbury took his force to the area of Chartres and then decided to attack the city of Orléans which he reached in October. Orléans was of major strategic importance. It was the last stronghold of the dauphin and the Armagnacs north of their capital at Bourges. If the English captured Orléans the dauphin's cause would be virtually lost. Salisbury began a long siege of the city. This important siege went on and on, with the English having insufficient troops to invest the city, and Salisbury dying of his wounds. Worse was to come when the Duke of Burgundy decided to withdraw his troops over a disagreement on the possible surrender terms.

Although the siege of Orléans was going nowhere for the English, the dauphin's situation at his small court in Chinon was far more desperate. He must have realized he had run out of credible options when he decided to pursue an incredible one. He gave an audience to an illiterate 17-year-old farm girl named Joan, who had developed the implausible story that she had been visited by saints, who had told her that God wanted her to drive out the English and have the dauphin crowned king, at Rheims Cathedral. The dauphin sent Joan to Poitiers to be examined by eminent theologians and members of his Parliament. Three weeks later they reported that Joan appeared to be genuine. The dauphin therefore granted Joan's request to accompany the army he had just mustered, to attempt to relieve Orléans. Joan's dramatic presence in armour, carrying her sacred banner, was an inspiration to the French troops. She also instilled fear in the besieging English soldiers who believed she had summoned demonic powers to support the dauphin's cause.

Joan's inspiring personality and bearing began to win the respect of the dauphin's commanders. They even started taking her advice to use extensive artillery and frontal assaults on the English fortified positions around Orléans. The success of these French assaults forced the English to abandon the siege and resulted in Joan being widely recognized as God's agent in bringing about the victory. With this clear proof of divine favour, Joan and the dauphin's army went on to capture several English strongholds along the Loire, then inflicted a resounding defeat on a combined English army under the Earl of Shrewsbury and Sir John Falstaff at the Battle of Patay. More than 2,000 of the 5,000-strong English force were killed and numerous men were captured, including Shrewsbury. This major disaster for the English cause opened the way for Joan to march on Rheims. On 16 July 1429 the dauphin was anointed as King Charles VII, at Rheims Cathedral. He could not actually be crowned because the French royal crown was in Paris, under English control. For all that, the ceremony was regarded by many as a coronation that confirmed his title to the crown of France.

After this Charles VII allowed Joan to lead an army to attack Paris. This did not go well. Joan's force was defeated, she was wounded and Charles and his army withdrew to the Loire Valley for the winter. The next year Joan led a force to help relieve the besieged town of Compiègne but was captured and taken prisoner by Burgundian forces. She was eventually sold to the English and taken to Rouen in January 1431 where she was put on trial for heresy. After a four-month trial Joan was convicted of witchcraft, on the grounds that she wore men's clothes. The fact that she had refused to wear women's clothes because she feared she would be raped by her gaolers was not regarded as an excuse. To save her heretical soul she was sentenced to being burnt at the stake, which was achieved on 30 May 1431.

Joan's horrifying death was a tragic end for an amazing person, but she had fulfilled her purpose. Her execution had been satisfactory in a number of ways. For the English and Burgundians, it removed someone whose success in battle had struck fear among their troops, who believed she was a witch who had utilised diabolical power against them. For Charles VII and his generals, it was a relief to be spared the strident opinions of a peasant girl who was being given all the credit for French victories. For the majority of the supporters of Charles VII, her death made her a saintly martyr and an inspiration for French nationalism against English occupation. For Joan herself it might have been some consolation had she known that the impact of her short life led her to being canonised almost four hundred years later, in 1920, and that she remains an inspiration to this day.

While Joan was still a prisoner the Duke of Bedford tried to reverse her greatest triumph. In 1430, on St George's Day (23 April), Bedford brought the young Henry VI to Calais, then took him to Rouen in preparation for being crowned King of France at Rheims Cathedral. Unfortunately, the English could not recapture Rheims, so it was decided to go to Paris for the ceremony. Henry entered Paris in state accompanied by his principal nobles and 3,000 horsemen. On Henry's tenth birthday, 16 December 1431, he was crowned King Henry II of France, in Notre-Dame Cathedral, by his great-uncle, Henry Beaufort. Despite the pomp, this was a hollow achievement. The coronation was a purely English affair and was not attended by any of the French nobility. There was no rejoicing by the Parisians, who were beginning to regard the English as an occupying power. Within a few days Henry returned to Rouen where he remained for a year, before visiting Calais and returning to London.

Joan may have been dead but her spirit continued to inspire the supporters of Charles VII and the Armagnacs, who wanted to avenge her death. Bedford's forces received a number of defeats and setbacks, including the loss of Chartres. Worst of all, the vital alliance with Burgundy was taking strain. Bedford's wife, Anne, the sister of the Duke of Burgundy, had died in November 1432. Two months later Bedford married Jacquetta of Luxemburg, a vassal of Burgundy, without telling the duke. The Duke of Burgundy was furious with Bedford for the disrespect shown to his sister. Relations between the two men began moving towards breaking point and Burgundy began to receive overtures from Charles VII, but the English-Burgundian alliance just managed to struggle on.

The winter of 1433 was very harsh with the Seine freezing over and bread being scarce in English-occupied Paris. The government in England was on the verge of bankruptcy caused by the never-ending war in France. The Calais garrison had not been paid their wages and mutinied. They seized the wool belonging to the Merchants of The Staple and ejected

Bedford's deputy, Sir William Oldhall, from the town. Bedford called a crisis meeting in Calais which was attended by Gloucester and their half-brother, Henry Beaufort, who had increased his power by having been appointed a cardinal. Bedford decided that the best way forward was to promise to pay the soldiers from the local wool customs. This ended the mutiny but as soon as the crisis was over Bedford withdrew the offer, arrested the mutineer leaders, executed four of them and banished the rest.

The Calais crisis was over but the problem of the lack of funding to prosecute the war continued, which persuaded Bedford and Gloucester to consider peace negotiations. The papal schism had been resolved and a single pope had been appointed, based in Rome, who called a peace finding conference at Arras in 1435. As might be expected this made no progress. The English delegation insisted on Henry VI's right to the French crown then temporarily withdrew, to await a response. While they were absent the delegates representing Burgundy and Charles VII finalized their master's informal agreement to end the Burgundian-Armagnac feud. This resulted in the Treaty of Arras in which Burgundy recognized Charles as King of France; in turn, Charles condemned the murder of Burgundy's father, promised to punish the perpetrators and transferred some lands to Burgundy for his lifetime. The English delegation returned to Arras to discover this fait accompli: while their backs had been turned their principal ally had become their enemy.

The defection of the Duke of Burgundy from the English alliance was the death knell of a dual Anglo-French monarchy. The Duke of Bedford died just before the end of the conference, which deprived England of a distinguished general and able regent in France, and 13-year-old Henry VI of a dependable uncle. He was left with his last remaining uncle, Humphrey, Duke of Gloucester and his great-uncle, Cardinal Beaufort, both of whom were vying to be his principal advisor. Divisions in advice to the king meant that it took six months of wrangling over who should succeed Bedford as regent of France, during which time the English forces in France were leaderless. Eventually Duke Humphrey won the contest and his appointee, Richard, Duke of York, was made regent. In the meantime, the English had lost territory in Normandy and then Paris. The Parisians had long been supporters of the Duke of Burgundy and opened their gates to his forces, which resulted in Lord Willoughby and the English garrison retreating to the Bastille and eventually surrendering. The loss of Paris was the end of any pretence that France was ruled by an English king. The Duke of York was forced to remove the seat of government to Rouen.

Calais itself came under threat. The Duke of Burgundy decided to bring all the Low Countries under his control, and that included Calais. Calais and the Calais Pale extended eighteen miles along the coast, from between Wissant in Picardy in the west, to Gravelines in Flanders in the east, and eight to ten miles inland. It was protected by its walls, moats and castle, together with the Rissbon fort at the entrance to the port. The Pale had a string of forts at Sangatte, Marck, Belingham, Guines, Hammes and Oye. Burgundy realized that the town and its outlying defences made a formidable military objective, so, in 1436, he began making extensive preparations for its capture. These preparations did not go unnoticed, and spies informed the English court in London of Burgundy's intentions. Duke Humphrey gathered a number of reinforcements – 2,000 men, 1,600 of them archers – and Sir John Radely, the Captain of Calais, was ordered to prepare to defend the town and the Pale.

Burgundy selected the civilian militias of Bruges and Ghent to conduct the siege and collected massive artillery and siege engines to overcome the defences of the town and its surrounding forts. Three very large cannon were transported all the way from Burgundy over forty-nine days, requiring roads and bridges to be reinforced because of their weight. The largest cannon was separated and travelled on two huge wagons, requiring forty-eight horses to pull the barrel and a further thirty-six to pull the chamber. The total weaponry transported by the Duke of Burgundy to the Calais Pale included ten bombards (mortars firing stone projectiles), sixty *veuglaires* (long barrelled breach loading cannon), 230 arbalests (giant crossbows), 450 culverins (handguns), several thousand cavalry lances and 450,000 crossbow bolts.[1]

Once the Duke of Burgundy had assembled a formidable force of 30,000 men, he began to attack the strongholds in the Calais Pale, in June of 1436. Soon the forts at Oye, Marck, Belingham and Sangatte had been captured and only the castle at Guines held out. By 9 June the duke's army was encamped before Calais, awaiting the arrival of a fleet of 35 ships and 1,400 marines from Sluis, to blockade the port. A contrary wind delayed the Burgundian fleet from sailing out of Sluis but on 25 June it arrived in Calais and then did little more than scuttle a few old ships in the harbour, in order to blockade it, before departing. As soon as it was low tide the English garrison went out into the harbour and removed the blockading ships. The harbour was clear for the English reinforcements to land, unopposed.

A couple of days later a sortie went out from the garrison and destroyed a wooded stockade manned by part of the Ghent contingent, killing the occupants. By this time word was circulating that English reinforcements were about to disembark, and the rest of the Ghent contingent decided it was time to return home. The next day the men of Bruges felt discretion was the better part of valour and departed so quickly that they abandoned their provisions and most of their artillery. The Duke of Burgundy was obliged to raise the siege and withdraw.

On 2 August Duke Humphrey arrived in Calais with 8,000 men and began an eleven-day raid into Flanders, burning villages and fields and driving herds of cattle into Calais. This was by no means a resurgence of English power in France, but it was a humiliation for the Duke of Burgundy that would make him think twice about any future attack on Calais. Duke Humphrey returned to England and resumed his feud with Cardinal Beaufort. Duke Humphrey, Richard Duke of York and the majority of the nobility wanted to continue the war with France, but Beaufort wanted peace. The young Henry VI was not a typical Plantagenet. He was a shy, scholarly, pious and trusting person who disliked bloodshed. In 1337 the king was recognized as being old enough to rule by himself. As a result, Beaufort held sway on English policy and there were no more major expeditions to France. Calais could continue as normal, although with its trade much restricted by the Duke of Burgundy.

The loss of revenue from Calais was a factor in Beaufort trying to find a settlement for the war in France. Beaufort travelled to Calais in May 1438 to try to launch peace negotiations. In January the next year he invited Duchess Isabella, the wife of the Duke of Burgundy, to Calais and during discussions reached an agreement, in principle, that the wool trade could be resumed. A larger conference took place six months later at which Charles VII was represented, but it was unable to find common ground for a lasting peace between England and France. Nevertheless, the conference resulted in a three-year commercial treaty with the Duke of Burgundy, which allowed the export of wool to continue as normal.

For his part, the Duke of Burgundy wanted to close the final chapter of the Armagnac-Burgundian feud through reconciliation with Duke Charles of Orléans, the nominal head of the Armagnac faction.

Duke Charles of Orléans was now a middle-aged 45-year-old, who had been held captive in England since Agincourt. As a sign of good will, Cardinal Beaufort agreed to release Orléans. During his twenty-five years in England Orléans had become an anglophile, and far from being a threat was prepared to be an agent for peace. He travelled to Calais, then to Flanders, to become reconciled with the Duke of Burgundy. He later married Marie, daughter of the Duke of Cleves, and returned to his estates in Orléans where he lived in peace to the age of seventy-one.

Duke Humphrey had been completely opposed to the release of Orléans and the power struggle between him and Beaufort was becoming increasingly bitter. The next year Beaufort found an opportunity to destroy Duke Humphrey's reputation. Humphrey had married his mistress, Eleanor Cobham, and Beaufort had received information that she had consulted astrologers about the health of the king. Eleanor denied this but was convicted of witchcraft, forced to divorce her husband, undergo a humiliating barefooted penance and then was permanently imprisoned on the Isle of Mann. This broke Duke Humphrey and he retired from public life.

Cardinal Beaufort's closest associate was William de la Pole, Earl of Suffolk, who gradually took over from Beaufort as chief advisor to Henry VI. In 1444 Suffolk was the main instigator of peace negotiations at Tours which resulted in a two-year truce with France, sealed by a marriage between the 24-year-old Henry VI and the attractive Margaret of Anjou. Margaret was the niece of King Charles VII, eight years Henry's junior, but confident and strong willed. Her father was René, Duke of Anjou, titular king of Naples, Sicily and Jerusalem. However, he had lost those lands and has been described as "a man of many crowns but no kingdoms". René was in debt and in no position to provide a dowry for Margaret, but Henry and Suffolk were so eager to end the war that they agreed that England would bequeath Maine and Anjou to Margaret, who would hold them as fiefs to the French crown.

Margaret was crowned Queen of England in 1445 but soon after their marriage Henry began to show early signs of mental illness. There followed a struggle to rule through a weak and compliant king. Duke

Humphrey was in retirement but was still popular with the people, so, to be on the safe side he was arrested for treason and died two days later. Humphrey probably died of a stroke but it was widely believed that Suffolk had arranged to have him poisoned. Humphrey's great rival, Cardinal Beaufort died soon after, and Suffolk assumed the role of Henry's chief councillor. But there were two other royal relations who sought power.

There was Edmund Beaufort, a grandson of John of Gaunt, who had been made Duke of Somerset while serving as Lieutenant of France during the 1444–8 truce, and then became Commander when war resumed. Then there was Richard, Duke of York, a grandson of Edward III on both his father's and mother's sides, who arguably had a stronger claim to the throne than King Henry himself. He was a popular figure who had fought with distinction in France and then had been made Henry's Lieutenant in Ireland, to keep him out of the way.

While these power struggles were taking place the English situation in France was deteriorating. Maine and Anjou had passed to Charles VII and provided the gateway to Normandy. Charles had matured into an effective king who put the royal finances on a firm footing and created a standing army with good military leaders. Having convinced most of the French nobility to acknowledge him, rather than Henry VI, as the true king of France, he marched into Normandy. Soon he had taken Rouen and by 1449 Henry VI had lost Normandy in its entirety. It should not be supposed that this loss was taken lightly in England. Most of the baronage and people were furious and blamed Suffolk, the king's principal advisor, who had been responsible for both the royal marriage to a French woman and for giving away the strategic counties of Maine and Anjou. In January 1450 Parliament began to impeach Suffolk for treason, while the population was calling for his execution. King Henry intervened to rescue one of his favourite advisors and commuted his sentence to five years banishment.

There was general fury that Suffolk had been reprieved from execution. Two thousand people assembled at St Giles to try to seize him as he was discharged, but Suffolk managed to escape to his estates. He then made his getaway, sailing in a small vessel from Ipswich for Calais. Suffolk's enemies heard of this and one of the largest ships in the navy was sent to intercept him and force him to come on board. As he stepped on deck he was received by the captain with the ominous greeting, 'Welcome traitor!'

Suffolk was then subjected to a mock trial, beheaded and his body thrown on the sands near Dover. Suffolk's savage murder was received with general approval as a fitting punishment for a man blamed for the loss of so much territory in France.

King Henry and his wife Margaret were angered by Suffolk's murder and threatened to punish the people of Kent for supplying the naval vessel that had captured him, their favourite. This in turn led to a serious rising in Kent under Jack Cade, which entered London but eventually dispersed after promises of pardon and redress for grievances. Needless to say, these undertakings were forgotten as soon as the rebellious army had disbanded, and Cade was later hunted down and killed. While Cade's rebellion had been short-lived it also had been potentially very dangerous and showed the growing opposition to a weak king and his French wife, who between them had lost so much of Henry V's hard-won domains.

Royal popularity was not enhanced when Henry and Margaret replaced Suffolk with the Duke of Somerset as their principal minister. Somerset had been the commander of English forces in France since 1448 and so had been more directly responsible for the loss of Normandy even than Suffolk. Richard Duke of York had been furious at the losses in France and had heartily disliked both Suffolk and Somerset. Indeed, he may well have been behind Suffolk's murder. In 1449 he had returned to England from his post as Lieutenant of Ireland and had brought with him a retinue of 600 armed men. Once back in England York established himself as leader of the opposition, which threatened his cousin, Somerset, and the increasingly unpopular royal government.

Henry VI had not produced an heir and it was assumed that he never would. Both Somerset and York began to hope that the king might nominate them as his heir. While they were competing for power, the situation in France went from bad to worse. Having taken Normandy, Charles VII turned his attention to removing the English from Gascony. The end came in 1453 when England's most experienced general, John Talbot, Earl of Shrewsbury, was defeated and killed at the Battle of Castillon. Bordeaux was lost soon after. Calais and the Calais Pale were all that remained of Henry VI's French domains. As well as being commander of the English forces in France, Somerset was also Captain of Calais, so he was responsible for England's last foothold in France. The decisive French victory at Castillon was the final battle of the Hundred

Years' War. Although the conflict continued, officially, for another twenty years, England had lost the war, and with crown debts of over £400,000,[2] was in no position to finance another army to attack France. Somerset had presided over the humiliating reversal of Henry V's great work.

Throughout the struggles for power in England, Calais had remained a vital commercial centre and the principal source of revenue for maintaining the occupation of France. The loss of Normandy enhanced the position held by Calais, and it reverted to being England's principal port on the French north coast. The loss of Bordeaux and the rest of France meant that Calais had become the only English port in France, and so the last bridgehead for a future re-conquest. It was not known at the time that such a re-conquest was never to occur, so Calais shone as a beacon of hope for the happy day when England would avenge its ignominious defeats and win back that which was hers, by right of conquest and treaty. The post of Captain of Calais became even more important than in the past, because its holder was head of what had become England's last remaining force in France.

The year of Castillon was also the year in which an heir, rather unexpectedly, was born to King Henry. The birth of this little Prince of Wales, called Edward, was not universally celebrated. It had been clear to all that Henry had been suffering from mental illness for some time, and it was thought this might have been inherited from his maternal grandfather, Charles VI. Henry was known to hate any physical contact and his enemies had believed that he was incapable of fathering a child. They assumed that the birth of Prince Edward was the result of adultery by his wife, Margaret of Anjou, possibly with Somerset. The pious Henry explained the conception as a miracle. Despite the king's delight at producing an heir, his condition suddenly deteriorated into a catastrophic mental breakdown. He became completely unresponsive, unable to speak, and had to be led from room to room. At first the Council tried to continue as normal, hoping that the king would recover, but by March the following year there had been no improvement and the Council decided to appoint a Lord Protector of the Realm. With Parliament so angry about the mismanagement that had led to the loss of France, it chose Richard, Duke of York, for the post, much to the consternation of Queen Margaret.

York assumed power in April 1454 and immediately had the unpopular Somerset impeached by Parliament, sacked as Captain of Calais, and committed to the Tower. York made himself Captain. A few months later the king made a partial recovery; he dismissed York as Captain and ordered that Somerset be released and his sentence commuted to five years banishment.

For some time, Henry's wife, Queen Margaret, had been taking the lead in royal affairs. Margaret was only 24 years old, but was now the mother of the heir to a throne occupied by her deranged husband. Margaret needed Somerset's support against the ambitious York and had him reinstated as Captain of Calais. Margaret called a Great Council in the name of her husband but did not invite York or his known supporters. The most prominent of these were the Earl of Salisbury and his son, the Earl of Warwick, who had married an heiress, Anne de Beauchamp, and become the greatest landowner in England. While some nobles supported Henry VI out of loyalty to the crown, there was little affection for the queen. Margaret was not seen only as an overbearing female who manipulated the king, but also a Frenchwoman, and was blamed for losing England's French territory and so depriving much of the English nobility of their French lands and possessions.

A weak monarchy, managed by an unpopular French woman, was unlikely to go unchallenged by a dissatisfied nobility that included the Duke of York, who had as strong a claim to the throne as King Henry VI himself. The scene was set for the chaos which would be called the Wars of the Roses, in which the country was split between supporters of the Lancastrian line of Henry VI, (the Lancastrians) and followers of the Duke of York (the Yorkists). This desperate period of strife was to last thirty years, with first one side gaining ascendency, then the other. Whoever was on top aimed to ensure that their supporters held the vital port and garrison of Calais.

York and his followers took up arms and defeated the royal forces at the Battle of St Albans in May 1455. The day had been won mainly by a charge led by the 26-year-old Earl of Warwick, which had taken the Lancastrians by surprise. The battle resulted in the death of Somerset and other leading Lancastrians, the arrest of King Henry, and York again becoming Lord Protector. That year the Duke of York made his powerful supporter, Warwick, the Captain of Calais. York was regent but the king and his formidable queen were still alive and York was ruling on their behalf. The situation became complicated when Henry temporarily recovered his wits and Queen Margaret ruled through him, but with York a major presence in the background. Henry Beaufort had inherited his father's title after his death at St Albans and had become Duke of Somerset and leader of the Lancastrian supporters of the king.

For the next three years attempts were made to reconcile the two factions of the royal family, but these came to naught. Margaret became the de facto ruler while York and his supporters continued to pose a threat to her rule. While York had his claim to the throne, Warwick was the far greater landowner, had a much larger retinue, was an equally successful soldier and would soon enjoy greater popularity. It was Warwick who was to dominate the politics of England for the next ten years. There was another reason why Warwick would eventually earn the nickname of the 'king-maker': as Captain of Calais, he controlled the closest thing to an English standing army, at that time.

Warwick fully exploited his position as Captain of Calais and began exerting the power it brought. In 1457 a French nobleman named de Bézé led an expedition from Honfleur in north-west France which sacked Sandwich, in Kent. De Bézé was known to be a supporter of Queen Margaret and this added to her unpopularity. Hoping to alleviate this she gave Warwick a three-year commission to command a fleet to protect the English coast. Warwick accepted this responsibility with enthusiasm, assisted by his cousin, Thomas Neville, who was already an accomplished military commander. However, funding was a problem. The royal coffers were bare, the Calais garrison was owed four years of pay in arrears, which amounted to £37,000.[3] In late 1458 Warwick used his fleet to attack merchant ships from Lübeck and Spain and used the plunder to pay his Calais garrison.

The success of this piracy resulted in Warwick being very popular with the garrison, and the merchants of London. They supported his action because it had removed foreign competitors for English trade with Flanders. The merchants of Calais were already extremely annoyed with Queen Margaret because she had raised money by granting licences to Italian merchants to sell English wool, without going through the Calais Staple. They were delighted with Warwick and his fleet for having achieved command of the sea so vital for secure commerce between London, Sandwich and Calais. Intentionally or not, Warwick was building loyal support from three important sources: the soldiers and sailors of Calais, the rich merchants of The Staple, and the City of London. Added to this, Warwick had made it his business to establish good relations with the Duke of Burgundy.

Despite all this, Warwick was not popular with Queen Margaret. She had been angered by Warwick's unauthorized attack of friendly foreign shipping and summoned him to London to explain himself before the king's council. When Warwick arrived in London violence broke out between his retinue and the royal household, and Warwick returned to Calais claiming that his life had been threatened. Margaret regarded Warwick's refusal to appear before the Council as defiance of Henry's authority and decided to bring matters to a head with York, Warwick and their followers. In June 1459 she summoned a council to Coventry, relying on her strong support in the Midlands. York, Salisbury and Warwick refused to attend because they rightly feared they would be arrested, so Margaret indicted them for rebellion.

In September 1459 a 5,000-strong Yorkist force raised by the Earl of Salisbury set out from Yorkshire, to link up with the main Yorkist army under the Duke of York at Ludlow Castle in Shropshire. Queen Margaret ordered Baron Audley to intercept Salisbury, which he did, at Blore Heath in Staffordshire. Audley's Lancastrian army of 10,000 was routed and Salisbury was able to reach Ludlow. Shortly afterwards, Warwick arrived in Ludlow to join them, together with his Calais contingent. The Wars of the Roses had resumed in earnest. But this Yorkist success did not last long. The combined Yorkist armies were met at Ludford, near Ludlow in Shropshire, by a much larger Lancastrian force, nominally under Henry VI himself, but commanded by the Duke of Buckingham. This was the first time King Henry had taken to the field in person. Thus, for the Yorkists to engage in battle was to take up arms against the anointed king, not just his advisers.

Among the troops Warwick had brought from Calais were 600 men led by Andrew Trollope, who decided he could not fight against his sovereign. That night Trollope took his men and others from the Yorkist forces, to defect to the king. Once this was discovered York, Salisbury and Warwick realized they faced certain defeat, so they deserted their army and fled to Wales. The leaderless Yorkist army then knelt in submission before King Henry and received his pardon. In his haste to escape York had not only deserted his army but also his wife and children, who were captured in Ludlow and placed under the care of the Duchess of Buckingham. York then returned to Ireland, and together with his eldest son, Edward the Earl of March, and Salisbury and Warwick, sailed to Calais. King Henry resumed his kingship with Queen Margaret running the country, but not for long.

King Henry was superficially back in control, York and Warwick were attainted as traitors, and Henry Beaufort, Duke of Somerset, was appointed Captain of Calais, to replace Warwick. Somerset crossed the Channel but was refused entry to Calais by Warwick's supporters. The Wars of the Roses had come to Calais. Somerset managed to capture the outlying fortress of Guînes and appointed Andrew Trollope as bailiff. This was followed by a number of skirmishes between the Calais garrison and the Lancastrians holding Guînes, until April 1460 when Somerset was decisively defeated at the Battle of Newnham Bridge (called Pont de Neullay then, and Pont de Neuilly now). Somerset returned to England leaving Calais and the Calais Pale in the hands of the Earl of Warwick and the Yorkists.

Somerset then decided to construct a fleet in Sandwich in preparation for another assault on Calais, but Warwick carried out a raid on Sandwich and made off with the ships. Soon after this a force from Calais under the leadership of Warwick's uncle, William Neville, the Baron Fauconberg, landed in Sandwich and overcame the Lancastrian garrison, which placed the port in Yorkist hands. Warwick now had a secure port for landing an invasion force from Calais.

In June 1460 Warwick, with his father, Salisbury, and Edward, Earl of March, landed in Sandwich with 2,000 men from Calais. Having received news of the invasion, Henry VI and his commander, the Duke of Buckingham, had taken a defensive position near Northampton. In the ensuing battle the Lancastrian army was routed, Buckingham and several other nobles were killed, and King Henry VI was captured. Henry was treated with respect and escorted to London. The Duke of York returned from Ireland and resumed the post of Protector. York made it clear to Parliament that he wanted the crown but it was finally agreed that he would be King Henry's heir, instead of Henry's son, Edward of Lancaster. One of the people who did not agree with this was Queen Margaret, who raised an army in the north under the young Duke of Somerset. On 30 December 1460 her Lancastrian army defeated the Yorkists at the Battle of Wakefield, killing both the Duke of York and the Duke of Salisbury. The next year Margaret followed this success by defeating Warwick at the second Battle of St Albans – and freeing her husband. With York dead and Warwick defeated, it seemed that the red rose of Lancaster had at last triumphed over the white rose of York.

King Henry was ostensibly back on the throne, but he was in a sorry state. When he had been rescued at St Albans he was found singing and laughing as the battle raged, and sadly his return to the throne did not result in his return to sanity. London refused to open its gates to Henry, fearing that Margaret's northern army would pillage the city. So, Margaret and Henry moved north with their army, while Warwick and Edward, Earl of March, were made welcome in London. The death of the Duke of York at Wakefield meant that his son, Edward, had become the leader of the Yorkist faction. Edward displayed all the attributes that one hoped to find in a king. He was of royal blood, brave, intelligent, energetic, affable and physically impressive, being handsome and 6 ft 4 in tall, which made a stark contrast to the devout, kind-hearted and mentally unstable Henry VI. Certainly, most Londoners felt that Edward's head would better fit the crown and proclaimed him 'King Edward VI'.

Having taken the crown, at least nominally, Edward and his Yorkist army moved north and met the Lancastrian force, led by Somerset, on 29 March 1461, Palm Sunday, at Towton in Yorkshire. Warwick was recovering from a wound so his large contingent was led by his uncle, Baron Fauconberg. Three-quarters of England's peers and about 50,000 men took part in ten hours of bloody hand-to-hand combat during a snowstorm, resulting in a crushing defeat for Somerset. Many among the Lancastrian army drowned as they fled under a hail of arrows across the flooded Cock Beck (a river), but some survivors managed to escape across a bridge of fallen bodies. It was probably the largest battle ever fought on English soil and was a resounding Yorkist victory. After the battle, Margaret and King Henry escaped to Scotland while Edward returned to London. After Parliament had formally deposed Henry, Edward was crowned King Edward IV. It seemed that the Yorkists had won the Wars of the Roses.

The only problem was that England now had two kings. Edward might be king, but King Henry VI was still alive, having fled to Scotland with Margaret. Try as she might, Margaret was unable to raise an army in Scotland where a power struggle was raging between the regent of the 8-year-old king and the Douglas family. Margaret decided to turn to France for help and despatched Somerset to request aid. King Charles VIII had died and his son, Louis XI, had become king. Louis was a cunning and devious person whom his subjects had nicknamed *'l'universelle aragne'* ('the universal spider'). Such a man was unlikely to be moved by the plight of Margaret and Henry, both of whom were his cousins. Somerset had no success with Louis, so Margaret herself travelled to France to beg for his support. While Louis was not moved by family loyalty, he seized the opportunity to further his self-interest. He reached an agreement with Margaret that Henry would surrender the rights of the English crown to Calais, in exchange for 20,000 livres. Of course, Calais was not Margaret's to give; it was under Warwick's control and therefore firmly in Yorkist hands. Nevertheless, it meant that Louis could take it, if Henry regained his throne, or claim it by right in a future military campaign. Margaret's treasonous action confirmed her enemies' worst prejudices against a French queen.

Margaret used the money from Louis to raise a 2,000-strong force in Normandy, and then landed them in north-east England and combined forces with Somerset. These efforts by Margaret ended in defeat in May 1464 at the Battle of Hexham. After the battle Somerset was captured in a barn and beheaded. Margaret managed to escape to France, but King Henry was captured and placed in the Tower of London. King Edward IV was now at last firmly on the throne, with his friend and principal ally, Warwick, the richest and most powerful peer in the kingdom, at his side. Much of the basis of Warwick's power had come from Calais. In November 1460 Warwick had been made Lord Warden of the Cinque Ports (a group of coastal towns in Kent, Sussex and Essex) and Governor of Dover Castle; he was also Keeper of the Seas and thus responsible for the royal fleet in the Channel. Later Edward agreed to Warwick becoming captain of all the separate garrisons on the Calais Pale, including Guînes and Hames. Warwick had ensured that only men who were personally loyal to him were placed in command, such as his uncle, Baron Fauconberg, who was made Earl of Kent and acted as his Deputy in Calais and as Keeper of the Seas. The Channel fleet consisted of royal ships and others which Warwick himself had acquired. Warwick fully exploited his post of Lord Warden to ensure the loyalty of the Cinque Ports, particularly Sandwich, which was the principal port for Calais. He also ensured that his influence extended to south-east England and maintained close relations with the City of London. Warwick had built up a small empire for himself, and the centre of that empire was Calais.

Warwick was feudal lord of extensive lands in England but the majority of those who might rally to his banner were not professional soldiers. England's nearest thing to a standing army was based in Calais and the Calais Pale. There was a garrison of 260 men for the town, a further 50 for the castle and 18 for the Rissbon fort which guarded the harbour. The Pale forts were also garrisoned, with 100 men at Guînes and 41 at Hames. In addition, Warwick had acquired a locally recruited force of 300 men,[4] plus a further 200 men who belonged to the retinues of the captains in the town and The Pale, who were answerable to him. To all this could be added the unknown number of privately hired soldiers of the Calais merchants and officials. For example, Sir John Paston has recorded that he hired four archers out of his own wages, who wore his own livery.

All these soldiers were experienced professionals, as was shown by their pay –eight pence per day (or £12 15s 8d. per year) for a man-at-arms or a mounted archer.[5] Accepting that an annual income of £10 a year was considered sufficient to allow the recipient to live the life of a gentleman, it will be appreciated that the soldiers in Calais were of very high quality. In short, as Captain of Calais, Warwick had at his disposal a substantial force that could be used to exert considerable military power in England. The Calais base and its force had already been a major factor in establishing Warwick as the 'king-maker' of Edward IV. It had had also helped him become King Edward's most powerful subject. This begs the question: for how long would Edward tolerate a subject so powerful that he could be a king-maker?

Chapter 6

The King Maker's Calais, 1464–85

With Edward IV firmly on the throne, Calais became England's centre of diplomacy with continental Europe in general, and France and Burgundy in particular. In this consular role Calais had its own diplomatic staff and its own pursuivant junior herald John Walter, who worked with Warwick's personal pursuivant. Warwick was often away from Calais and when his uncle, Baron Fauconberg, died in 1463, Warwick appointed the loyal Lord John Wenlock to replace him as Lieutenant of Calais, and to supervise Warwick's diplomatic initiatives in his absence.

One of these initiatives was to arrange a French alliance by negotiating a marriage for Edward IV to Bona of Savoy, who was the sister-in-law of King Louis XI of France. These arrangements were progressing well, only for Warwick to find that Edward had secretly married the beautiful Elizabeth Woodville. Warwick was furious that Edward had married behind his back and made him look a fool to the French. Over time Warwick and other nobles would become increasingly incensed when Edward showered honours and wealth on Elizabeth's numerous family members. Her father was made the First Earl Rivers and became Lord Treasurer, and her immediate family garnered two dukedoms, three earldoms and one baronage.

On the same day that Edward informed his council about his marriage he informed them that he intended to debase the coinage by lowering the gold and silver content of coins. The devaluation had a major impact on England's trading partners in Flanders, and the Duke of Burgundy retaliated by banning the purchase of English cloth. This in turn had a major impact on the cloth and wool merchants of London and Calais. Edward's finances were already bad enough without losing vital revenues from the Calais Staple. For the next couple of years there was intense diplomatic activity while France and Burgundy tried to reach a solution, complicated by the fact that a civil war was being waged between Louis XI and Duke Philip of Burgundy.

An added complication was that Louis had offered to support Queen Margaret to regain Henry VI's throne, in exchange for Calais. In order to counter the alliance between Louis and Margaret, Warwick continued to press for an alliance with the French, while Elizabeth Woodville's father, the increasingly powerful Earl Rivers, wanted an alliance with Burgundy. King Edward supported Rivers against Warwick and when Duke Philip died in 1467, Edward concluded an alliance with his son and heir, Duke Charles I ('Charles the Bold') which was sealed by the marriage of Edward's sister, Margaret, to the young duke. By the end of September that year the trade embargo had been lifted, much to the relief of the members of the Calais Staple. Rejoicing by The Staple was soon marred by Edward passing the Act of Retainer which made The Staple solely responsible for the payment and maintenance of the garrison. As this amounted to an annual £12,000 in peacetime, and £19,000 in times of war, it was a most unwelcome drain on the finances of The Staple.[1]

Earl Rivers and the Woodville family had become Edward's favourites and were displacing Warwick and his followers. As early as 1465 Rivers had been appointed to replace Warwick as Keeper of Seas, but Warwick had not easily relinquished his power. He retained his personal fleet and Rivers was largely ignored, so strong was Warwick's influence, particularly in Sandwich, and of course in Calais. Warwick received another setback when his brother, George Neville, Archbishop of York, was dismissed as Chancellor. Relations between Edward and Warwick deteriorated further, to the extent that in the winter of 1467-8 Warwick stayed away from court and kept to his estates in the north. Other nobles had begun turning against Edward and his Woodville favourites, who were particularly disliked for having supported the Lancastrian side in the civil war. Chief among the dissidents was George, Duke of Clarence, Edward's younger brother and the heir to the throne, at that time.

Edward realized that opposition was building against him when he learnt that John, Lord Wenlock, Warwick's Deputy in Calais, was involved in a Lancastrian conspiracy. Two years later, Warwick's brother-in-law, the Earl of Oxford, was found to have been scheming with the Lancastrians. Warwick instigated an uprising in Yorkshire which gave him and the Duke of Clarence an excuse to assemble a force, ostensibly to put down the rebellion. King Edward realized that his brother and Warwick were plotting against him, so when Clarence announced that he wanted to marry Warwick's eldest daughter, Isabella, Edward refused to allow the match. In July 1369, in defiance of the king, Warwick and Clarence travelled to Calais where Clarence was married to Isabella by Warwick's brother, the Archbishop of York, at the church of St Nicholas. Clarence, Warwick and the archbishop then issued the Calais manifesto condemning the king's covetous advisers and then sailed back to England with a Calais contingent, intending to link up with a rebellion that Warwick had orchestrated in Yorkshire.

London opened its gates to Clarence and Warwick, and they then moved north against King Edward who was in Northampton. Their advance guard joined the Yorkshire rebels near Banbury and confronted a Welsh army under the Earl of Pembroke which had come to reinforce the king's army. A battle took place at Edgecote Moor in which Clarence and Warwick's forces were victorious. In the pursuit after the battle, Pembroke was killed, Earl Rivers was executed, and King Edward was captured and held prisoner. Clarence and Warwick attempted to rule in the king's name but did not receive the backing of the majority of the nobility. Riots ensued in London and the country was becoming ungovernable. Clarence and Warwick were forced to release the king so they could use his authority to raise levies, to quell the uprisings that were threatening Warwick's estates in the north. Once released King Edward pardoned Warwick, Clarence and the other rebels, but the precarious entente was short-lived. Warwick incited a rebellion in Lincolnshire which was crushed by the king. Warwick was dismissed as Captain of Calais, fired from his other appointments, and he and Clarence were declared traitors. Finding themselves abandoned by most of their previous supporters, the two gathered together some of Warwick's ships and sailed for Calais.

When Warwick and Clarence arrived at Calais, they were refused entry by Lord Wenlock. However, Wenlock sent word in secret to Warwick, saying that he remained loyal to him but feared for Warwick's safety because the marshal of the garrison had come out in support of King Edward. Having lost their secure base, they eventually sailed to the Seine estuary where they were granted refuge by Louis XI. Louis knew that Edward was considering attacking France with his new ally, Duke Charles of Burgundy, so decided to use Warwick and Clarence against Edward. Queen Margaret, Louis' cousin, was still in exile in France with her son, Edward, Prince of Wales. Margaret hated Warwick but Louis eventually persuaded her to use Warwick as an ally. Clarence and Warwick agreed to change sides and invade England on Margaret's behalf, to restore Henry VI to the throne. The alliance was sealed by the marriage of Warwick's younger daughter, Anne Neville, to Prince Edward.

Assisted by King Louis, Warwick gathered a force and in September sailed from La Hogue to Devon. On arrival, Warwick marched to Bristol where he was joined by the Earl of Shrewsbury and Lord Stanley. Warwick's army rapidly increased in number as some Lancastrians and his former Yorkist allies joined his standard. King Edward was in Yorkshire with a small force when he learnt that Warwick's brother, the Marquis of Montague, was behind him and he was completely outnumbered by Warwick's advancing army, which was ahead of him. Edward decided his only option was to flee and on 2 October sailed with his friend and chamberlain, William Lord Hastings, and a few other supporters from Bishops Lynn, for the Netherlands. That same day Warwick was welcomed into London. The sad and pitiful figure of Henry IV was released from the Tower where he had spent the last five years and he was restored to the throne, but not to power. Warwick indeed had become the 'king maker'. He re-occupied the powerful position of Captain of Calais and Clarence became Lieutenant of Ireland. Warwick led an interim government, ruling in Henry's name, until such time as Queen Margaret and Prince Edward felt it safe enough to return to England. Calais remained firmly in support of Warwick and visitors noted that nearly all its citizens were wearing Warwick's badge – the bear and ragged staff. It seemed that, with Warwick's help, the Lancastrians had finally won the Wars of the Roses.

This restoration lasted a mere six months. Warwick overreached himself and joined Louis in declaring war on Burgundy. This prompted Duke Charles of Burgundy to remember that his brother-in-law, Edward IV, was in Holland and could be used to cause civil war in England. Edward gratefully accepted the duke's offer to provide money, ships and men for an invasion. In March 1471 Edward sailed from Flushing for England with his Burgundian-financed force and landed in Yorkshire. On arrival Edward declared that he had returned not to seize the crown, but merely to take back his confiscated lands. He soon gained the backing of the House of Percy and other important northern families, and Clarence decided to desert Warwick and re-join his brother. Edward and his increased army advanced on London where he was warmly received by the city, and took Henry VI prisoner, once again. Warwick gathered contingents from his brother Montague, the Earl of Oxford and the Duke of Exeter, then advanced to north London and confronted Edward's force at Barnet. In thick mist on the early morning of 14 April 1471, a battle commenced that would help decide the monarchy of England.

The Earl of Oxford overcame Edward's left wing under Baron Hastings, and after pursuing the fleeing Yorkists returned to the battle. Montague was commanding the Lancastrian Centre but due to the thick mist mistook Oxford's banner for the Yorkist flag and attacked them. Montague was killed in the chaos, Oxford's men fled, and Edward's brother, the Duke of Gloucester, who had been commanding the Yorkist Right put the rest of the Lancastrian army to flight. Warwick was killed in the rout, so the great leader and king-maker was no more. It was ironic that on the very day of the battle Queen Margaret at last landed in England, at Weymouth, with her son and reinforcements for Warwick's army. She had expected to make a triumphal entrance into London but soon learned that her husband was a captive, again, the Lancastrians had suffered a major defeat, and her powerful ally, Warwick, was dead. Having lost her main general, Margaret was obliged to lead her own troops. She rallied what Lancastrian forces she could and having gained recruits from Wales, raised an army of about 6,000 men. Margaret's force was intercepted by Edward, with a force equal in size, at Tewkesbury on 14 May. The subsequent battle was a devastating defeat for Margaret. Her army was routed and those who sought sanctuary in Tewkesbury Abbey were slaughtered. In the aftermath of the battle Queen Margaret was captured and the 17-year-old Prince of Wales was killed, while begging for mercy from Clarence, who had sworn loyalty to him only months earlier.

Edward entered London and Henry IV died in the Tower on the same day. Official statements indicated that Henry had died of grief, but there was little doubt that he had been murdered. Queen Margaret was a broken woman; in the space of a few days, she had lost her husband, son, crown and liberty. The king's body was put on display for a brief time, to prove that there had been no foul play, but this did not go well as blood stains were clearly visible. Henry's body was then placed on a barge with a guard of honour comprising soldiers from the Calais garrison, taken down the Thames, and silently interred at Chertsey Abbey. It made sense to use Calais soldiers to escort the dead king; the Calais garrison had loyally supported Henry by following Warwick's lead when he changed his allegiance to the Lancastrians. Nevertheless, it was ironic that earlier, under Warwick, Calais had been a vital Yorkist base and the nucleus of the army that had enabled Edward to usurp the king – for whose body the Calais soldiers were providing an honour guard.

The Lancastrian line of Plantagenet kings had come to an end, and was followed by fourteen years of the Yorkist dynasty. Edward IV was every inch a king. Tall, and regarded as extremely handsome, he had proved himself a brave and charismatic leader in battle. He made an impressive sight in armour and in the extravagant clothes for which he became famous. Having finally secured the throne, Edward decided to make the most of the fruits of his victory by establishing one of the most extravagant courts in Europe. This display of magnificence came at a time when the royal coffers were empty and the government survived by means of loans, only, particularly from the London branch of the Medici bank. Opportunities to raise taxes were limited, as the country would take a considerable time to recover from the civil war. Taxes paid by the Calais Staple normally amounted to about a third of royal revenue and would have been particularly valuable, had they been available.

Despite the death of Warwick and Edward's crushing victory at Tewkesbury, Calais remained loyal to Warwick's new Lancastrian cause. Warwick's deputy, Wenlock, had left Calais to join Queen Margaret as she prepared to set sail for England, leaving Sir Walter Wrottesley in charge of Calais. Wenlock had been killed at Tewkesbury so Wrottesley sent Sir George Brook, with a contingent of 300 men from the Calais garrison, to fight against Edward IV. This force was transported to England by the remains of Warwick's fleet under Thomas Neville, the bastard son of Fauconberg. They landed in Kent and tried to advance on London but were beaten back and forced to return to Calais. Meanwhile Edward had decided to entrust the vital town of Calais to his loyal supporter, Baron Hastings. Although Edward trusted Hastings, he was determined to avoid giving anyone the power that Warwick had been able to wield as Captain of Calais. Hastings was therefore given the less powerful post of 'Lieutenant of Calais'. Hastings arrived in June but found that Wrottesley had defended Calais against him. The consequent siege of Calais lasted for two months before Wrottesley came to terms and surrendered in exchange for pardons.

The vital fortress of Calais was finally in Hastings' possession and Edward was at last reasonably safe upon his throne. Having taken control of Calais, Hastings was only an occasional visitor to the town for the rest of Edward's reign. He left it in the safe hands of his deputy, John Howard, aided by his own brother, Ralph Hastings. The Lancastrian faction was now completely defeated, and Edward could concentrate on indulging his appetite for feasting, mistresses and splendour. Unfortunately, Edward's hedonistic idyll was haunted by Warwick, the man who had made him king and then taken the crown from him. Warwick of course was dead, but it was necessary to resolve the matter of his huge estates which had made him so powerful. Warwick had left no surviving son, so his estates should have passed to his wife, Anne. Needless to say, this was not allowed, and Anne was bundled off to be confined in the north of England, while Clarence claimed the inheritance, having married Warwick's eldest daughter, Isabella, in Calais.

King Edward IV was less than enthusiastic about his ambitious brother Clarence amassing such considerable power. Edward's other brother was Richard, Duke of Gloucester, who, unlike Clarence, had been unfailingly loyal to him. Gloucester had his own ambitions and insisted on having a share of the Warwick estate. Warwick's younger daughter was Anne Neville, who had been married to Henry VI's son, Prince Edward, who had died at Tewkesbury. In order to provide Gloucester with some legitimacy for his claim to the Warwick estates, Anne Neville was forced into marriage with him. It looked as though the conflict between Clarence and Gloucester might result in civil war, but their brother, King Edward, managed persuaded them to agree on the division of the estate, with Clarence receiving the larger part.

Once Edward had defused the dangerous situation between his brothers he could return to the enjoyments of a lavish court. He soon felt it was not enough to display the magnificence of a great monarch and wanted to express his success in deeds. So, he turned his attention to France and the need to regain the lost English territory, and the crown itself. It was not just a matter of honour to reclaim what was rightfully English, but also an opportunity to avenge Louis for having supported Queen Margaret and Warwick. Edward already had fought, personally, in ten battles and had never lost; he had every reason to believe that he could emulate his grandfather Edward III's French success. The circumstances were ripe for a successful campaign. In the previous year, 1473, he had not only resolved the destabilising feud between his brothers but had established a truce with the Scots. Furthermore, the powerful Duke Charles of Burgundy was his brother-in-law and wanted to break from France and establish himself as king of his large and prosperous territories. The situation was brought to a head when Duke Charles and his ally, the Duke of Brittany, formally asked Edward to align with them against King Louis XI.

Edward had Calais as a secure base from which to launch an attack on France in conjunction with his new allies, Burgundy and Brittany, who had been joined by the Count de St Pol, the Constable of France, in their coalition against Louis. But Edward lacked the money to raise a large army and transport it to Calais. Fortunately, Parliament was enthusiastic about another war with France; the lords saw it as an opportunity to regain their lost French lands and to amass booty from conquest. Parliament granted Edward a number of huge subsidies, including one for £31,460, and the right to raise further funds at his own discretion through benevolences (forced loans). Having accumulated plenty of money, and supported by an aristocracy eager for war, Edward soon assembled an army of 1,500 men-at-arms and 15,000 archers.[22] On 22 June 1475 this great force departed from Sandwich and arrived safely in Calais. An army of this size under an experienced soldier such as Edward, allied with Burgundy and Brittany, should have been enough to make Louis tremble on his throne. A kind providence had ensured all that was necessary for England to take back the crown of France, by force of arms.

Having arrived in Calais Edward wanted to make his intentions clear to Louis. He despatched his senior herald, the Garter King of Arms, with a letter, to Louis. The herald was received by King Louis who read the letter, which was nothing less than Edward's demand for the crown of France. Many would assume that Louis responded with angry defiance – but that was not the case. Instead, Louis took the herald politely to his privy closet and there, in the most courteous manner, told him he was sorry for this misunderstanding with the king of England, that for his part he had the highest respect for King Edward and wanted to be on amicable terms with him, and he realized that the present situation had been stirred up by the Duke of Burgundy and the Constable St Pol, who would be the first to abandon Edward as soon as it suited them. Louis then put it to the herald how much better it would be for England and France to be on good terms, giving weight to this argument by placing a purse of 300 crowns in the herald's hand. Louis then assured the herald that if he used his influence to preserve peace between the two kingdoms, he would add an additional 1,000 crowns.

The herald was captivated by Louis' manner and reasons for good relations, so promised to do all he could to promote a peace. The interview ended with the herald being despatched at once back to King Edward, but only after he had been publicly presented with some rolls of scarlet cloth, as though this was the only payment for his embassy. While the herald had been away, Edward's campaign had not prospered. The Duke of Brittany had sent Edward 2,000 archers only, rather than a substantial army. Duke Charles of Burgundy had become distracted by mounting a military expedition against the Duke of Lorraine, and when he finally appeared at Edward's camp with a small retinue only, rather than a large army, he explained that he would be unable to provide any forces for that campaign season.

Edward was angered at this major setback but decided to press on and advanced to Saint-Quentin. The Duke of Burgundy accompanied Edward and assured him that Constable St Pol, who held Saint-Quentin, would open the gates to them on their arrival. Not only did Saint-Quentin not open its gates, it proceeded to fire arrows at Edward's troops from its walls. Edward was furious and made his feelings known, so forcibly, to Duke Charles, that the latter retired in haste from the English camp. Duke Charles had proved himself a useless ally; not only had he failed to provide a large army, but none of the Burgundian towns of Flanders, Artois and Picardy had admitted Edward's army within their walls. For Edward the Saint-Quentin debacle was the last straw that broke the Burgundian alliance.

It was at this juncture, with Edward fuming at his brother-in-law, that his herald returned from his visit to Louis. The herald's report of Louis' offer of friendship was well received by Edward and provided an agreeable way of punishing his perfidious allies. Edward called a council which concluded that with winter approaching, supplies low, and lack of assistance from allies, it was prudent to launch peace negotiations with

Louis. Negotiations took place over the following two months, during which Louis made sure that the English plenipotentiaries had sufficient French gold to encourage a favourable outcome. That outcome was the Treaty of Picquigny, signed near Amiens in August 1475. The treaty agreed a seven-year truce and that Louis would pay Edward 75,000 crowns immediately, and a further 50,000 crowns a year, during their joint lives. As an additional bonus, Louis agreed to pay a further 50,000 crowns for the ransom of Queen Margaret, who had spent the last four years in the Tower. This once spirited and formidable lady was by then a shadow of her former self. She was escorted to Anjou where she spent the next seven years of her life as one of Louis' neglected poor relations, until she died at the age of 51.

An additional undertaking, to further bind the French-English alliance, agreed that Edward's eldest daughter, Elizabeth, would marry the dauphin when they both came of age. This allowed Edward the satisfaction that his daughter would one day be Queen of France and a grandchild would succeed to the French crown. Although the treaty was in many ways advantageous to Edward, there was nothing in it to recompense the nobles and soldiers of his army. Louis was aware that the treaty would be unpopular with the majority of Edward's army who had crossed the Channel in high hopes of conquest and plunder, and he therefore took great pains to sweeten the pill. Three hundred cartloads of his best French wine were sent to the English camp to help quench the bloodthirsty English soldiers. Louis made a particular effort to win over the English nobles. He invited them to Amiens where they were richly entertained. Those who had supported the treaty were rewarded, and those who had not were given gifts of money, plate or horses. One of the people who had been a strong supporter of the treaty was the Captain of Calais, William Lord Hastings, and Louis promised him an annual pension of 2,000 crowns, a substantial income even for a rich man like Hastings.

Louis' charm offensive had been expensive but it worked well for him. He is reported to have remarked that whereas his ancestors had been forced to fight to get the English out of France he had done it with gifts of wine, cheeses and pâté. For his part, Edward marched his army to Calais, and they returned to England – but without the hoped-for plunder or occupation of French territory, let alone the Crown of France.

Despite these efforts by Louis, there was little doubt in the minds of most Englishmen that Edward had sold his honour, and that of the nation, for a French pension. It is true that King Edward, in his anger with the Duke of Burgundy, had been manipulated by King Louis. Also, his actions were hardly in keeping with the chivalric standards of his war-like ancestor, Edward III. That said, with the campaign season coming to an end and with no support from his allies, Edward had little option but to return his army to England. He had at least obtained money from Louis to cover the cost of the campaign and an annual French payment. This was actually of far more value to the royal exchequer and the nation than the vast military expense of a further campaign in a country as large as France, in the hope of gaining territory which would be near impossible to retain.

For the remainder of his reign King Edward concentrated on enjoying the luxuries of monarchy, his many mistresses and a magnificent court. Edward knew that such a lifestyle needed major financial support, so he ordered a rigorous implementation of crown revenue by fully exploiting the collection of customs duty, clergy tithes and feudal dues. He also converted his transport ships (designed for moving troops from place to place) into trading vessels. This merchant navy took with it tin, cloth and other merchandise to be traded in ports as far away as the Levant and returned to England with products from the east. So successful was this venture that after a couple of years Edward became the wealthiest monarch in Europe. This emphasis on trade rather than costly warfare was particularly welcome in Calais. The commerce of the town had suffered continual disruption during the Wars of the Roses, and with hostilities at an apparent end, and a seven-year truce with France in place, merchants were at last able to prosper. Of course, Calais was no longer able to make money from the provision of accommodation, food and supplies to an invading English army, but it was spared the huge additional costs of paying for a wartime town garrison.

At home in England Edward's brother, Clarence, remained a problem. He was hated by the queen, understandably, having been responsible for the death of her father and brother, and for continuing to plot against her Woodville relations. Clarence was immensely rich, having taken over the bulk of Warwick's estate, had become very powerful, and still harboured ambitions of wearing the crown. In January 1477 Duke Charles of

Burgundy died in battle at Nantes, in his war against the Duke of Lorraine. Charles' only surviving child, 19-year-old Mary, the daughter from his first marriage, inherited his extensive empire. That empire extended from the county of Holland in the north to the counties of Mâcon and Charlais in the south. Suddenly Mary had become the most prominent heiress in Christendom. Clarence's wife, Isabella of Warwick, had died a month earlier, but he quickly overcame his grief and requested Mary's hand in marriage. Such a marriage would make Clarence one of the most powerful rulers in Europe and would immensely strengthen any future attempt to secure the throne of England.

Following Charles' death, Burgundy was ruled on Mary's behalf by his widow, Duchess Margaret, the sister of Edward and Clarence. Margaret supported a potential marriage between her brother, Clarence, and her step-daughter but Edward was completely opposed to so much power passing to his ambitious brother. Edward was persuaded by Queen Elizabeth, his wife, to put forward her brother, Lord Rivers, as a candidate for Mary's hand. This match was immediately rejected by the court of Burgundy as Rivers was considered too low-born, so Margaret looked to France and Austria for prospective suitors for Mary. Clarence was furious that his ambitions had been thwarted by Edward and Elizabeth and did everything in his power to undermine them.

There followed a period in which Clarence was as difficult and obstructive as he could be, but then he overstepped himself and accused the queen of sorcery. This resulted in Clarence being arrested and being escorted to the Tower by Edward himself, to await his trial for treason. The trial was never concluded as Clarence suddenly died in mysterious circumstances: it was said that he had drowned in a butt of Malmsey wine. Clarence was known to be partial to Malmsey (a sweet Madeiran wine) and this description of the manner of his death was probably said as a joke. It is also probable that Clarence's convenient demise was greeted with some glee by his two brothers. Edward would have been delighted that his increasingly irritating brother was no longer a threat to his crown; and Richard, Duke of Gloucester, would have been equally pleased that he had become the closest royal adult in line for the throne.

Meanwhile, the vital matter of Mary of Burgundy's marriage was being settled. Louis XI of France had put forward his son, Charles, as a suitor for Mary. This was much to the annoyance of Edward IV – in doing so,

Louis had reneged on his earlier promise that the dauphin would marry Edward's daughter, Elizabeth. Louis also exploited Burgundy's instability by invading and capturing the Duchy of Burgundy itself. Accordingly, the Duchy, which originally had been ceded by John II, great-great-grandfather of Louis, to Philip, his younger son, reverted to the crown of France. Unsurprisingly, this robust method of wooing did not go down well with the Burgundian court, and Duchess Margaret decided that Mary should marry Maximilian Hapsburg, the son of Frederick, the Holy Roman Emperor. Mary married Maximilian in 1477 and, consequently, all the Burgundian lands surrounding Calais (the counties of Flanders, Artois and Boulogne) fell under the control of Austria and its Hapsburg rulers. This was not an immediate problem as, despite the marriage, Margaret, Dowager Duchess of Burgundy, continued as its effective ruler, managing the Burgundian lands through her stepdaughter, Mary.

Louis XI continued with his attacks on the Burgundian lands and Margaret turned to her brother, Edward IV, for help. She visited him in London in the summer of 1480 to renew the Anglo-Burgundian alliance. This resulted in some improved trade between England and Burgundy but did not provide any practical military help against Louis. Two years later, in 1482, having been badly injured in a riding accident, Duchess Mary died and the Duchy was inherited by her 4-year-old son, Philip. Margaret clung to power but her position was much weakened. The Burgundian nobles would not accept Mary's husband, Maximilian, as regent for his son, and weary of war with France they concluded the Treaty of Arras with Louis in December 1482. The treaty gave Louis the counties of Picardy and Boulogne and Margaret and Maximilian had to accept it as a fait accompli.

Maximilian decided that he could not continue his war with France and concluded his own peace with Louis. They agreed that Maximilian's young daughter, Margaret, should marry the dauphin and provide as part of her dowry the county of Artois. In this way the situation regarding Calais underwent a fundamental change. Its nearest neighbours were the counties of Picardy, Boulogne and Artois, which were part of the Burgundian empire and so under the rule of a traditional ally. If a king of England wanted to invade France he would require not only a secure disembarkation port in Calais, but also that the surrounding area be in allied hands. As a result of the Treaty of Arras and the Artois dowry, an invading army would be in hostile French territory the moment it crossed the perimeter of the Calais Pale.

As it happened, Edward IV did not intend to invade France, despite being furious with Louis for his attacks on Burgundy, and for having reneged on the original marriage agreement. Although Edward blustered about an invasion for some time, in the end he concluded that the annual payment of 50,000 crowns from Louis was enough to satisfy his personal pride and reverted to his life of regal excess. By this stage Edward was no longer the tall, handsome soldier but an overweight, debauched, glutton. He loved food and would eat as much as he could, then take an emetic, vomit, and return to the table to eat more. This excess may well have undermined his health and at Easter 1483 he fell ill and died soon after, aged only 41. His unexpected early death meant that his heir, his son Edward, was only 12 years old at the time. However, just before Edward died, he appointed his brother, Richard, Duke of Gloucester, as Protector during young Edward's minority.

At the time of Edward's death, Richard of Gloucester was in the north of England having been fighting in Scotland. Richard immediately paid homage to his nephew Edward and travelled with his army from the north to escort Edward to London for his coronation. Young Edward was in the Welsh borders with Earl Rivers and his mother's other Woodville relations, who began to escort him to London. Rivers and his son Lord Grey rode ahead of young Edward and his followers, to meet Richard and his 20,000-strong army near Northampton. Richard welcomed Rivers and offered a declaration of lasting friendship – then arrested Rivers and his son the next day, as they arrived at the camp with young Edward. Rivers and Grey were executed shortly afterwards. Richard then arrested young Edward's close servants and took the prince into his care.

With due deference, Richard took Edward to London and led him in a royal procession to the Tower, to await the boy's coronation. Things then moved fast. Queen Elizabeth had sought sanctuary in Westminster Abbey with her younger son, the Duke of York, but was tricked into agreeing that he be placed in the Tower for his own safety. Then, using lies, threats and guile of the highest order, Richard persuaded the people of London to offer him the crown, on the grounds that Queen Elizabeth was a sorceress, that her marriage to Edward IV was invalid and that her children were therefore illegitimate. Within two months of the death of

Edward IV, Richard had been crowned King Richard III. No more was heard of the princes in the Tower; not then, and not since.

Richard had become king and there were no other prominent royal Yorkists to challenge him. The main Lancastrian line had died with Prince Edward at Tewkesbury, but there was a minor line from John of Gaunt, whose descendant was Margaret Beaufort. Margaret had married Edmund Tudor, Earl of Richmond, but soon after their marriage he died of the plague, leaving a 13-year-old widow who was seven months pregnant. The child of that marriage was Henry Tudor, Earl of Richmond, who had been visiting the Duke of Brittany at the time of Edward IV's death. Richmond had only a tenuous claim to the throne, but nevertheless was seen as a threat by Richard. Indeed, Richard had been taking steps to ensure all potential opposition to him was neutralized. He gave honours and gifts to his supporters and removed any persons of note whose motives were suspect. One of the many people who fell into this category was Lord William Hastings. He and Richard had long been friends, and Hastings had warned him of the Woodville's plans to escort Prince Edward to London. Nevertheless, Richard felt he might harbour loyalties to Prince Edward and so, during a council meeting, he had Hastings arrested, dragged outside and beheaded on a nearby log. This and similar displays of Richard's ruthlessness ensured that few people felt it prudent to oppose him.

Hastings had held the post of Lieutenant of Calais and, although largely absent from the town, his brother, Ralph Hastings, was lieutenant of the Calais Pale fortress of Guînes and acted as his representative. Richard knew how important Calais was to the security of the crown and rapidly removed Ralph and installed Lord John Dynham as Lieutenant of Calais. Dynham had been a long-term supporter of Edward IV, a prominent member of his council, and the commander of naval forces for Edward's brief invasion of France. He was very familiar with Calais, having spent time in the Yorkist base there during the Wars of the Roses. But the principal reason for Dynham's appointment was that Richard could trust him to be unswervingly loyal.

At much the same time that Richard was usurping the English throne, King Louis XI of France died leaving his 13-year-old son, Charles VIII, as his heir, and the boy's elder sister, Anne, as regent. The French crown had been greatly strengthened during the reign of Louis XI, who had regained the Duchy of Burgundy and put the royal finances on a sound footing. That said, any kingdom with a minor as its sovereign was bound to be vulnerable. Under different circumstances a successful soldier such as Richard III would have been tempted to launch an attack on France in an attempt to regain the French crown, but Richard was fully occupied with securing his own throne. Soon after his coronation he heard that his key supporter, the Duke of Buckingham, was inciting the nobles to depose him, rescue Prince Edward from the Tower and crown him as King Edward V. Richard countered this by letting it be known that Prince Edward and his brother had died. As a result, the planned insurrection was abandoned. Buckingham and other disaffected peers then thought they should champion Henry Tudor, Earl of Richmond as their future king.

At the same time, Margaret Beaufort, Countess of Richmond, used the services of a go-between to contact Queen Elizabeth in her Westminster sanctuary. Margaret's message proposed that Queen Elizabeth's daughter, also Elizabeth, should marry Margaret's son, Henry, and so unite the York and Lancastrian families and their factions. The dowager queen agreed to the match and sent a messenger to Henry in Brittany, informing him of the arrangement and urging him to return to England, in time for an insurrection being organized by Buckingham, for 11 October.

Richard got wind of this threat and had Buckingham declared a traitor. Despite this the uprising began, but soon collapsed. Flooded rivers prevented Buckingham from reaching his fellow rebels, they lost heart and dispersed, and several of their leaders fled to Brittany. Henry had sailed from Saint-Malo but was delayed by bad weather. When he eventually arrived on the Devon coast it was to hear that the rebellion had failed and Buckingham had been captured and executed. There was nothing for him to do but return to Brittany. Then, completely confounding Henry's plans, Richard decided to marry Elizabeth of York to his own son, the 10-year-old Edward, Prince of Wales. Just as it seemed Richard had finally secured his throne, tragedy struck and his son died, followed by his queen, Anne Neville. Richard then considered marrying his niece, Elizabeth of York, but abandoned the idea when he realized the strength of opposition against it.

While King Richard had begun to face mounting discontent, Henry Tudor was gaining support from Richard's opponents, who travelled to join him in Brittany. These opponents came not just from England but also from Calais, and included Sir John Fortesque, the Master Porter, (in charge of the port of Calais). In fact, the entire garrison of Hames castle in the Calais Pale defected to Henry, but it was recaptured by Lord Dynham, which proved that Richard had made a wise choice when he appointed him Lieutenant of Calais. More importantly, Anne, the French regent gave her support to Henry and in August 1485, with a 3,000-strong army, he sailed from Harfleur in a fleet provided by France and Brittany. He landed at Milford Haven and gained more support as he marched through his homeland of Wales. Richard hurried from the north to intercept Henry, whose force had increased to about 6,000 men. On 21 August the two armies camped opposite each other at Bosworth, outside Leicester.

Richard's army numbered about 12,000 men and it seemed that Henry Tudor's hopes were about to be shattered. However, many of Richard's captains had lost faith in their monarch and some began deserting to Henry. One of these was Lord Stanley who, with his brother, Sir William Stanley, commanded a force of 5,000 men. Secretly Lord Stanley informed Henry that he would come over to his side, but not until the battle had commenced, as Richard was holding his son hostage. Accordingly, when the confrontation began Lord Stanley did not move his troops to join Richard, and Sir William Stanley wheeled his men round and attacked Richard's centre, causing chaos and dismay. Despite Richard leading a number of charges and even killing Henry's standard bearer, he was cut down and killed. After the fighting, the coronet that Richard had worn on his helmet was found in a hawthorn bush and given to Lord Stanley – who then placed it on Henry Tudor's head. The Tudor dynasty had begun.

Chapter 7

Tudor Bling, 1485–1520

After the Battle of Bosworth Henry Tudor entered London in state and was recognized by Parliament as the rightful king. A little later he married Anne of York and by doing so united the dynasties of York and Lancaster; but this happy union did not bring a complete end to the Wars of the Roses. Too much blood had been spilt for there to be universal amity. Much of Ireland and the north of England remained predominantly Yorkist, and barons such as Viscount Lovell, who had prospered under Richard III, now feared for their estates and indeed their lives. There were also those with a far stronger claim to the throne than Henry VII. It was generally assumed that the 'Princes in the Tower' were dead, but Clarence's son, to whom Richard III had given the title Earl of Warwick, and Richard's nephew, John de la Pole, Earl of Lincoln, were still alive.

Above all there was Richard's sister Margaret, the Duchess of Burgundy. Her husband had died and the actual Duchy of Burgundy had been lost to France, but the rest of the demesne covered an area larger than modern Belgium, Netherlands and Luxembourg. Margaret's young stepdaughter, Mary, had inherited the duchy and married Maximilian Hapsburg, but had died as the result of a riding accident, leaving her 4-year-old son, Philip, as her heir. The Burgundian nobles regarded Margaret as regent, so she held considerable power and was prepared to use it to support her Yorkist family in ousting Henry Tudor from the throne.

Following the Battle of Bosworth, the Earl of Lincoln was reconciled with Henry VII and allowed his freedom, but the young Earl of Warwick was placed in the Tower. Despite appearing loyal to Henry, Lincoln and other diehard Yorkists began conspiring to oust Henry from the throne. A Yorkist priest found a 10-year-old boy named Lambert Simnel who bore a strong resemblance to the Earl of Warwick. Having taught the boy some royal etiquette he took him to Ireland where the Yorkist sympathiser, the Earl of Kildare, was Lord Deputy. The conspirators put about the story that Simnel was the Earl of Warwick, who had escaped from the Tower, and that the person being held in the Tower by Henry was an imposter! Kildare welcomed Simnel believing him to be Warwick, the rightful Yorkist heir to the throne. At the same time Lincoln escaped to Burgundy to seek the support of his aunt Margaret of Burgundy. Viscount Lovell was already at Margaret's court, having fled there after leading an earlier failed Yorkist rising. It is unlikely that Margaret of Burgundy believed that Simnel was the real Warwick, but she probably supported the conspirators in the hope that were Henry VII to be defeated, either Lincoln or the real Warwick might end up wearing the crown.

Other Yorkists soon gathered at Duchess Margaret's court at Mechelen. Among them was Thomas David, a captain of the Calais Garrison. Calais, of course, had been Yorkist under Richard III who in March 1485 had made his illegitimate son, John of Gloucester, Captain of Calais. Richard had known the importance of Calais and wanted to ensure that it remained in loyal hands, so who better than John, who Richard describes in the patent for the appointment as 'our dear bastard son'. John was only about seventeen at the time of his appointment but had lived in Calais for several months, previously, and it must be assumed that he took proper control of the colony. John was removed from office soon after Henry VII seized the throne, but rather than being persecuted, was given an annual pension of £20, possibly at the instigation of his cousin Elizabeth, Henry's wife. In March 1486 Henry put Giles Daubeney in charge of Calais. He was a former Yorkist who had changed allegiance to Henry Tudor. Following the failure of Buckingham's rebellion, Daubeney had fled to Brittany with Henry and had been attained by Richard III. Having proved himself fiercely loyal to Henry VII, he was made a baron and given the important job of running Calais, but with the lesser title of 'Lieutenant' rather than 'Captain.'

Daubeney was also Master of the Mint and used by Henry on diplomatic and other tasks, so was unable to spend all his time in Calais. This probably meant that his appointment did not immediately stamp out the traditional Yorkist sympathies at Calais. It could explain why Thomas David, one of the garrison captains, was able to take some of his men and join the Yorkist conspirators at Margaret's court at Mechelen. With the arrival of the Calais contingent and others, Margaret of Burgundy decided to launch an operation to overthrow Henry. She provided

Lincoln with money, ships and 2,000 Flemish mercenaries who, together with the other Yorkists, set sail for Ireland. When this force arrived in Ireland it joined the 4,000 troops already raised by the Earl of Kildare in readiness to invade England for the Yorkist cause. After a ceremony in which Simnel was crowned 'King Edward VI' in Dublin Cathedral, the Yorkist force sailed for England and landed in the area of Furness in Lancashire.

Having made a safe landing, Lincoln headed towards York to try to increase his army, which grew to about 8,000. At Tadcaster, Viscount Lovell and 2,000 men conducted a night attack which overwhelmed 400 Lancastrians under Lord Clifford, but that was to be the limit of the Yorkist success. Lincoln's force was met by a 12,000-strong army, raised by Henry VII, at the village of East Stoke near Newark. On 14 June 1487 a ferocious battle began which lasted three hours and ended in a complete and bloody victory for King Henry. Most of the Yorkist leaders were killed, including Lincoln, but Lovell escaped, never to be heard of again. Simnel was captured but Henry realized he had been a mere puppet and granted him clemency, at the same time showing his contempt by employing him as a scullion in the royal kitchens.

The rebellion crushed, Henry turned his attention to France. Henry's old ally, Duke Francis of Brittany, had died, leaving a 12-year-old daughter, Anne, as his heir, just at the time that King Charles VIII of France had invaded Brittany. Before his death Duke Francis had begged for Henry's help, and Parliament had voted the money to provide an army to go to Brittany's defence, but Henry had merely pocketed the money and done nothing of consequence to help his old ally. Anne was besieged at Rennes by Charles and rather than surrender she agreed to marry Charles, thus transferring Brittany to the French crown. Emperor Maximilian was furious at this, because King Charles had jilted his daughter, to whom he had been engaged to be married. English barons were up in arms about Charles VIII's behaviour and the loss of Brittany to France and feelings were running high. Parliament voted more money for a confrontation with France and Henry felt obliged to prepare for war. An English force was assembled and landed in Calais in October 1492 in readiness to attack France. But it was all a sham.

Prior to leaving England Henry had already come to some arrangement with Charles VIII. Henry's force consisted of 25,000 foot and 1,600 horse, quite sufficient to give the French a bloody nose. The English army advanced from Calais to besiege Boulogne. While there, Henry received word that the emperor was unable to send an army to join him, and as the campaign season was drawing to a close, he decided to make peace with Charles. Giles Daubeney, the Lieutenant of Calais, travelled to Charles at his base in Étaples to negotiate peace. Daubeney knew exactly what Henry wanted – he wanted to be bought off. Henry had become obsessed with the accumulation of wealth, so the eventual agreement between Henry and Charles, which became known as the Peace of Étaples, was very favourable to Henry – but it was an affront to English honour. It was agreed that Charles should retain Brittany but pay Henry 620,000 gold crowns in exchange for peace, an additional 125,000 gold crowns as arrears for the pension Louis XI had granted to Edward IV, and an annual pension of 25,000 gold crowns (total £159,000).[1] The nobility who had joined the expedition to France were less than pleased that instead of winning back French territory and enriching themselves with plunder, they returned empty handed to Calais and then to their estates.

The Peace of Étaples contained a remarkable clause concerning a boy named Perkin Warbeck. Yorkist refugees in Flanders court had decided to find a young boy who, in age and aspect, would be able to impersonate Richard, Duke of York, the younger of the Princes in the Tower, whom they would claim had escaped. They alighted on Perkin Warbeck who was the same age as Prince Richard would have been, had he been alive, and who bore a strong resemblance to Edward IV. Indeed, he may even have been an illegitimate child fathered by Edward during his time in Flanders. While Warbeck had a natural charm and aristocratic bearing, he was nevertheless deliberately groomed, to the extent that be became so plausible an imposter that he was accepted by Duchess Margaret of Burgundy as her nephew and given the full trappings and treatment befitting a prince. Warbeck was sent to Cork in Ireland but found little support there, so travelled to France with introductions from Margaret of Burgundy to Charles VIII. He was welcomed with open arms by the French king and celebrated as Richard, Duke of York, the rightful king of England.

Warbeck provided Charles with an ideal opportunity to threaten Henry VII and was given royal accommodation and his own bodyguard. Charles evinced the strong likelihood that he would join with Margaret of Burgundy to invade England, to put Warbeck on the throne. This may or may not have been the case, but it gave Charles a useful bargaining point during negotiations for the Peace of Étaples. Charles was able to engineer the removal of English troops from French soil simply by paying off Henry with gold and promising not to harbour his enemies. Warbeck left France and returned to Flanders; but that was not the last of him.

Margaret of Burgundy received the returned Warbeck as King Richard IV of England. This infuriated Henry who made a formal complaint to the 14-year-old Philip Hapsburg, the Duke of Burgundy. When young Philip explained that he had no jurisdiction over Margaret's territory, Henry placed an embargo on trade with Burgundy. The ensuing disruption of trade was very unpopular and, coupled with Henry VII's exorbitant tax demands, resulted in serious opposition to the king. So strong was the feeling against Henry that in 1494 some of his closest supporters, led by Sir William Stanley, the Lord Chamberlain, began plotting against him. Stanley and the other conspirators decided to rebel against Henry and replace him with the pretender Warbeck. However, one of the conspirators developed cold feet and informed Henry of the plot. As a result, the conspirators were quickly apprehended. Like Stanley, most of them were executed, but those who had been less involved were imprisoned. The latter group included Baron Fitzwater who was sent to the castle of Guînes in the Calais Pale. Fitzwater attempted to escape by bribing a guard but was discovered and taken to Calais town where he was beheaded. Henry became concerned that Calais might be used as a base for opposition to the crown, as had been the case in Warwick's time. Consequently, all those whom he suspected of harbouring support for Warbeck were arrested and indicted for treason, the most prominent among them being Sir Thomas Thwaytes, the Treasurer of Calais. But this too was not the last that was heard of Warbeck.

The next year Margaret of Burgundy funded Warbeck to launch a rebellion and landed in Kent with a small force, but Warbeck was beaten back when he attempted to land at Deal so he sailed to Ireland to obtain support from the Earl of Desmond. When he and Desmond failed to take Waterford, Warbeck fled to Scotland. King James IV of Scotland was no friend of Henry VII and not only welcomed Warbeck, but arranged for him to marry his own kinswoman, Catherine, the daughter of the Earl of

Huntley. Their marriage was celebrated in some style, with feasting and a tournament.

King James now had an excuse to invade England in support of Warbeck as 'King Richard IV', England's rightful monarch. In the autumn of 1496 Warbeck and the Scottish army crossed the Tweed, then retreated to Scotland when an English army approached. James began peace negotiations with Henry VII but had begun to find Warbeck an embarrassment, so he packed him off to Ireland, again. On his return to Ireland Warbeck made another unsuccessful attempt to besiege Waterford and then fled – with two ships and just 150 men – home to Flanders.

The next year (1497) Margaret of Burgundy financed Warbeck for an expedition to Cornwall, where its citizens were up in arms over Henry VII's high taxation. Warbeck landed and swiftly built a 6,000-strong Cornish force which advanced on Taunton. When he heard that a strong army was approaching, led by Baron Daubeney, the Lieutenant of Calais, he deserted his men and fled to Beaulieu Abbey for sanctuary. Having been promised that his life would be spared, Warbeck surrendered and was taken to London and ensconced in the Tower. Once he had confessed to being an imposter he was released and allowed to attend court and even royal banquets, but always under guard. After eighteen months of this surprisingly pleasant existence, he tried to escape, but was captured and returned to the Tower, together with the Earl of Warwick. Warbeck persuaded some of his guards to allow the two of them to escape, but the plot was discovered and they were subsequently tried and sentenced to be executed. Warwick was despatched with an axe (beheaded) on Tower Hill, as befitted a member of the Yorkist Royal family, while Warbeck met his end via a noose at Tyburn, as befitted the greatest con-man of his age.

Margaret of Burgundy would live until 1503; but without any remaining real or imposter Yorkist claimants to the English throne, she was unable to trouble Henry VII further. While Henry had been occupied with the irritation of Warbeck and raising exorbitant taxes and fines from his subjects, major events had been taking place in mainland Europe. In 1493 Maximillian Hapsburg had become Holy Roman Emperor and the next year Charles VIII of France claimed the throne of Naples. He crossed the Alps with 25,000 troops and swiftly advanced to Naples where he established himself as king.

This power grab by the French horrified much of Europe which responded by forming a league against France, composed of several Italian states together with Maximilian and Ferdinand of Spain. The league drove Charles VIII out of Italy and he took the remnants of his army back to France. For the next half century, the politics of Europe would be dominated by the struggle in Italy between the Valois kings of France and the Hapsburgs of Spain and Germany.

Despite his setbacks in Italy, Charles began to prepare for another campaign to regain Naples, but this was not to be. Charles died at the age of 28 – not, as might be expected, on the field of battle but in a commonplace accident. He was hurrying to watch a game of tennis when his head struck a low lintel and he fell into a coma and died. Charles had no surviving children, so the French throne passed to his cousin, Louis, Duke d'Orléans, who became King Louis XII. The new French king soon showed that he was no less ambitious than his predecessor. His first step was to marry Queen Anne of Brittany, widow of Charles VIII, to ensure that the duchy remained under the French crown. Having secured control of a united country, he invaded Italy in 1499, laying claim to both the Duchy of Milan and the throne of Naples. Once again, the status quo of Europe had been threatened by French expansionism.

But what of Calais during these few eventful years? For some time, England's export in raw wool had been somewhat overshadowed by the sale of broadcloth. Trade in woven cloth had been largely with the Low Countries and had been negatively impacted by Henry VII's trade embargo against Philip of Burgundy. The Merchant Adventurers – the London guild authorized to sell woven cloth to Flanders – had relocated from Antwerp to Calais, thus giving extra impetus to the Calais economy. As it happened, the Calais Staple was doing reasonably well at this time. In fact, it had reached sales of about 8,937 bales per annum in the 1490s,[2] which, although well below the annual sales of 16,000 bales at the start of the century, was still a substantial amount. For the avaricious Henry VII, it was a particularly welcome source of royal revenue. Calais was also the place of receipt of the various annual payments to Henry by Charles VIII, under the Peace of Étaples. Transportation of the half yearly shipments of 25,000 francs fell to Baron Daubeney, as Lieutenant of Calais and the diplomat who had engineered the Étaples agreement. Daubeney had prospered in the years following the Peace of Étaples; he had become

Henry VII's principal general and had been made Lord Chamberlain after the execution of Sir William Stanley. However, despite these and other appointments, Henry VII probably valued Daubeney most for his diplomatic skills, and it was in that capacity that he accompanied the king to Calais in 1499.

Henry's reason for going to Calais was to meet with Philip of Burgundy. Philip was then 21 years old and was becoming a prince of some consequence. He had not yet inherited the Burgundian Netherlands, and Margaret of Burgundy was to live for another three years, but his father was now Emperor Maximilian of the Holy Roman Empire, and Philip was his heir to the Archduchy of Austria and the Hapsburg territories. In addition, Philip was married to Princess Joanna of Spain.

The marriage of Ferdinand of Aragon and Isabella of Castile and their conquest of Moslem Granada had created a unified Spain, making it a leading power in Europe. It was also a power with strong interests in Italy, where Ferdinand's cousin – Frederick IV, also known as Frederick of Aragon – was the king of Naples, although that crown was again being claimed by France. Maximilian also had a major interest in Italy as he was a claimant to the duchy of Milan which had just been invaded by Louis XII of France. In short, Philip was eager to meet with Henry to persuade him to join his father and father-in-law in a war against the French aggressor.

Henry's reason for wanting to meet with Philip was to re-establish good commercial arrangements, now that Perkin Warbeck was no longer a source of friction. Henry invited Philip and his retinue to visit Calais as his guests while negotiations took place. Philip declined the invitation; he did not trust Henry and thought there was a danger that Henry might detain him in Calais as a hostage. This did not augur well; it seemed the talks were unlikely to take place in an atmosphere of mutual trust. It was eventually agreed that the meeting would be held in the town of Saint-Pierre outside the Calais Pale. When Henry and Philip at last sat down to negotiate the result was little more than a slight improvement in relations: Philip had failed completely to win Henry's agreement to join the war against France. This was hardly a surprise, as the rapacious Henry was far more interested in keeping his shipment of French gold from the Peace of Étaples, than depleting his wealth by warfare. Henry returned to Calais and then England, to concentrate on negotiating a rich dowry for the marriage of his eldest son, Arthur.

Henry, like the Hapsburgs, had recognized the growing power of a united Spain and was negotiating for his son, Prince Arthur, to marry Catherine, one of the four daughters of Ferdinand and Isabella. Marriage negotiations had begun in 1489 but became protracted by long haggling over the dowry. The wedding of 15-year-old Arthur and 16-year–old Catherine had taken place eventually in 1501, but six months later Arthur had died. Not wishing to lose the hard-won dowry, Henry obtained Ferdinand's agreement that the widowed Catherine would marry Arthur's younger brother Henry, who had become the heir to the English throne. Henry VII then turned his attention to arranging peace with James IV of Scotland, now that Perkin Warbeck was no longer an issue. The principal aim of Henry's peace negotiations was to decouple Scotland from its traditional Auld Alliance with France. Henry had no intention of invading France, but he wanted to ensure peace with Scotland and to seal the agreement through the marriage of his daughter, Margaret, to James IV.

James IV also was ready for peace and in 1502 the 12-year-old Margaret Tudor was affianced to King James in an agreement rather optimistically called the 'Treaty of Perpetual Peace'. It need hardly be said that this turned out to be a misnomer, but the wedding took place the following year (1503). Henry VII died of tuberculosis in 1509, secure on his throne, at peace with his foreign neighbours, and with a full treasury. However, it could be said that the future union of the English and Scottish crowns was his most important legacy. Although war was to break out between Scotland and England just eleven years after the Perpetual Peace, the treaty would result in the two countries being united under one sovereign when Margaret's great-grandson, King James VI of Scotland, succeeded to the throne of England in 1603.

Henry VII had not been held in any affection by his subjects, but despite being feared he was also respected. His son, the new 18-year-old King Henry VIII of England, was a good looking, affable and generous young man, who swiftly did away with the gloomy regime of his father. Like most teenagers who inherit considerable wealth, he began to spend it freely. One of his first acts was to end the long haggling over a dowry and marry Catherine of Aragon, which was followed by magnificent joint coronation. This at last confirmed the increasingly important Spanish alliance.

Catherine's elder sister, Joanna, had inherited the throne of Castile and was the heir to Aragon, but her husband, Archduke Philip, had died of typhoid fever. This meant that Charles, the 9-year-old son of Joanna and Philip would eventually inherit the Netherlands, Spain and its territories, as well Austria and the other Hapsburg lands from Philip's father, Emperor Maximilian. The Hapsburgs were on their way to dominating Europe, and Henry was their ally.

The young Henry wanted to pursue military glory and the traditional battleground on which to achieve this was France. As Henry VII had established friendly relations with all the main rulers of Europe, including France, the new Henry VIII could not easily change the situation. Nevertheless, he began to dream of regaining England's lost French territory and Calais remained vital to any such aspirations. Baron Daubeney had died the year before Henry had acceded to the throne, so the vacant post of Lieutenant was given to Sir Gilbert Talbot, an ultra-loyal soldier who had led the Lancastrian right wing at the Battle of Bosworth. The first friction with Louis XII began early, when the French king stated his reluctance to continue the £80,000 annual payment that he had agreed with Henry VII. However, it was not this, but affairs in Italy, that resulted in young Henry opening hostilities with France, and the attack was launched not through the secure base of Calais but from a landing near San Sebastian.

This strange turn of events had come about because young Henry was quite simply duped by his older, more experienced fellow rulers. Pope Julius II felt that Louis XII was threatening his papal lands and so established an alliance with Ferdinand of Spain and the Emperor Maximilian, to drive France out of Milan and expand papal power. Julius gave the alliance the pious title 'The Holy League'. He wanted to bring England into the alliance and offered to transfer the papal honour, 'Most Christian King', from Louis to Henry. The appeal to Henry's vanity worked and Henry joined the League. He then concluded an additional alliance against France, at the behest of his wily father-in-law, Ferdinand, who made the irresistible suggestion that Spain and England should launch a joint attack on south-west France, to enable Ferdinand to annex Navarre and Henry to reclaim Aquitaine. So Henry sent a herald to Louis demanding that the French king surrender Anjou, Maine, Normandy and Guienne, as Henry's rightful inheritance; to which Louis replied with laughter. As a result, preparations were made for an English invasion of south-west France.

In 1512 Henry despatched an army of 10,000 men, commanded by the Marquis of Dorset, which landed near San Sebastian in preparation for a joint attack on France. Frederick had never had any intention of assisting Henry and invaded Navarre, which he then occupied and took the crown, to add to the crown of the Kingdom of Naples, which he had snatched from Louis XII eight years earlier. Pope Julius perceived the war as a success because it had enabled the soldier pope and his Swiss mercenaries to drive Louis back over the Alps. But for England the whole expedition had been a complete failure. Dorset returned with his army diminished by disease and the lack of supplies, while the English fleet had suffered major losses in an engagement with the French off Brest. Henry VIII's first attempt to retrieve England's territories in France had not gone well, but another opportunity would soon arise.

The next year Pope Julius II died, content that he had enlarged the Papal States and never having had cause to ponder whether leading his forces into battle had been the precise function of Christianity's spiritual leader. He was succeeded as pope by the less belligerent but equally wily Giovani Medici, who became Pope Leo X. The new pope is reported to have said, 'God has given us the papacy, let us enjoy it.'[3] And enjoy it he did, with an unsurpassed extravagant lifestyle for himself and his family, which helped to finance some of the great art of the Renaissance. In 1513 Pope Leo revived the Holy League with the purpose of a four-pronged attack on France: Maximilian was to attack from the east, Ferdinand from the south-west, Leo from the south and England from the north. Henry VIII was delighted with this prospect of Louis' certain defeat, and once more becoming master of the English lands in France. With youthful enthusiasm he even agreed to loan Maximilian 100,000 gold crowns for his eastern invasion. The only problem was that neither Maximilian nor Ferdinand had any intention of invading France.

Maximilian was happy to take Henry's money and do little, while Ferdinand had decided to devote his military efforts to strengthening his position in his new kingdom of Navarre. Indeed, this was not the end of Ferdinand's perfidy – he made a secret alliance with Louis in conjunction with King James of Scotland. Clearly, for James, the Auld Alliance with France meant more than the Treaty of Perpetual Peace which he had signed with Henry VII, eight years earlier. It was with this unhappy state of affairs that the unsuspecting Henry launched his attack on France. In June 1513 Henry and his fleet crossed to Calais with a 25,000-strong army. Having despatched his vanguard to besiege the town of Thérounne, Henry remained in Calais with his courtiers, engaged in a round of gaieties. When Thérounne had not fallen after a month, he moved to join the siege. At Thérounne Henry was met by Emperor Maximilian with just 4,000 horsemen. But Maximilian played on Henry's vanity, saying he would serve under Henry's command and even wear his badge of the Tudor rose and the cross of St George, and Henry immediately forgave him.

Henry's pleasure at being so honoured by the Holy Roman Emperor was somewhat dashed when a herald arrived with a declaration of war from King James IV of Scotland. At much the same time a large French army commanded by the Duke of Angoulême advanced to relieve Thérounne. A battle ensued in which the French cavalry attacked, then pretended to retreat, to lure the English into pursuing them into the French main body. But this feint went badly wrong. The French main body thought it was a real retreat and fled the field, leaving Henry and Maximilian as the victors. The alacrity of the French flight resulted in the engagement being named the Battle of the Spurs.

Thérounne soon capitulated and the obvious action for Henry was to make a rapid advance on Paris. Instead, Maximillian persuaded him to lay siege to Tournai. Although the city fell after only eight days, the initiative presented by the victory of the Battle of the Spurs was lost. Henry did not appear too concerned by this missed opportunity and enjoyed entering Tournai with all the pomp of a great conqueror. He marked his new power in the city by getting the pope's agreement to make his new advisor, Thomas Wolsey, the Bishop of Tournai. His vanity was fed even further when he was joined by Charles, the young Duke of Burgundy, and other leaders from the Netherlands, all wishing to pay their respects to the victorious English king. They were indeed grateful to Henry, as their Burgundian/Netherland border had been strengthened against France at no cost to themselves.

Having enjoyed basking in his military acclaim, Henry returned to Calais and then to England where he found another victory to celebrate. While he had been in France, King James IV of Scotland had invaded

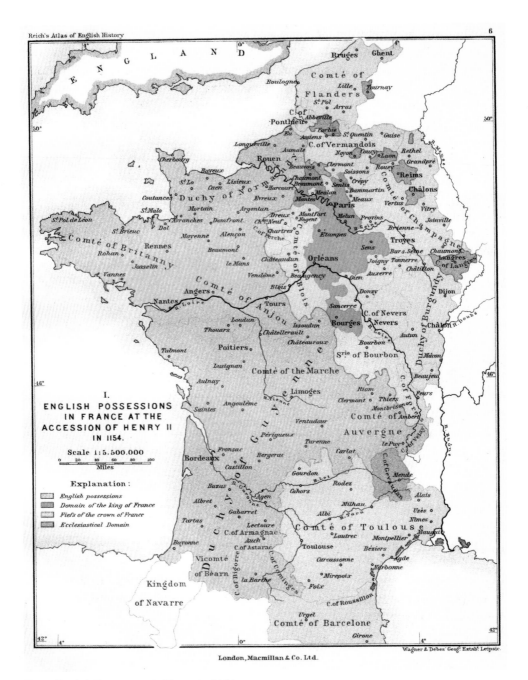

Fig 1: English Possessions in France in 1154.

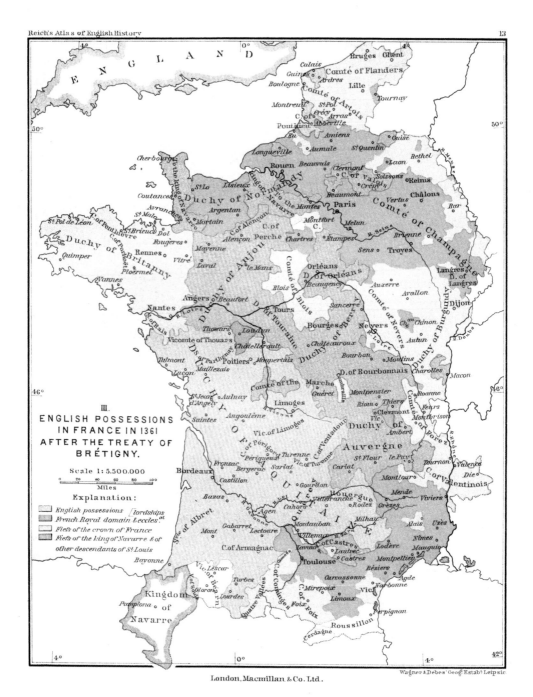

III.
ENGLISH POSSESSIONS
IN FRANCE IN 1361
AFTER THE TREATY OF
BRÉTIGNY.

Scale 1: 5.500.000

0   20   40   60   80   100
Miles

Explanation:

English possessions   lordships
French Royal domain &eccles⁻al
Fiefs of the crown of France
Fiefs of the king of Navarre & of
other descendants of S.ᵗ Louis

London, Macmillan & Co. Ltd.

Wagner & Debes' Geog. Establᵗ Leipsic

Fig 2: English Possessions in France in 1361.

Fig 3: North-west France in 1477 showing the Calais Pale and neighbouring counties.

Fig 4: King Henry V. Charles VI made him heir to the French throne.

Fig 5: Sir Richard (Dick) Whittington, Lord Mayor of London and Mayor of Calais, with his cat.

Fig 6: King Edward IV seized the crown, helped by the Calais army of Warwick the Kingmaker.

Fig 7: Queen Mary I. Her support of her husband Philip's war against France resulted in the loss of Calais.

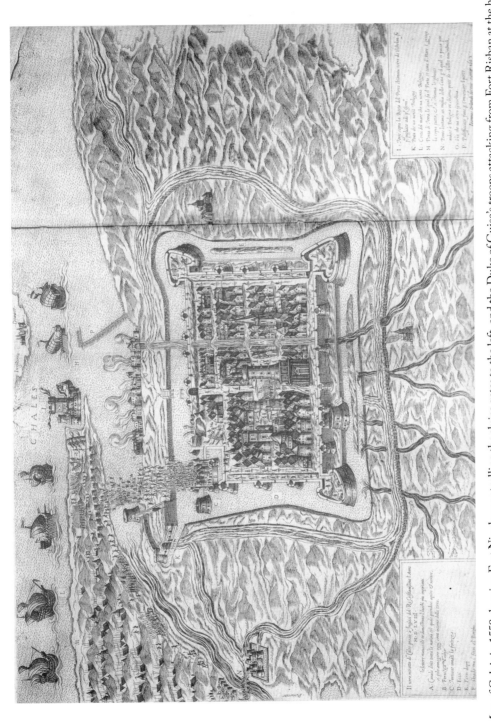

Fig 8: Map of Calais in 1558 showing Fort Nieulay controlling the sluice gates to the left, and the Duke of Guise's troops attacking from Fort Risban at the harbour.

Fig 9: The Armada portrait of Elizabeth I; behind her are the fire ships that scattered the Spanish fleet at Calais.

Fig 10: George (Beau) Brummell who fled to Calais to escape his creditors.

Fig 11: Lady Hamilton, Lord Nelson's beautiful mistress, who died penniless in Calais.

Fig 12: The 1802 French plan for a Channel tunnel to invade England, with air shafts and lit by candles.

Fig 13: Soldiers evacuated from Dunkirk arrive at Dover 1940. They might not have made it if the Battle of Calais had not bought them precious time.

Fig 14: German soldier in Calais after the British surrender in 1940.

Fig 15: Preparing to launch V-1 flying bomb from Pas de Calais.

England with 60,000 men, but had been defeated at the Battle of Flodden, in Northumberland, by the Earl of Surrey. The battle had been very bloody and had resulted in the death of King James and much of the Scottish nobility. Flodden had been a major disaster for Scotland, and had left the crown to James' heir, a 1-year-old boy. The child became King James V, with his mother, Henry VIII's sister Margaret, as regent. The only consolation from the Scottish point of view was that Surrey's army had suffered such high casualties that it had been unable to invade Scotland.

Henry must have felt proud of his first few years of kingship, but any hubris was soon replaced by rage. Instead of being able to control Scotland through Margaret as regent, the Scottish nobility invited the Duke of Albany, the closest adult male relative of the young king, to be regent instead. Albany had been born and brought up in France and supported the Auld Alliance. Margaret was obliged to hand over little James VI and then fled to her brother in England. The more immediate setback for Henry was, despite the long-time engagement of Charles of Burgundy, Maximilian's grandson, to Henry's sister, Mary, the emperor made peace with France and agreed that Charles should instead marry Renée, the daughter of Louis XIII. Louis used one of his noblemen who had been held captive in England after the Battle of the Spurs to further capitalize on this situation. The nobleman reminded Henry how he had been let down by his allies; Ferdinand had provided no support in the war against France, and Maximilian had broken his promise regarding a marriage between Charles and Mary. Henry was persuaded that he should discard such unfaithful allies and align himself and England with France.

In late 1514 Henry cemented an alliance with France by a marriage between Louis, whose wife had died, and Henry's sister, Mary. Mary may not have been enthusiastic about this match; the 16-year-old girl was already in love with the handsome Duke of Suffolk and Louis was 53 years old and in poor health. Fortunately for Mary, the marriage lasted only a couple of months before Louis died in January 1515, whereupon Mary returned to England and married Suffolk. Louis XII had produced no male children, so the throne passed to his son-in-law and cousin, Francis, who became Francis I of France. The new French king was 23 years old and just as eager as Henry to seek fame, and looked to Italy to find it. In 1516, a few months after having been crowned, Francis invaded Italy and defeated the combined army of the Papal States and the Swiss Confederacy at the Battle of Marignano, near Milan.

So great was Francis' victory that he took possession of Milan and concluded advantageous peace agreements with both the Swiss and the pope. Francis had made his presence felt in Europe. However, there was another newcomer to the European scene who was about to have even greater impact. In the same year as as the Battle of Marignano, (1516), Ferdinand of Spain died. His crowns were inherited by Charles of Burgundy, who became Charles V, alongside his mother Joanna. This made the 16-year-old Charles V ruler of a united Spain, Navarre, Naples, Sicily and Sardinia, together with the new Spanish lands in the West Indies, as well as the Duchy of Burgundy, which included the present Belgium, Luxembourg and the Netherlands. However, Joanna was suffering from a mental illness, so Charles took over her position as sovereign. Three years later his grandfather, Maximilian, died and Charles V became also the Archduke of Austria. This conglomerate of territories virtually surrounded France and was to lead to a deadly rivalry between these two young men.

Maximilian, like the Hapsburgs before him, had been elected Holy Roman Emperor. Francis put himself forward as a candidate for election as the new Holy Roman Emperor, in opposition to Charles. However, Charles gave bigger bribes to the electors and so won their vote, adding the prestige of the imperial crown to his many titles. This setback for Francis only made him more determined to contest the hegemony of Europe with Charles. The site for this contest was Italy, where Francis was dominating the north and Charles the south, with the Papal States between. Both rulers needed another country to tip the balance in their favour and looked to England for assistance. Francis was already ahead of the game. The year before Charles had become emperor, Francis had made a treaty with Henry VIII. The treaty had been arranged largely by Thomas Wolsey, who had become both a cardinal and Henry's principal minister. Wolsey had been bribed to facilitate the treaty, by agreeing that England should return Tournai to France and give up its bishopric, in exchange for an annual pension of 12,000 livres, from Francis. It was also agreed that Henry would receive 600,000 gold crowns in exchange for Tournai. Further, a treaty of friendship between the two countries would be sealed by the eventual marriage of Henry's 2-year-old daughter, Mary, to Francis' newly born son, also named Francis.

One of the conditions of the Anglo-French treaty was that Henry and Francis should meet in person to discuss further cooperation. After some delay, this meeting was set for some time in the year 1520. Since the excitement of 1513, with Henry's visit and the Battle of the Spurs, Calais had returned to its routine as a busy commercial centre. That was about to be disrupted by the forthcoming summit which would become one of the major events in the town's history. The unprecedented magnificence of the setting of this meeting would become known as the 'Field of the Cloth of Gold', because of the amount of gold embroidery on the tents and banners and the attire of those who attended. Extensive preparations started many months before the event, which was the talk of Europe.

Among the people who were less than pleased to hear of these preparations was Charles V. He had no wish to be upstaged by Francis at wooing Henry into an alliance, so he decided to pre-empt the summit by meeting with Henry, just before Henry met with Francis. Charles' ambassador arranged this with Wolsey, and it was agreed that the conference between their masters should appear to be completely unplanned. Accordingly, in May 1520 Charles stopped off at Hythe on his way to his coronation as emperor. Word was circulated that Charles had suddenly decided to divert his voyage because of his regard for Henry and he wished to pay his respects to him and his aunt, Queen Catherine of Aragon. Henry feigned surprise at the news that Charles had landed in England and sent Wolsey to meet him and conduct him in state to Dover Castle, where he was joined by Henry. This visit by Charles lasted four days, during which he was magnificently entertained by Henry. No treaty was agreed during the visit, but Charles continued his journey feeling reasonably confident that he had built on the good relations between England and Spain, exemplified by Henry's marriage to Catherine of Aragon. Charles had also seduced Wolsey into supporting him, by giving him the revenue of two bishoprics and hinting that he would support him as a candidate for the papacy.

Soon after the departure of Charles V, Henry, his queen and most of the court sailed to Calais. On reaching Calais they hardly stopped but pressed on to Guînes to be ready for the great meeting with Francis, four days later. The castle and walled town of Guînes guarded the southern border of the Calais Pale, but the actual location selected for the meeting was just outside Guînes at a place now called Balinghem. The terrain encompassed a number of open fields, equidistant between English Guînes and the French town of Ardres. King Henry and Queen Catherine were not accommodated at Guînes castle but at an amazing temporary palace that had been erected in front of the castle, especially for the event. It comprised four blocks with a central courtyard, with each side measuring 100 metres in length. It was constructed of brick work two metres high, above which were 10-metre-high walls of cloth or canvas on wooden frames, made to look like stone or brick, and topped with battlements. The roof also was made of canvas, painted to resemble slate, and had impressive brick-built towers at each corner. The structure had many large glass windows and was beautifully decorated with *trompe-l'oeil* statues and other embellishments. The sumptuous, richly furnished interior was hung with tapestries and velvet and led to the courtyard where a fountain of red wine flowed.

Preparations for the event had taken months of work, with Cardinal Wolsey masterminding the arrangements in liaison with the French. He had been assisted by Sir Richard Wingfield who had just resigned as Lord Deputy of Calais, to become ambassador to King Francis. In early March 1519 a workforce of 2,000 men, including 500 carpenters and 300 masons, had arrived in Calais from England, to start work on the site. Every effort had been made to ensure equality between the two kings and their contingents. The valley for the first meeting had been landscaped to provide equal elevations, so that no side could look down on the other. Ornate pavilions had been constructed for the various activities during the summit, including a tiltyard with magnificent stands for tournament viewing. In addition to the edifices that had been contrived specially for the meeting and the accompanying festivities, there were 2,800 tents for the less senior members of the English retinue. The French had an equal number of tents and pavilions, and both sides had to erect the working and sleeping accommodation for their small armies of servants, cooks, waggoneers, and horses. Each of the national contingents numbered about 6,000 people.

The express stated purpose of the meeting was to strengthen the bond of friendship between the two countries, within the context of the call from Pope Leo X for a universal peace between European rulers. The papal injunction was Rome's response to the recent Ottoman conquest of Egypt and Syria. From Francis' point of view, it provided an opportunity for a personal meeting with Henry, to gain support for his military ambitions in Italy. Although the event had been choreographed to demonstrate a display of amity between England and France, there was an underlying tension. At the time Henry was 28 years old and Francis was 25; both of them were, intelligent, athletic, dashing and accomplished young men, and both of them were eager to show the world they could outshine the other.

The summit began on 7 June 1520. Cardinal Wolsey and his splendid retinue rode to the magnificent palace at Arles, which had been specially constructed for Francis. He then escorted Francis to the ornate marquee midway between Guînes and Arles where Francis and Henry met and embraced, for the first time. So began a period of eighteen days of lavish entertainment, with magnificent banquets and masques hosted by each king in their respective temporary palaces, and a variety of events, from tournaments to archery displays and wrestling. It was an amazing spectacle with its gorgeous tents, marquees and pavilions, the attendees and their horses attired in their finery, and fluttering above all, the numerous flags and banners.

The summit concluded with a High Mass celebrated by Cardinal Wolsey on Sunday, 24 June in an outdoor chapel above the tiltyard. As the Mass ended an enormous kite – a fire breathing dragon – appeared in the sky, soaring above the crowd in a dramatic finale. Both sovereigns left the meeting well content with the event and the manner in which they had projected their individual wealth, power and accomplishments. But, for all that, there was little to show for the summit. Despite the numerous displays of Anglo-French friendship, no treaties had been signed, and, as we shall see, the universal peace celebrated by this great event lasted barely a year.

The Field of the Cloth of Gold has gone down in history as no more than a display of self-indulgent extravagance to feed the egos of two rulers. However, it was an event of such magnitude and magnificence that it is still remembered today. This is a testament to the imagination, organisation and sheer hard work by those who created one of the greatest shows on earth. The honours for having made this endeavour such a success were shared equally by the English and the French. The sheer magnitude of the task to achieve this spectacular event is hard to grasp, but some facts and figures about the formal dinners may give us some idea. Food served at the banquets comprised three courses with 50 dishes for each course. Accounts show that the English contingent, alone, used 99,050 eggs, 29,518 fish, and 6, 475 birds, including storks, swans and peacocks, and more than one million planks of firewood for the ovens [4]

Calais and the Calais Pale provided the majority of the work required to arrange and manage the English contribution to this huge event. For example, the Calais breweries provided all the beer, and it was from Calais that the four or five thousand craftsmen were recruited, to construct the palace, the elaborate tents and pavilions, and undertake the massive logistical task of providing food and shelter for the English entourage of 5,832 people and 3,217 horses, for nearly three weeks. The summit may have changed little in diplomatic terms, but nothing can detract from its success as an unrivalled, glittering event, and for that Calais and the Calais Pale must take the credit.

Chapter 8

Religious Strife, 1520–1542

The finale of The Field of the Cloth of Gold did not mean a return to normality for Calais and the Pale. It had been a very busy period, receiving all the nobles and their followers in the town and then preparing to ship them, with all their horses and baggage, back to England. There was also the significant task of dismantling the temporary palace and taking down all the English tents and the various pavilions and structures that had been erected for the great event. Deciding how to dispose of the various components must have been a challenge in itself. Some of the structures and their valuable contents and embellishments had been borrowed and needed to be returned to their owners; others had been assembled for the occasion only, and everything, from the rich hangings to wooden frameworks had to be sold at a good price. Winding up the event's finances was an important part of the deconstruction process, and included payment of various amounts, large and small, owed to the numerous builders, craftsmen, grocers, butchers, vintners, waggoneers and the rest. Another factor added to the frenzied activity: one summit was over, but another was about to begin.

Henry had not immediately returned to England. He remained in Calais with about half his courtiers, preparing for another royal meeting. On 10 July all was ready and Henry, accompanied by Cardinal Wolsey, set out with a splendid retinue to meet with Charles V. The venue for this summit was Gravelines, just outside the Calais Pale but within Burgundian territory. Charles met Henry and his entourage en route to Gravelines and escorted him into the town with every display of honour. He continued to offer magnificent hospitality and friendship to Henry, to eclipse that shown by Francis, a few weeks earlier. Later, Charles and his enormous train of courtiers were escorted by Henry, when they made a reciprocal visit to Calais. Once again, no effort or expense was spared to impress Charles and his nobles during this Calais summit.

After a brief period of lavish entertainment in Calais, Charles V and his followers returned to Burgundy and Henry sailed home to England. No treaties had been signed, but both rulers no doubt were pleased with the outcome. Henry would have been flattered that Charles, the Holy Roman Emperor, had gone to extreme lengths to seek his friendship, which enhanced his status at home and abroad. Charles would have been pleased that his charm offensive appeared to have earned Henry's support. As a bonus, having continued to dangle the prospect of backing Wolsey for the papacy, Charles would have been reasonably confident that Cardinal Wolsey would return his support.

Shortly after these summits the antipathy between Charles and Francis became so extreme that war appeared inevitable. The issues of dispute were numerous and ranged from the occupations of Milan by France, and Navarre by Spain, to questions of homage for Flanders and Artois. Charles suggested that Henry VIII should act as a mediator, and Francis reluctantly agreed. It was confirmed that the mediation would be conducted on Henry's behalf by his chief minister, Cardinal Wolsey, and that it would take place in Calais. Accordingly, Wolsey landed in Calais in July 1521, with a huge and splendid entourage. Charles' imperial ambassadors arrived early and secretly agreed with Wolsey that he would give them his support. The French delegation arrived the next day and discussions began, with Wolsey at pains to show his impartiality as a prince of the church. Two weeks later the negotiations reached an impasse, because Charles' senior diplomat had been ordered not to make any concessions without the emperor's approval. Wolsey proposed that the negotiations be suspended until he had visited Charles at his Imperial Court in Bruges, to obtain more flexible terms. The French reluctantly agreed to this.

On 12 August Wolsey left Calais in style, attended by the imperial ambassadors and a retinue of 400 prelates, nobles, knights and gentlemen. He was received with honour by Charles V and remained in Bruges for almost a fortnight. Little of this time was spent on finding a way forward for the Calais negotiations. Wolsey used the time to strengthen the emperor's support for his bid for the papacy, and the emperor used the time to make a secret pact with Wolsey against France. They agreed that Charles should visit England on his journey to Spain, at which time war against France would be declared.

Wolsey then returned to Calais and resumed his mediation, while maintaining his pretence of impartiality. Meanwhile fighting had broken out between France and the Holy Roman Empire in the Ardennes. Wolsey insisted that the belligerents put down their arms and when France demurred, he pronounced them the aggressors. The peace conference broke up and the French departed Calais, leaving Charles' ambassadors free to agree with Wolsey further schemes against France. Their plan was that Henry, Charles and Pope Leo X would invade France in the spring of 1523. Further, if Francis had not concluded a peace with Charles V by the time the emperor visited England, then Henry would declare war on France. Calais had become the setting for the diplomatic deception and intrigue which led to the conflict named the Four Years' War.

By the time Wolsey returned to Dover, the forces of Charles V and the pope had managed to eject France from Milan. Leo X had no sooner celebrated this victory with a *Te Deum* than he died, suddenly, in December 1521. Poison was suspected, but not confirmed. Wolsey had fully expected, with support from Charles V, that he would win the election for the papal triple-crown. But it was not to be – Charles did not raise a finger to help him. In January 1522 Adriaan Boeyens became Pope Adrian VI, for a short time, to be followed by Pope Leo's younger brother, Giulio Medici, who became Pope Clement VII in November 1523. When Pope Leo X died Francis suspected that Wolsey would feel let down by Charles and launched a charm offensive to coax Wolsey and Henry into an alliance with him. When this failed Francis tried applying pressure and placed an embargo on English shipping. This put Henry in such a fury that he declared war against France.

Five days after the declaration of war Charles V arrived in England and began a state visit that lasted a month and a half. Amid the full programme of feasting, hunting, tournaments and general pageantry, a treaty was signed. The treaty built on the agreements made in Bruges and Calais and both sides undertook to invade France with 40,000 men, with Henry attacking from the north and Charles from the south. The treaty ignored the fact that Henry's daughter, Mary, was already affianced to Francis' son, the young dauphin, and confirmed that the 5-year-old girl would be affianced to her 21-year-old cousin, Charles V. In early July Charles bade farewell to his aunt, Queen Catherine, and his new best friend, Henry, and sailed for Spain to prepare for war.

The next four years of the Italian wars brought France to its knees. It began when a combined Anglo-Spanish fleet of 180 ships, under the command of the Earl of Surrey, ravaged the north-west coast of France, burning coastal towns and villages. By the following year sufficient revenue had been raised to fund an army for a full invasion. In August 1522 the Earl of Surrey landed in Calais with 15,000 men. They were joined by a cavalry of about 1,000 horsemen from Charles' Spanish, Flemish and German lands. Surrey's army marched through Artois and Picardy, destroying and looting as they went. A French force harassed them constantly, but they avoided a full engagement. However, bad weather and a bout of dysentery among his troops obliged Surrey to return to Calais. While Surrey's expedition had obtained some plunder and caused some damage in north-east France, it had made no lasting gains; nor, for that matter, had Charles' army in the south. Nevertheless, France was still in deep crisis, surrounded by powerful foes.

Unbeknown to Francis, this crisis was even worse than it first appeared. The Duke de Bourbon, Constable of France, had been alienated by Francis and had made a secret agreement with Henry and Charles. He had agreed to lead a rebellion in central France at the same time that England and Spain invaded, from the north and south respectively. Once Francis had been defeated, France would be carved up between them. Bourbon would have Provence and Dauphiné with which to form a small kingdom; Charles would have Languedoc, Burgundy, Champagne and Picardy; and Henry would have the rest of France. For Henry this was an almost God-given opportunity to reclaim the dominions of his ancestors. In August 1523 Henry's brother-in-law, the Duke of Suffolk, and a new army landed in Calais. He was joined by troops from the garrisons of Calais, Hames and Guînes, increasing the force to 13,000 men. About three weeks later Suffolk led his army out of the Calais Pale and joined imperial troops from the Netherlands, which made a combined force of 20,000 men. More imperial troops were on their way from Germany, and everything pointed to a quick and decisive victory.

Unfortunately, far from being quick and decisive, Suffolk and his allies lost momentum through indecision. Instead of hastening to join the imperial force from Germany, they remained under the walls of Saint-Omer for a month, debating whether or not to besiege Boulogne instead. This gave Francis time to arrange for an army, commanded by the Duke of Guise, to interpose itself between Suffolk and the German imperial force. Suffolk and the allied army decided to advance on Paris and came within 20 miles of the capital, to the panic of its citizens. Just when it looked as though they might take Paris, news arrived that the German imperial force had been defeated by Guise and was in full flight. Worse was to come. Guise began attacking Suffolk's flanks and threatened to cut the vital supply link to Calais, and illness was spreading among the troops, so Suffolk and his allies decided to retrace their steps. The return march suffered mounting sickness and torrential rain, which made the roads almost impassable. Many of the imperial troops deserted and when Suffolk at last reached Calais, in December, his army was greatly reduced. What should have been the glorious campaign of 1523 had ended in utter failure.

It might have been expected that Suffolk would resume an invasion of France, from Calais, at the start of the 1524 campaign season. It had been agreed with Charles that an English force would launch a diversionary attack on Picardy. Consequently, the Duke of Bourbon, in command of Charles' army in Italy, attacked Francis' remaining troops in Italy, and Charles invaded Languedoc. In fact, Bourbon not only drove the French troops out of Italy – he crossed the Alps and besieged Marseilles. But neither Henry nor Charles had conducted their promised invasions, while Francis had raised a large army which drove Bourbon back over the Alps. Bourbon raised a new army in Germany, returned to Italy and confronted Francis at Pavia in February 1525. A ferocious battle took place in which the French army was heavily defeated, many of its nobles were killed, and Francis himself was captured. Charles V was now dominant in Italy and Francis was taken to Spain as a prisoner. France was at Charles' mercy and, in the absence of its king, was ruled by Francis' mother, Louise of Savoy.

Cardinal Wolsey had become disenchanted with Charles V the previous year, when Pope Leo X had died and he (Wolsey) had not been elected to the papacy, and Henry had begun tentative peace negotiations with France, when news of the Battle of Pavia arrived. With France suddenly on its knees, Henry decided to exploit the situation. He immediately sent ambassadors to Spain to congratulate Charles on his great victory and to begin talks about the partition of France. But Charles had no interest in carving up France with or for Henry, whose small army had remained in

Calais for over a year doing precisely nothing. The English ambassadors returned from Spain with a frosty reply from Charles. Enraged by this snub, Henry entered into a peace treaty with the French regent, Louise, which committed France to pay Henry the sum of 2,000,000 écus over 20 years.[1] Meanwhile, Charles was engaged in forcing Francis to agree to humiliating terms for his release, including relinquishing his claims to Milan and Naples and renouncing his sovereignty over Artois and Flanders. Francis accepted these terms and was released, but, as soon as he was safely home on French soil, he claimed he had agreed under duress, and the terms were therefore null and void.

For the previous two years Henry had dreamt that with military backing from Charles he could launch an army from Calais and conquer England's lost French territories. His recent alienation from Charles meant that his hopes were at an end. Indeed, France and England moved to become allies against Charles V. The new pontiff, Pope Clement VII was concerned about the growth of Charles' power in Italy and established a league against him, comprising several Italian states, France and England. Francis again invaded Italy and the Italian Wars resumed. England played no part in the wars but strengthened its treaties with France, culminating in the 1527 Treaty of Westminster, which committed the two countries to perpetual peace. By this time Charles' armies had sacked Rome and Pope Clement had been forced to take refuge in Castel Sant'Angelo, surrounded by imperial forces. Also, by this time Henry had become less interested in the Italian wars and more interested in producing a male heir to continue the Tudor dynasty.

Henry VIII had become convinced that his failure to father a legitimate male heir was God's punishment for having married his brother's widow. He wanted his marriage with Queen Catherine annulled so that he could find a new bride. Henry instructed Wolsey to obtain an annulment from Pope Clement, but this was more easily said than done. Clement had escaped from Sant'Angelo to Orvieto but was still being threatened by Charles' Imperial troops who remained in possession of Rome. Charles V was Queen Catherine's nephew and had already made it clear that Clement was not to annul Henry's marriage to his aunt. Meanwhile Henry had fallen in love with a tall, attractive and vivacious brunette named Anne Boleyn. Anne's sister, Mary, previously had been one of Henry's mistresses and in normal circumstances Anne would have merely taken her place. However, Anne had no interest in being a mistress and made it clear that she would not consummate her relationship with Henry out of wedlock.

For the amazingly long period of six years this impasse continued – Anne refused to be seduced and the pope refused to grant a divorce. During this time the pope sent a legate to England to try the case, and the legate refused to agree to an annulment. Wolsey was blamed and fell from power; Queen Catherine was banished and Anne took ownership of her rooms; and Henry began planning to break with Rome. Against this background Henry wanted to find allies against Pope Clement and Charles V, so, naturally, he turned to Francis. On 23 June 1532 at Westminster a new treaty was signed with France. It was agreed that the two monarchs should seal the new accord by meetings at Calais and Boulogne.

This twin location summit was not in the same league as the Field of the Cloth of Gold but it was still a grand affair which required considerable preparation in both Calais and Boulogne. Henry asked Francis to bring his own mistress to the summit, so that he could bring Anne Boleyn with him. The summits began in December that year, after four months of preparation. The usual pageantry, banquets and masques ensued, which fostered the personal relationship between the two kings and confirmed Francis' support for Henry's marriage to Anne. While in Calais Henry must have told Anne that he intended to marry her, and she finally allowed him to consummate their union. An amorous night in Calais resulted in Anne becoming pregnant with the future Elizabeth I. Henry straightaway took steps to marry Anne, thus defying the pope. Immediately after returning to Dover in January 1533 Henry and Anne were secretly married. Things began to move fast. Henry appointed Thomas Cranmer to the vacant position of Archbishop of Canterbury, and a few months later Cranmer pronounced that Henry's (first) marriage to Catherine was invalid and that his (second) marriage to Anne was legitimate. On 1 June that same year Anne was crowned queen.

At last, the star-crossed lovers were united as king and queen, but they would not live happily ever after. Anne gave birth to baby Elizabeth, a girl, much to Henry's disappointment. Further pregnancies were unsuccessful and did not produce living infants, let alone a male heir. In early 1536 Anne celebrated the news that Catherine of Aragon had died, but her triumph was short-lived. Henry had already tired of Anne and his eyes had settled on the attractive and gentle natured Jane Seymour. The king indicated to Thomas Cromwell, his principal minister at the time, that he wanted to be rid of Anne and marry Jane. Accordingly, Cromwell arranged a series of trumped-up charges against Anne, including incest with her brother, and Anne was charged with high treason. The outcome of the case was never in doubt, but Henry decided to show some compassion for his former love. At that time the official sentence for a woman convicted of treason was to be burnt at the stake. Henry commuted the sentence to having Anne's head 'cut off', as opposed to being beheaded. 'Beheading' required severing the head from the body by means of an axe, which often took several blows. 'Cutting off' required severing the head from the body by means of a sword, in a single stroke. Even before the official guilty verdict had been returned, Henry had arranged for a trained swordsman from Calais to effect Anne's execution.

Henry's consideration for his wife went even further. He ordered that the execution should take place inside the Tower on Tower Green, rather than the customary venue, outside the walls, on Tower Hill, in front of baying crowds, Finally, he gave specific orders relating to the Calais swordsman's clothing. It had become the norm for executioners to wear garish clothing, rather like jesters, to ensure they stood out in a crowd, and to add an element of theatre to what was usually a well-attended public spectacle. Henry's instructions required the swordsman to wear a sombre outfit – so that Anne would not be able to identify him from the scaffold – to avoid alarming her.[2]

Anne's execution was carried out on 19 May 1536, but not entirely as Henry had ordered. The scaffold had been hastily erected outside the White Tower rather than on Tower Green and the gates had not been closed, so crowds of spectators had gathered there to join the group of ambassadors, peers and officials. Anne delivered a short speech, was blindfolded, then knelt, upright, her head held high. The Calais executioner, in his indifferent attire, had hidden the sword under the straw so that Anne would not see it. Silently he picked it up, swung it above his own head a few times, to gain some momentum, then severed Anne's head with a single, clean, stroke. It was a job well done.

The next day Henry, in a joyous mood, became betrothed to Jane Seymour. They were married ten days later, on 30 May 1536.

In 1523 Calais had been the base from which the Duke of Suffolk had launched his invasion of France. Twenty years would pass before the town and the Pale would be used again for that purpose. Although there were periods in which England was officially at war with France, these military actions took place in Italy. An important defensive development for Calais in this period was the building of Fort Nieulay in 1525, to protect the sluice gates at Newnham Bridge at the mouth of the River Hames. The sluice gates had been constructed so that by closing them the River Hames could be diverted to flood the land south of Calais Town. The south of Calais was already marshland, but diverting the Hames made a land attack on the town almost impossible. Control of the sluice gates was vital to the protection of Calais and building the four-towered Fort Nieulay represented a significant defensive enhancement.

Since the signing of the Treaty of Westminster in 1532, England and France had been allies, and there was no question of Henry invading France. Calais had its garrisons and while they had to be ready for a sudden change in the political situation, the town had resumed its primary role as a commercial centre. Unfortunately, the commercial centre was past its best; wool exports had been overtaken by undyed broadcloth, for which the Company of Merchant Adventurers, who had moved out of Calais and back to Flanders, held the monopoly. In the period 1526 to 1530, the Calais Staple had sold approximately 4,800 sacks of wool a year, only. This figure was reduced to 3,000 sacks per year, over the next five years.[3] This circumstance affected not only the prosperity of Staplers but meant that the vital Staple revenue for the crown was much reduced, which made it more difficult for Henry VIII to afford to send an army abroad.

The long serving Lord Deputy of Calais, Baron Berners, had died in 1953 and had been replaced by Arthur Plantagenet, Viscount Lisle. Arthur was the bastard son of Edward IV but had entered Henry's VII's household through his half-sister Queen Elizabeth. By the time Henry VIII had come to the throne, he and Arthur had become close companions, despite Arthur being almost thirty years older than Henry. It may have been that Henry found his uncle a more approachable father figure than his own dour parent. By virtue of having married an heiress, Arthur had become a major landowner; through the patronage of Henry VIII, he had been created Viscount Lisle, had become a Knight of the Garter and a member of the Council, and then vice-admiral of England. Lisle was almost 70 years old, but in many ways was a good choice for Lord Deputy of Calais. He had been born there, had visited the town during the Field of the Cloth of Gold, and many other times since, as admiral. Most of all he was loyal and could concentrate on his role in Calais and his related appointment as Lord Warden of the Cinq Ports. His predecessor, Baron Berners, had been far superior to Lisle in intellect and talent, but having been Chancellor of the Exchequer as well, had meant that he spent most of his time at court, rather than in Calais. Lisle was a steady individual who would be permanently based in Calais and better able to keep on top of the serious tensions that had begun to disrupt the town.

Sixteen years earlier, in 1517, a German priest and theologian named Martin Luther had nailed to the door of Wittenberg castle church, his *Ninety-Five Theses*, an academic disputation criticising the sale of indulgences and other abuses by the clergy. Since then, Luther had been excommunicated by the pope but had not been silenced. His pamphlets and translation of the Latin New Testament in German had been widely circulated, thanks to the introduction of the printing press. Luther's writing and preaching soon went beyond criticising church abuses. He formulated a new Christian doctrine which rejected the pope and placed the bible at the centre of a simple worship, with salvation being achieved through faith rather than good works. Lutheranism became an organized separate church, increasingly popular across Northern Europe.

By 1529 many of the rulers of the German states had adopted Lutheranism, which prompted the regent in Germany at that time, Ferdinand, the younger brother of Charles V to call the princes of the empire to the Diet of Speyer. At the meeting Ferdinand pronounced Lutheranism heretical and forbade the rulers from supporting it. This resulted in the Lutheran rulers signing a document 'protesting' at the regent's ruling. The term 'Protestantism' was born and leaders of important states such as Saxony, Brandenburg and Hess found themselves in conflict with both the pope and their emperor. Two years later (1531), at Schmalkalden in Germany, they formed the Schmalkaldic League to protect themselves from any attempt by the emperor to force Roman Catholicism upon them. The shock waves of German Protestantism began to be felt across Europe.

In England, although Henry VIII had defied the pope he still held to Catholic doctrine, but interest in Protestantism was growing in his court.

Henry's principal minister, Thomas Cromwell, had protestant sympathies and even Thomas Cranmer, the Archbishop of Canterbury, had been married in secret. For all that, while the king remained a Catholic, few would dare openly to declare themselves protestant.

Calais was located in mainland Europe and geographically was closer to the German Lutheran states. Furthermore, Calais was a commercial centre and thus a place where new religious ideas could be exchanged, as much as goods. It was not only Lutheran books and pamphlets that were being read and discussed in Calais. In time a number of separate groups emerged, espousing different protestant dogma, such as those of the French humanist lawyer, John Calvin, and the Swiss preacher, Huldrych Zwingli. In a deeply religious age, it was vital to decide whether your immortal soul would be saved by clinging to the traditional dogma of the Catholic Church, or by adopting one of the protestant teachings. For several years Calais had been in religious ferment, and Viscount Lisle faced the challenge of keeping the lid in place on this highly combustible situation.

In 1537, a year after his marriage to Jane Seymour, Henry VIII broke completely with Rome His compliant parliament had passed the first Act of Supremacy in March 1534, which made him 'Supreme Head on Earth of the Church of England'. This was followed by the Treason Act in December 1534, which made it punishable by death to disavow the Act of Supremacy. That was no idle threat and when Henry's friend and Chancellor, Thomas More, refused to accept the Act of Supremacy, he was executed. These were dangerous times for anyone close to the king who remained loyal to the pope. It made life even more complicated for Viscount Lisle in Calais, where the heated antagonism between ardent supporters of Roman Catholicism and those with new protestant beliefs had been dangerously swirling around for some time. What was more, Calais was becoming a focal point for spreading protestant beliefs to England. This was happening through pamphlets printed in the protestant states reaching Calais and then being sent across the Channel, and also by word of mouth of the protestant-minded garrison soldiers, and merchants, returning to different parts of England. It was Lisle's unenviable duty to suppress Protestantism and also enforce the law against those displaying continued allegiance to the pope. He was a man content to bend with the wind and do his duty to his sovereign, but his wife, Honor Grenville, remained steadfast in her spiritual allegiance to Rome. Honor was not foolish enough to express her views openly, but her strong Catholicism was known at court and so cast a doubt on her loyalty, and by extension, that of her harmless husband.

In England, the Act of Supremacy, Cromwell's introduction of changes to traditional church practices, and the dissolution of smaller monasteries, had seriously divided the church. It also had brought unrest in many parts of the country. The most significant of these was in the north in what was called the 'Pilgrimage of Grace'. This was a peaceful march to London to request the king to abandon the new changes and return to the traditions of the Catholic Church. Some 40,000 people had joined the pilgrimage by the time it reached Lincoln, and to Henry it had all the appearances of a major rebellion. The marchers were ordered to disperse and did so, having been promised a pardon, and knowing that the Duke of Suffolk (with an army) was advancing against them. Once the marchers had dispersed it was relatively easy to hunt down the ring leaders and summarily execute them for treason. Henry VIII had restored obedience with ruthless efficiency

It was against this background that in October 1537 an event occurred that brought a brief respite from the gloom caused by unrest and bloody repression. There was general rejoicing when it was announced that Queen Jane Seymour had given birth to a boy. The child was christened Edward, possibly in memory of Edward III, whose great exploits in France had included the capture of Calais. Henry was ecstatic and ordered great celebrations and a magnificent christening. Queen Jane, whose health had never been robust, had endured a difficult birth. In a very frail state, she was obliged to attend the prolonged christening banquet which proved too much for her and she died soon after. Henry was distraught by her death and donned mourning but was soon distracted by foreign affairs. He had become increasingly concerned about his relations with Francis I, after the French king had openly criticized the execution of Anne Boleyn. Intelligence had been received that Charles, Francis and the pope were moving towards a peace agreement that might lead them to unite against England. In June the next year (1538) this proved to be the case, when the Truce of Nice agreed a ten-year cessation in the Italian Wars.

Both France and Spain needed a pause in hostilities. Francis had allied with the Ottoman Turks but their combined attack on Genoa had been repulsed. Charles had been forced to pull back from his attack on Provence, and desperately needed a peace so he could concentrate on defending Hungary from the Ottomans. Negotiations for the truce were not an amicable affair. Charles and Francis hated each other so much they refused to be in the same room, so Pope Paul III had to facilitate the negotiations by moving to and fro between the two. The one point on which Charles and Francis did agree was to urge the pope to excommunicate Henry. With France and Spain at peace, there was a sudden danger that either one of them could decide to invade heretical England. When Henry heard the terms of the truce he ordered the strengthening of harbour defences and ordered the navy and the Calais garrison to be ready to attack.

Thomas Cromwell realized that the king needed allies in the event of an invasion and looked to the protestant states of Germany, who had rebelled against Charles V. The two most prominent members of the protestant military alliance of the League of Schmalkalden were its leader, the Duke of Saxony, and the Duke of Cleves. Cromwell had heard that the Duke of Cleves had an attractive, blonde daughter named Anne, whose sister was married to the Duke of Saxony. If Henry married Anne of Cleves he would not only create a counterbalance to any Franco-Spanish threat but would have a new queen and the prospect of her giving him a 'spare' heir. The king accepted Cromwell's advice but, before confirming a treaty, wanted to be sure of Anne's good looks. As a result, the court artist, Hans Holbein, was despatched to paint Anne's portrait. When Henry saw Holbein's depiction of Anne he was delighted with her appearance, and an alliance was agreed with the German Protestants. Preparations were started for Henry's marriage to Anne.

Arrangements had been made for Anne of Cleves to travel to Calais before being escorted across the Channel to England. Viscount Lisle and his staff would have been very busy making sure that Calais provided a suitable welcome and stay for Anne and her entourage. The task of escorting Anne to England had been given to the Lord Admiral, the Earl of Southampton, who arrived early in Calais to receive the future queen. Anne remained in Calais for a few days probably as the guests of Viscount Lisle and his wife at The Staple Inn, the official residence of the Lord Deputy. On 27 December 1539 Anne and her party embarked for Deal, attended by the Earl of Southampton, escorted by a fleet of fifty ships.

On landing Anne was taken to Rochester Abbey. Henry had decided it would be a romantic gesture to surprise her by arriving in disguise. This did not go well. Henry had expected to meet a beauty but found Anne exceedingly plain. He was also less than pleased that she appeared to take little interest in him when he removed his disguise and revealed himself as king. The fact that Anne spoke German only did not help this initial encounter. Henry rode back to the Palace of Greenwich without his future wife.

Henry was furious at having been put in the position of marrying someone he regarded as unattractive and graceless. On 6 January the marriage went ahead – it was unthinkable to do otherwise without causing offence to Henry's new German allies. The angry king summoned both Cromwell and the Earl of Southampton. Cromwell was blamed for not having obtained accurate information about Anne's looks, and Southampton for not having notified Henry that she was plain, when he had met her in Calais. Southampton was a longstanding friend of the king and won Henry's grudging forgiveness when he insisted that he had not been involved in choosing Anne and was merely carrying out orders to escort her to England. Although Henry's full anger descended on Cromwell, he did not dismiss him as his principal minister; Cromwell was too valuable to him as his general fixer. Cromwell's power and protestant leanings had brought him many enemies, the most important of whom was the Duke of Norfolk, the leader of the Catholic faction. Norfolk decided the time was right to exploit Henry's anger and engineer Cromwell's downfall.

During the next few months Cromwell seemed to have regained the king's trust, but all this would change when Henry sent the Duke of Norfolk on an embassy to King Francis. The purpose of the embassy was for Henry to offer himself as a mediator in outstanding disputes between Francis and Charles V. When Norfolk reported that the proposal had been favourably received, it demonstrated to Henry that neither France nor Spain were plotting to attack him, and so Cromwell's alliance with the Germans and Henry's marriage to Ann of Cleves had been unnecessary. Henry had lost patience with his principal minister and on 10 June 1540 Cromwell was arrested, charged with high treason and imprisoned in the Tower. On 24 June Queen Anne of Cleves was banished to Richmond where she was informed by Norfolk of the king's intention to end their marriage. Cromwell's titles and offices were withdrawn, his property was confiscated, and he was executed without trial on Tower Hill on 28 July. On the same day Henry VIII married the Duke of Norfolk's niece, Catherine Howard.

Anne of Cleves sensibly agreed to an annulment of her marriage and in exchange was given Richmond Palace as her residence, together with Hever Castle and a large income from lands confiscated from Cromwell and the Boleyns. Instead of being Queen, Anne was given the title of the 'The King's Beloved Sister', and precedence over all ladies in the realm, other than Queen Catherine Howard, and Henry's two children. When Henry first visited her after the annulment, he found she was a changed person. She bore no animosity towards him, was rather good company, and enjoyed her privileged life without queenly responsibilities. Indeed, over time the two became friends; Anne was a frequent and popular visitor to court and close to princesses Mary and Elizabeth, both of whom came to hold her in great affection. Anne lived happily until 1557 when she died at Chelsea Old Manor, having outlived Henry and all his wives.

The king's wrath against those responsible for his unnecessary marriage to Anne had destroyed Cromwell and may have included others. Henry may have considered his uncle, Viscount Lisle, at fault for not having warned him of Anne's looks while she was staying in Calais. If that was the case it could not have come at a worse time for Lisle, as a plot to betray Calais to the French had just been discovered. Lisle's wife, Honor, was known to have papist sympathies, and this was not just court gossip. Three years earlier she had written to Archbishop Cranmer asking him to intercede on behalf of Roman Catholic priests who had been arrested in Calais. As a result, she had received a warning from Cromwell to stop meddling. If Honor was a papist sympathiser her husband might share the same sentiments; and if so, he was quite likely to plot to turn Calais over to the Catholic French. Lisle found himself in a very dangerous position. He was the much-liked uncle of the king; but a king who was prepared to execute his own wife on trumped-up charges was likely to be merciless to anyone whom he suspected of betrayal.

The origins of what became known as the 'Botolf Plot' date back to spring 1538. It was at that time that two young men arrived in Calais from England to take up posts in Viscount Lisle's household. One was Gregory Botolf, who had arrived as one of Lisle's three personal chaplains.

The other was Clement Philpot, who had joined Lisle's household as an esquire. Boltof was an ambitious, smooth-talking cleric who became known in Calais as 'Gregory Sweet Lips'. He was also a secret papist and his manipulating eloquence soon had Philpot under his spell. A month after the two arrived in Calais there was another arrival of note, a Lutheran preacher named Adam Damplin. Calais was already experiencing serious religious ferment and the Catholicism of Henry's Church of England was being challenged by a growing number of reformists, influenced by Luther or Calvin. Despite this, Lisle had given Damplin a licence to preach and before long Damplin's sermons gained a significant following among the reformists. When this came to the attention of England, Lisle was ordered to arrest Damplin and send him to London for examination by English bishops. Damplin was found to have been spreading heresy against England's official religion and executed. However, that was not the end of the matter.

Damplin was dead, but his sermons had inflamed religious unrest in Calais, which had led some people in England to cast doubts on Lisle's competence as Lord Deputy. In fairness, it should be said that Lisle had granted Damplin a preaching licence having been guided by Cromwell, the chief minister. Although Henry had broken from Rome it was not known whether he would adopt some of the Lutheran reforms advocated by Cromwell, or retain adherence to the Catholic doctrine, as advocated by the Duke of Norfolk. In the spring of 1539 Henry decided to support Norfolk, and that summer the Statute of Six Articles was passed, affirming Catholic beliefs and practices. Meanwhile the situation in Calais had deteriorated to the point of there being violence in the streets. In early 1540 the Duke of Norfolk urged Henry to establish a commission to investigate the governance of Calais and stamp out protestant heresies. Henry agreed and appointed Norfolk's son, the Earl of Surrey, as head of the commission.

A few weeks before this, Lisle had granted Botolf, Philpot and another member of his household, John Woller, permission to go to England on business. On 5 February the three met in a Calais tavern and made all around them aware that they were about to embark for England on the 2 am tide. In fact, Philpot and Woller did set sail, but Botolf slipped away from them in the darkness and crossed into France. From there he travelled to Rome and sought an audience with Cardinal Pole, a grandson of George, Duke of Clarence. Pole had opposed Henry over his divorce from Catherine of Aragon and had then travelled abroad, calling on the Roman Catholic princes of Europe to depose Henry for having broken from Rome. Botolf was granted an audience with Pole and the pope and described his plan to betray Calais to the Catholic French. He explained that Philpot and a dozen co-conspirators in the town would overcome the watch and allow Botolf and five hundred men waiting outside with ladders to scale the twenty-foot walls, using ladders. They would then overpower the soldiers guarding the main gate to allow a French force to enter and seize the town.

The pope gave Botolf and his plot his blessing, together with 200 crowns, and Botolf returned to Calais. He arrived on 17 March, one day after Surrey arrived with the commissioners. Botolf then travelled in secret to a nunnery in Gravelines, in Flanders, where he met with Philpot who had just returned from England and explained the plot in detail. Botolf then left for Ghent to make final arrangements with papal contacts and Philpot returned to Calais. But, while Botolf was in Ghent, Philpot had time to develop cold feet. On 2 April Philpot decided to save himself by asking to see the commissioners. He threw himself on their mercy by confessing the whole plot, naming Botolf and all who were involved, most of whom were members of Lisle's household.

The king was informed and ordered Lisle to return to England immediately. On arrival Lisle was treated as normal and even sat on Henry's left at the installation of Garter Knights at Windsor on 9 May. In the meantime, Botolf had been extradited from Flanders. He ended up in the Tower with Philpot and six other members of Lisle's Calais household. On 17 May Lisle was summoned to the Council and questioned about his knowledge of the Botolf conspiracy. The day after that he was questioned by the king himself. Henry must have had misgivings about his uncle, for the next day Lisle was arrested and committed to the Tower. His wife, Honor, and two daughters were arrested and placed in Calais gaols. It goes without saying that Botolf, Philpot and the other suspected conspirators were soon executed. Lisle's life hung by a thread but there was no hard evidence against him, and even the ever-suspicious Henry may have doubted that his almost 70-year-old uncle would organize a papist plot.

Time went by with Lisle and Honor languishing in their respective prisons. In the spring of 1541 Henry decided to empty the Tower by releasing or executing its prisoners, in order to make room for others. The reason for this was to take his revenge on Cardinal Pole by executing his relations, including Pole's 67-year-old mother, Margaret, Countess of Salisbury. Once this reign of terror was over Lisle was released from solitary confinement and permitted to walk on the Tower's walls. This might have indicated that a pardon was on its way, but Henry had become preoccupied by information of his wife's adultery with a courtier. He invoked the Act of Attainder to justify her execution and on 13 February 1541 Catherine Howard was beheaded, by axe – no sword for her! Four days later Henry was being rowed down the Thames when he saw Lisle on the Tower wall, calling to him for mercy. Henry decided to release Lisle and granted him a full pardon and the restoration of his lands and titles. Lisle was informed of this news the next day and was so overcome with joy that he had a heart attack and died two days later, before leaving the Tower. His wife, Honor, was released from her Calais prison and returned to live at her estate in Cornwall for another 24 years, but she had already become insane.[4]

In Calais, neither Sussex's commission nor the appointment of Lord Maltravers as the new Lord Deputy proved any more successful than Lisle at quelling religious disturbances. This was unfortunate, and before long England was again at war with France.

Chapter 9

The Last Hurrah, 1540–57

I n 1540 Henry Fitzalan, Lord Maltravers, had been appointed Lord Deputy of Calais to replace Lisle. He was the eldest son of the Earl of Arundel and a consummate courtier who had been a page to Henry VIII and had accompanied him to Calais in 1532. He had become an MP, attended the trial of Anne Boleyn and was a strong Catholic, which made him acceptable to the now dominant Duke of Norfolk. He was also an energetic 28-year-old, as compared with the elderly and rather doddery Lisle. Maltravers took over at a time when the town and the Pale were in religious upheaval and the Wool Staple was in decline. The decline in the fortunes of The Staple meant that there was less money with which to pay wages for the garrison and the upkeep of the defences. The religious turmoil that was taking place across Europe was being felt in Calais. Religious disputes were becoming civil disturbances, causing The Staple to devote its limited funds to pay the garrison, and thus ensure its loyalty, rather than pay to maintain the fortifications. The fortifications had become neglected, so Maltravers set about repairing them, with his own money.

The repair of Calais' defences assumed increasing importance while Henry moved towards war with France. King Francis still had unfinished business regarding his claim to Milan. In preparation for war, he made alliances with the religious enemies of Charles V – the protestant states of Denmark, Sweden and Cleves, and Suleiman, Sultan of the Ottoman Empire. In July 1542 the Italian Wars resumed when Francis again invaded Italy. By then Charles' aunt, Catherine of Aragon, had been dead for some time, so it was possible to heal the rift between Charles and Henry. The two entered into a secret alliance to attack France in 1543, having agreed to demand that Francis end his alliance with the Turks and make reparations for the damage caused in his recent campaigns. If Francis rejected these terms, as they knew he would, it would be an excuse to declare war. Once Francis had been defeated, Charles would seize the duchy of Burgundy, and Henry would regain the French territories of his ancestors. All round it was a most attractive proposition.

Whenever England contemplated war with France it was normal practice to ensure that Scotland would not launch an attack over the border, while the English army was engaged across the Channel. Henry's sister, Margaret Tudor, was the mother of King James V of Scotland, and Henry hoped that he might come to terms with his young nephew. But James was by then 30 years old and very much his own man. He was a strong Roman Catholic who followed his godfather, Francis of France, rather than his heretical uncle, Henry VIII of England. Indeed, in 1537 James had travelled to France to marry Francis' daughter, Madeleine, and renew the Auld Alliance. Madeleine died soon after their return to Scotland, but James retained the French connection by marrying Mary of Guise the next year.

In September 1541 Henry had travelled to York for a meeting with his nephew, but James had not arrived at the venue. An angry Henry returned to London only to find that James had further insulted him. Henry had recently assumed the title 'King of Ireland', but James had been in contact with Irish chiefs who agreed that he should be known as 'Lord of Ireland'. When Henry's sister, Margaret, died in October 1541, there was no longer any incentive for peace, and war broke out with Scotland. Border skirmishes led to the defeat of a small English force, and in November a Scots army of about 15,000 men advanced to the River Eske in England. They were met by a 3,000-strong English army at Solway Moss, but arguments among the Scots concerning their leadership led to confusion and a Scots defeat, which resulted in 1,200 prisoners being taken, several of them nobles. King James had not been at the battle but had withdrawn to Falkland Palace, humiliated, with a fever, in a very depressed state. Soon after the fever took hold and he died at the age of only 31. A few days before his death he heard that his wife, Mary of Guise, had given birth to his only heir, a girl named Mary, who would become known to history as 'Mary Queen of Scots'.

Henry's northern army was far too small to capitalise on the instability caused by the death of King James, in order to dominate Scotland. Mary of Guise and the Roman Catholic faction among the Scots nobility were outmanoeuvred by the protestant Earl of Arran, who became regent. A struggle for power soon turned into armed conflict. Henry decided to exploit the situation by trying to win Scotland by marriage rather than force of arms. Negotiations began with Arran for baby Mary to be affianced to Henry's son Edward. If agreed, this would not only end the Auld Alliance but also unite the crowns of England and Scotland. The prospect of this agreement made Henry feel that he could invade France without fear of a Scottish attack. He declared war and sent a force of 6,000 under Sir John Wallop to reinforce Charles V in Flanders. Henry did not lead the army himself as he was preoccupied with wooing a sixth wife, an attractive and accomplished 30-year-old widow named Catherine Parr. Henry and Catherine were married in July 1543. By the time the campaigning season had come to an end, Wallop's forced had been seriously depleted and had returned to Calais with nothing to show for its deployment.

In December, with Scotland still disrupted by power struggles, the Scottish Parliament rejected the proposed marriage of little Queen Mary to Henry's son, Edward, and Henry immediately ordered the invasion of Scotland. A fleet of a hundred ships commanded by the Lord High Admiral, John Dudley, appeared in the Forth accompanied by a strong army. The army was commanded by Edward Seymour, Earl Hertford, the brother of Queen Jane Seymour and uncle to Edward, Henry's heir, who had risen to a position of power. Hertford's force landed at Leith and informed the Scottish authorities that they must immediately hand over the 1-year-old Queen Mary, to be taken to England in preparation for her eventual marriage to Prince Edward.

When the Scots rejected this 'rough wooing', Hertford burned Leith and went on to sack Edinburgh and the surrounding area but could not take the castle. The Earl of Arran gathered a Scottish army which caused the English to withdraw, leaving destruction in their wake. Dudley sailed down the east coast, raiding towns and villages as he went, and Hertford's army returned to England, burning and looting along the way.

Hertford was Lord Warden of the Scottish Marches, so he remained in the north of Scotland where he was kept busy. The Scots had not appreciated being ravaged by the English, so they conducted a number of border raids during the early part of 1544. At home in London Henry was preparing to launch an invasion of France in 1545 and intended to lead the attack himself. The latest strategy agreed between Charles and Henry was that Charles should invade France from Champagne and

Henry from Picardy, but rather than stop to besiege towns they would advance to Paris, take the city in a combined attack, and then dictate peace terms to Francis. Once again, a very attractive scenario. It could hardly go wrong.

Calais was crucial to the expedition, so it was a little inconvenient when the Earl of Arundel died, early in the new year. Maltravers, the Lord Deputy, was Arundel's heir and returned to England to assume the earldom. Henry must have thought Maltravers had done a good job in Calais as he was made a Knight of the Garter. The new Lord Deputy appointed by Henry was George Brooke, Baron Cobham. Cobham was an experienced soldier who had fought with distinction in the Calais area in the 1520s and had been one of Hertford's commanders for the invasion of Scotland. Cobham was rapidly installed as Lord Deputy, to direct the major task of preparing Calais to receive the invasion force.

In May Hertford was able to send word to Henry that he had quelled the border raids, and there was no immediate threat from Scotland. Henry felt he was now safe to invade France without being attacked in the north by the Scots. As the imperialist forces had already gone into the field, Henry ordered that the invasion be launched as soon as possible. The next month an army of 20,000 men arrived in Calais, commanded by the Dukes of Norfolk and Suffolk, with Maltravers, now Earl of Arundel, as a subordinate commander. On 14 July Henry arrived in Calais and was soon joined by 15,000 of Charles V's imperial troops. This large, combined force advanced into Picardy at the end of the month. All was set to implement the agreed strategy of a rapid advance to take Paris. Unfortunately, neither Charles nor Henry kept to the plan.

Charles decided that his advance should include the capture of Luxembourg, Ligne and Saint-Didier. Not to be outdone, Henry turned aside to besiege Boulogne and Montreuil. Charles captured his three towns quite quickly and continued his rapid advance, only to find that his English allies were still in position outside the walls of Boulogne and Montreuil. Henry had decided personally to take command of the siege of Boulogne, and once Henry had set his mind to something, he stuck to it with tenacity. In vain did Charles send ambassadors to urge Henry to abandon the towns and advance on Paris; Henry doggedly continued the sieges for the next two months. On 14 September Boulogne fell but Montreuil still held out. By this time Charles was already just a few miles from Paris but there had been enough time for Francis to place a blocking force between Charles and Henry. A great opportunity had been lost, and the frustrated Charles agreed to come to terms with Francis.

Both Charles and Francis needed a breathing space. They were seriously short of funds and Charles was concerned about unrest among the German protestant princes. This situation resulted in the Treaty of Crépy, agreed on 18 September 1544, which returned to the status quo of 1535, with Francis again renouncing his claims to Naples, Artois and Picardy, and Charles renouncing his claim to Burgundy. On the face of it the treaty had changed nothing, but it included the promise of a marriage alliance between relatives of Charles and Francis, and a secret clause that they would support each other against England. Henry had been stabbed in the back by his nephew. Francis and Charles had temporarily sorted out their differences, but Henry was still at war with Francis. What was more, the Duke of Orléans and his army were bearing down on Montreuil.

Henry directed Norfolk to ensure that Boulogne was strongly defended, then returned to England, regarding himself as something of a hero for having captured Boulogne. While it was a good thing that England had taken Boulogne, it was a minor achievement when the purpose of the invasion had been to force Francis to agree to restore to England all the lost English territories in France. As it was, Boulogne was by no means safe. Orléans and his army were about to descend on the English besiegers at Montreuil, so Norfolk ordered the siege to be abandoned and the force to return to Calais. Orléans was able to relieve Montreuil and then turned his attention to Boulogne.

Norfolk believed that Boulogne could not hold out for long against concerted French attacks, so he pulled back most of his troops to the safety of the Calais Pale, leaving Boulogne with only a 4,000-strong garrison. This was a sensible move but risked encouraging a French attack on the town, and Orléans needed little encouragement. He began to invest the town and then, on 9 October, launched a major attack. His troops had almost succeeded in capturing the town but had become distracted by looting, and a firm English counterattack drove them back. Orléans decided to abandon the siege, but it had been a close-run thing. While Norfolk's gamble had paid off, Henry was furious with him for having put his newly won town at risk. Norfolk was uncle to two of Henry's former wives and had enjoyed a glittering career. He was Lord Treasurer, a senior general and one of the most powerful peers in the kingdom, but he would soon learn that annoying King Henry VIII was not a good career move.

The year 1545 began with England in control of Boulogne but with Francis intent on retaking Boulogne and also capturing Calais. England and France were still at war, but no action was planned by either side until the start of the campaign season in the spring. Francis had decided that before attacking Boulogne and Calais, he would bring the war to Henry's own shores, but doing so would take time. A large invasion force had to be assembled, together with the ships necessary to transport them and their supplies to England. Francis' immediate objective was to destroy the English navy and capture Southampton. He requisitioned supplies from various ports, from Brest to Marseilles, to gather the necessary galleys, war ships and troop transports. In July all was ready and a French fleet of 200 ships carrying 20,000 soldiers arrived in the Solent. An English fleet of 60 ships under Dudley, and 12,000 soldiers, prepared to defend Portsmouth, watched by Henry from the shore.

A naval battle took place in the Solent during which the English ship the *Mary Rose* foundered and was lost. Despite this, the outcome was inconclusive, and the French withdrew to attack the Isle of Wight. This attack was repulsed and, running out of supplies, the French returned to their own waters. During this return the French fleet conducted a raid on the English coast and made a half-hearted attempt to blockade Boulogne, but the approach of Dudley's fleet made them abandon the blockade and the ships returned to their ports. Francis had intended his attack on Portsmouth to be the precursor to an attack on Boulogne and then Calais, but its failure meant that the two English possessions were temporarily safe. In fact, while Francis had been busy preparing for his invasion a considerable amount of work was being carried out on Boulogne's defences by 1,200 stone masons, craftsmen and labourers, transported from England.

Although England and France technically remained at war for nearly another year there were no military engagements of any consequence. A situation of stalemate existed between Henry, Francis and Charles, all of whom were financially exhausted and short of troops. The period was one of diplomatic manoeuvring that came to nothing. In January 1546 Henry sent the Earl of Hertford to Calais with some more troops. The intention was to mount an attack on France and break the deadlock, but the plan never got off the ground. It became clear that the only way forward was to negotiate with Francis for a peace which would include England's retention of Boulogne. Dudley was sent to Calais to open negotiations with emissaries sent by Francis. The result was the Treaty of Camp on 7 June 1546; it was signed by Dudley and the French delegation in a tent in French territory, just outside the Calais Pale fortress of Gûines.

The location for signing the treaty was very close to the site of the Field of the Cloth of Gold which had taken place 26 years previously, but this event was obviously very low key after the grandeur of its predecessor. However, it did at least result in a more lasting peace. France undertook to pay Henry the arrears of the pension that had been agreed in earlier treaties and it was agreed that Boulogne should remain in English hands until 1554 when it would be handed over, in exchange for 2,000,000 French gold crowns (£750,000).[1]

Further, the agreement stated that neither the English nor the French should build any additional fortifications for the town of Boulogne or the surrounding area. Finally, the French remembered their Scottish allies and obtained agreement that England would carry out no more attacks against Scotland without 'due cause'.

Henry must have been happy that Boulogne was to remain in his hands for eight years, and that it was unlikely that the French would ever have the enormous sum of 2,000,000 crowns with which to buy it back. This appeared to be a success of sorts and brought the recent war with France to an end. Unbeknown to Henry, future events would mean that the recently ended war would be the last time, ever, that an English monarch would invade France to claim the French crown. Calais, which had been the vital secure port for an English invasion force would never again be used for that purpose. Calais also was in decline; its other *raison d'etre*, as the Wool Staple, had been reduced to selling about 4,500 sacks a year. This was higher than some previous years but was still a significant reduction from the boom times of the past.

In England the cost of £650,000[2] for the war against France had meant that the Treasury was deep in debt. Henry imposed crippling levels of taxation and debased the coinage, which caused much dismay across the kingdom. Henry was then only 46 years old but more than feeling his age. He had become grossly obese, could no longer walk and had to be carried about in a litter. In addition, his bloated legs had become painfully ulcerated. As his health declined, so his temper increased, as did his suspicion of his courtiers. Henry realized it was unlikely that his son would reach adulthood before he died and began to consider the arrangements for a council to govern during Edward's minority. The two most prominent courtiers were the Duke of Norfolk, who led the Catholic faction, and the Earl of Hertford, who had strong protestant sympathies, both of whom jockeyed for position. The outcome was to be decided in 1546.

Henry had not fully forgiven Norfolk for disobeying his orders and pulling back his force from Boulogne to Calais and, in his pain-induced paranoia, became convinced that Norfolk's son, the Earl of Surrey, intended to usurp the crown. This perception seemed to be confirmed when Surrey, in a moment of foolish vanity, added the traditional coat of arms of King Edward the Confessor to his own coat of arms. In December 1546 Norfolk and Surrey were charged with high treason and Surrey was executed on 19 January 1547. Norfolk's execution was arranged for 28 January but did not take place because King Henry VIII died on that day, 28 January 1547.

With Henry dead the crown passed to the 9-year-old Edward, who became King Edward VI. Although Norfolk's life had been saved by the king's death, he was still sentenced to imprisonment in the Tower. With the leader of the Catholic faction out of play, the protestant Earl of Hertford became the most prominent English peer. Hertford had kept the king's death a secret for sufficient time in which to position himself to take over the government. He moved fast and managed to persuade the Council to appoint him as Lord Protector of the Realm for the young king's minority. He also arranged the distribution of lands and titles among his supporters: the Lord Admiral, John Dudley, became Earl of Warwick, and Hertford himself became Duke of Somerset.

With Henry out of the way, Hertford, now Somerset, was able to be openly reformist and began introducing protestant practices into the church. Edward VI may have been young, but he knew his own mind, and his mind was reformist. Henry VIII had been moving towards Protestant Reformation of his Church of England, cautiously encouraged by Archbishop Cranmer. Edward had become supportive of this Reformation through the influence not only of his uncle and the

Archbishop but also his protestant-leaning stepmother, Catherine Parr. As Edward grew older so did his protestant zeal, and it was with the young king's enthusiastic backing that Somerset and Cranmer began pushing through parliament various protestant reforms, such as the removal of Catholic ritual. Over the next few years these reforms would transform England into a fully-fledged protestant state.

Having set in train the English Reformation, Somerset turned his attention to foreign affairs. An unresolved earlier matter was the desirability of Edward marrying Mary Queen of Scots. Somerset sent a letter to the Scottish nobles asking for their agreement to the marriage. When this was rejected England returned to its policy of 'rough wooing' by invading Scotland, in direct contravention of the Treaty of Camp. In September an army led by Somerset and Warwick inflicted a devastating defeat on the Scots army of the Earl of Arran, at the Battle of Pinkie, near Musselburgh. Somerset's victory enabled his army to establish garrisons which dominated most of Lowland Scotland. Despite this, Arran would still not agree to the marriage.

The English invasion moved Scotland even closer to their traditional allies, the French. King Francis outlived his old adversary, Henry VIII, by two months only, and died on 31 March 1547. The new French monarch was the dashing 28-year-old King Henry II, who wanted to unite Scotland with France and was eager to have Mary Queen of Scots betrothed to his 3-year-old son, the Dauphin Francis. This plan had the added attraction of providing a claim to the throne of England, as Mary was the great-grandchild of Henry VII. Mary's mother, Mary of Guise, naturally supported the French match, and the Earl of Arran was persuaded to agree by the promise of a French dukedom and military assistance against the English. In June 1548 a French force arrived at Leith and eventually forced the English invaders to abandon the strategic town of Haddington. Mary's betrothal to Francis was agreed and in August a French fleet arrived at Dumbarton and escorted the 5-year-old Mary to France, where she would remain for the next fourteen years.

These events in England and Scotland naturally had an effect on Calais and the new English possession of Boulogne. During the reign of Henry VIII, it had been difficult to know whether the Church of England was to remain basically Catholic in doctrine or would embrace Protestantism. With the accession of Edward VI, it was becoming clear that the Lord

Protector and Archbishop were pressing ahead with protestant reforms, such as allowing the marriage of priests. All became crystal clear when Cranmer introduced the English Book of Prayer, in 1549. This, coupled with agricultural hardship following the enclosure of common land, led to uprisings in the West Country and a more serious peasant rebellion led by Robert Kett, which captured Norwich. The Earl of Warwick took an army of 14,000 men and destroyed Kett's rebels in a bloody encounter that restored peace to the kingdom.

There was obviously heightened religious tension in Calais at this time, between devout Catholics, religious conservatives, and avowed Protestants. However, it was clear which way the wind was blowing. Lord Cobham, the Lord Deputy, favoured Protestantism and ensured that religious reforms were enforced in Calais. Numerous clergy were at work in Calais, in the twenty-five parishes of the Pale, in religious houses, or as chaplains to the garrisons, and among prominent citizens. They had to decide whether to go along with the protestant reforms or risk losing their livelihoods. In tandem with this religious upheaval there was an increased military threat. With the Auld Alliance back in prominence, and French troops fighting the English army in Scotland, military friction increased in the areas around Calais and Boulogne. One of the provisions of the Treaty of Camp was that neither side should create or improve fortifications in the Boulogne area. Following the strong deterioration of Anglo-French relations over Scotland, both sides began accusing the other of building fortifications. In May 1549 France launched an attack on Boulogne.

The attack on Boulogne meant that Somerset had to summon troops from other garrisons in Scotland to defend the town. The Earl of Huntingdon was appointed commander of a force comprising a number of mercenaries and 3,000 English troops, to thwart the French assault. Boulogne was temporarily saved, but with French reinforcements en route, its long-term prospects did not look encouraging. Somerset may have considered his actions successful, but this view was not shared by the Council. There was a growing belief that Somerset was guilty of mismanagement – he had kept a very expensive garrison in Scotland that had achieved nothing. Later that year he was criticized for his handling of the uprisings in the West and in Norfolk. In October the council had Somerset arrested and imprisoned in the Tower.

By January 1550 Warwick had emerged as leader of the Council and had sent a delegation to France to negotiate a peace. During the winter, the French had begun to blockade Boulogne and had managed to cut its all-important land link with Calais. Supplies had run low in Boulogne and the Earl of Huntingdon had insufficient troops to restore communications with Calais. There was not enough money to raise an army to relieve Boulogne. Two years of war had cost £350,000, at a time when the annual Crown revenue was only about £150,000.[3] The country could not afford to be fighting on two fronts, Scotland and France, so Warwick had to accept the inevitable. In March the Treaty of Boulogne was signed, confirming that Boulogne would be handed over to France in exchange for 400,000 gold crowns (far less than the 2,000,000 agreed at the Treaty of Camp). A further related treaty with Scotland agreed to the withdrawal of all English forces from the country. England was at last at peace with Scotland and France. There followed protestations of lasting friendship: Henry II was awarded the Order of the Garter and Mary of Guise landed at Portsmouth and was entertained by King Edward and his court. A long period of peace and prosperity appeared to be beckoning.

There was indeed to be a period of peace in which Calais could return to its commercial activities without the disruptions of war. Had the French been able to take Boulogne their next objective would have been Calais. The Treaty of Boulogne removed French troops from the area and meant that Calais was no longer under threat. In 1550 Cobham, the Lord Deputy, a supporter of Warwick, resigned his post to return to England to take up membership of the Privy Council. Cobham was replaced by Baron Willoughby, a courtier and soldier who had served with distinction under Warwick during Kett's rebellion. Unfortunately, this appointment was not a success. Willoughby was involved in a dispute over authority with the Captain of Gûines, who happened to be Warwick's brother, Sir Andrew Dudley. The dispute became so acrimonious that Warwick dismissed both Willoughby and Dudley and ordered their return to England in 1553.

In early 1550 Warwick had become Lord President of the Council. Over the next year he further extended his power by orchestrating the trial and execution of his rival, Somerset, and became Duke of Northumberland and de facto regent for King Edward. There followed a period of peace and stability with the intelligent young king taking an increasing interest in government. In February 1553 the promising 15-year-old Edward was about to embark on a royal tour when he was struck down with an illness, which may have been smallpox. Whatever it was, he had barely recovered when he fell prey to tuberculosis. Edward made a will, and being a staunch Protestant decided that, should he die without an heir, his successor should not be his Catholic sister, Mary Tudor, but the resolutely protestant Lady Jane Grey, the granddaughter of Henry VII's daughter, Mary Duchess of Suffolk. Edward had ruled out his Protestant stepsister Elizabeth, as she had been declared illegitimate. At much the same time Northumberland had arranged the marriage between his younger son, Guildford Dudley, and Lady Jane Grey. When Edward died on 3 July 1553, Northumberland obtained agreement from the Council to proclaim Lady Jane Grey the queen.

The Protestant succession and English Reformation seemed secure. However, this belief did not take into account Princess Mary, who soon showed that she was her father's daughter. She knew that she was generally regarded as the rightful heir to the throne and immediately travelled to her estates in East Anglia to raise an army. Northumberland was unprepared for this but rapidly gathered a force of 3,000 from London and advanced against Mary and her supporters. By this time Mary's force had grown to 20,000 strong. The Council realized they had backed the wrong horse and proclaimed Mary as the true monarch of England. Northumberland was arrested, tried and executed. Mary, a pious Catholic, was now Mary I, Queen of England.

Mary had received considerable public support as Henry VIII's eldest living child and daughter of the popular Catherine of Aragon. The protestant changes had come too quickly for much of the population who felt deprived of the time-honoured Catholic traditions and holidays. Mary was a known Catholic and many welcomed the prospect of her gently returning religious life to normality. What may not have been expected was that she would reintroduce Catholic doctrine with such severity that over 280 unrepentant Protestants would be burnt at the stake. Protestant reforms were put into reverse throughout her lands, including, of course, Calais.

Mary wanted a reliable Catholic to take over the vacant post of Lord Deputy of Calais and chose Baron Thomas Wentworth, a soldier who had made his name at the Battle of Pinkie and had recently become one of her trusted advisers. Wentworth therefore had the difficult task of implementing a Counter Reformation in Calais. It was more difficult in Calais than in most parts of England because the geographical position of Calais meant that it had been influenced by the Protestant Reformation in Germany. Indeed, for some thirty years Calais had been receiving protestant literature from the new printing presses, as well as from reformist priests from Germany and the Low Countries. This gave Protestantism far deeper roots than had been formed in England during the short reign of Edward VI.

At least Wentworth did not need to be greatly concerned by a French attack on Calais. In 1551 Henry II had once again allied with Suleiman the Magnificent of the Ottoman Empire and declared war against Charles V, in the hope of regaining land in Italy. The war had begun in the Mediterranean, but despite having persecuted Protestants himself, in January 1552 Henry allied with protestant princes who were rebelling against Charles V. Military operations spread to Lorraine and Tuscany, still far enough away from Calais. Henry had been pleased when Jane Grey had become queen as he hoped England would join the German Protestants against Charles. He was disappointed when she was replaced by Mary, who was not only a Catholic but also a cousin of Charles V, and therefore more likely to ally with Spain than with France. Despite the uncertainty of future alliances, in 1553 England and France remained at peace while Henry was focused on supporting Siena against Florence and its Hapsburg allies.

Mary's right to the throne was generally agreed, but there was no getting away from the fact that she was a woman. There had only been one queen of England previously – the Empress Matilda in 1135, which had resulted in nineteen years of civil war. A female monarch was by and large considered dangerous and a journey into uncharted waters. Much would depend upon her husband, who would receive the title 'king' and become joint ruler of the kingdoms of England and Ireland. In 1553 Mary was 37 years old, and greatly in need of a husband if she were to produce a Catholic heir. She looked to her cousin Charles V for advice, and not surprisingly, he recommended marriage to his 24-year-old son, Philip of Spain. The Council announced its agreement for the match, but the proposed union was not greeted with universal rejoicing.

Some people feared being ruled by a Spaniard, others feared that the devoutly Catholic Philip would persecute Protestants. These fears coalesced into an uprising led by Sir Thomas Wyatt, in league with the Duke of Suffolk and the French ambassador. In early 1554 Wyatt gathered a 3,000-strong force, captured Rochester, and then advanced on London. An army of about 20,000 men was raised by Mary and prevented Wyatt's entry to London, after which his force melted away and he surrendered. Wyatt, of course, was executed, as was Suffolk and also his daughter, Lady Jane Grey, although she had known nothing of the plot. Protestant resistance was over, and the wedding of Mary and Philip took place in Winchester Cathedral on 25 July 1554. The marriage treaty contained certain provisions to protect England from foreign domination. It had been agreed that Philip would be king only during Mary's lifetime, and that England would not have to provide military support for Philip's father, Charles V, in any war. The question was, would these important provisions last the test of time?

Mary and Philip had met for the first time just two days before their wedding. Almost immediately, Mary fell deeply in love with her young husband. Sadly, this was not reciprocated. For Philip the marriage was a duty only, and being a dutiful person, he carried it out punctiliously. As joint monarch he co-chaired the Council, opened parliament, and tried hard to make himself liked as king. He must have felt that his marital duties had been rewarded when, in the April following their wedding, Mary announced that she was pregnant. Mary was not in good health, but she was overjoyed. Tragically for her, three months later it was found to have been a phantom pregnancy.

At much the same time Philip's father, the mighty Charles V, decided to abdicate and spend the rest of his days in a monastery, engaged in gardening, clock making and religious devotion. Charles handed Austria's Hapsburg Empire and the Holy Roman Empire to his younger brother, Ferdinand. Philip was given the rest, and the rest was a lot. Philip's 'inheritance' included the kingdoms of Spain, Sardinia, Naples, Sicily and Jerusalem, the whole of the Netherlands, the duchy of Milan and the Spanish lands in the Americas.

In September 1555 Philip sailed from Dover to begin assuming control of his new scattered domains. Mary was too ill with dropsy to see him off. She was heart-broken at his departure and was already entreating him to return as soon as possible. She found solace in putting what energy she had into continuing her efforts, supported by Philip, to return England to Catholicism. One of her first actions as queen had been to release the ageing Catholic leader, the Duke of Norfolk. Later she welcomed back to England as Papal Legate her father's *bête noir*, Cardinal Reginal Pole. Cranmer had been removed as Archbishop of Canterbury and was replaced by Pole, who had become chief councillor to Mary and Philip. In February 1556 the first Protestant was burnt at the stake, under Mary's reinstated Heresy Acts, followed the next month by the burning of Cranmer. More and more trials of protestant 'heretics' took place and resulted in 220 men and 60 women being burnt alive over the next three years.

Calais, like the rest of England, was convulsed by Mary's imposition of Catholicism and implementation of the reinstated Heresy Acts. The situation was more complicated than on mainland England because many Protestants had fled abroad to escape Mary's persecution. Their first port of call was usually Calais because it was the shortest distance to the Continent, and it was known that a large percentage of the population was Protestant. The Calais authorities had to tread the difficult balance of appearing to implement anti-heretic policy while not unduly alienating a significant proportion of the Calais population. Indeed, Mary herself trod carefully, and although she did establish some Dominican nuns in the town, of the 26 clergy in Calais only two were removed and replaced with Catholic priests.[4]

Philip was fortunate that he had left England to visit some of his new territories at the time of a five-year truce with France. However, few would have expected the truce to last, least of all Philip, when he heard that the pope was calling on France to eject Spain from Italy. Henry II of France began breaking the truce and Philip returned to England in March 1556 with the sole purpose of persuading Mary to join Spain in a war against France. Mary was overjoyed at his return and would willingly have done anything for her husband, but her Council, including Cardinal Pole, were strongly against being dragged into an expensive Spanish war. Their view was to be changed by the actions of Henry II, first in Calais and then in England itself.

For some time Henry had been using the protestant Sir Henry Dudley to destabilize England. Dudley was a cousin of Lady Jane Grey and a relative of the Duke of Northumberland. He was a successful soldier who had become Captain of the Guard at Boulogne and had led a diplomatic mission to the French court. In December 1555 he visited Paris and was well received by Henry II who persuaded him to organize an insurrection of Protestants in England, against Mary and Philip, and to place Princess Elizabeth on the throne. This plot had been abandoned because of the truce, but Dudley had then been given the task of assembling a group of Protestants from Calais and the Pale in a conspiracy to betray the castles of Hammes and Gûines to France. Careless talk among the conspirators led to the plot being reported by an informer. Realising that their plot was compromised, Dudley and the other conspirators fled to France.

Knowledge of the Calais conspiracy had made the Council aware of Henry's hostile intent, but this was made manifest by an attempted invasion. With Henry's encouragement, Thomas Stafford, a grandson of the late Duke of Buckingham, assembled a small army in Dieppe. The purpose was to use French ships to land in England and start a Protestant insurrection against Philip and Mary. The small force comprised English, Scottish and French soldiers and landed in Scarborough in Yorkshire. Stafford and his force captured Scarborough castle but received no support from the local gentry. The Council despatched an army which arrived at Scarborough and surrounded the castle, obliging Stafford to surrender. Stafford was taken to London for vigorous interrogation at the Tower and confessed that the King of France had provided the money, ships, supplies and manpower for the expedition. Stafford was beheaded in May 1557 and his main followers were hanged at Tyburn. These events were quite sufficient for the Council to agree to Philip's call for war against France. Having attained his objective, Philip left immediately for Flanders. Neither Mary nor England would ever see him again.

In July an English army of 7,000 men under William Herbert, Earl of Pembroke, followed Philip to Flanders. Once there they marched to join Philip's multi-national force from Hapsburg nations under the command of the Duke of Savoy, the governor of the Spanish Netherlands. The combined allied army numbered 60,000 men and was poised to attack north-west France. At home in England many would have thought this was just another army sent abroad in the long-running wars against

France. Optimists may have hoped that the size of the combined allied force would result in winning considerable plunder and quite possibly more French territory. Pessimists may have regarded it as an unnecessary waste of English money and manpower in a foreign cause. Even the most pessimistic would never have dreamt that the war would result in the loss of Calais.

Chapter 10

Loss and Aftermath, 1557–88

E ngland's new war with France had required funding for two operations, a land army that was sent to Flanders, and a naval operation to menace French ports. The naval deployment was quite ambitious; it entailed attacks on French ports as far as Bayonne but, as it turned out, was to achieve little other than the plunder of a few defenceless coastal villages. Nevertheless, mounting the two operations had stretched the Exchequer to the limits and beyond. In order to victual the navy *all* the corn in Norfolk had been seized by the crown, without payment, and forced loans had been extracted from the city of London and some of the wealthy nobility, together with levying the second year's subsidy voted by Parliament a year earlier. Before there had been any military engagements, Philip's war with France had left the government of England deep in debt.

It was under these strained financial circumstances that the Earl of Pembroke's English force marched to join Philip's Hapsburg army while it was besieging Saint-Quentin, in Picardy. Henry II had sent the Constable of France with an army of 26,000 men to relieve the town. The French force was heavily outnumbered, so it attempted a surprise approach to Saint-Quentin, through a marsh, but their army became divided and was ambushed by the Hapsburg multi-national force. The battle took place on 10 August, the day of the Feast of St Lawrence. It resulted in 3,000 French soldiers being killed on the battlefield and over 7,000 being captured. Philip's army lost 1,000 dead. It was a major defeat for France and provided the opportunity for Spain to win the war. Paris was only 95 miles from Saint-Quentin and the main French army was miles away in Italy, advancing towards Naples. A swift advance to take Paris was likely to force Henry II into a humiliating peace. As Philip was king of England, the peace terms would probably include the transfer of large amounts of English reclaimed French territory for the English crown. But this was not to be.

The battle of Saint-Quentin had resulted in massive slaughter. Philip was so moved by the magnitude of his bloody victory that he decided to commemorate St Lawrence, on whose saint day it had occurred. St Lawrence is associated with a gridiron on which he was roasted to death, so Philip ordered that a new royal palace in the shape of a gridiron should be built in the mountains north of Madrid. The palace became known as El Escorial. The more immediate result of Philip's revulsion at the mounds of dead and dying was to desist from further conflict. As soon as the town of Saint-Quentin had been captured, he ordered his great army to return to the Netherlands, where it moved into winter quarters. The opportunity to strike a decisive blow against France was lost.

The Earl of Pembroke's English force had arrived just too late to engage in the battle itself but took a major part in capturing the town of Saint-Quentin. As Philip's army was returning to the Netherlands, Pembroke took his force home to England, leaving a rather depleted garrison in Calais. Henry II's response to the defeat at Saint-Quentin was to abandon his operations in Italy and recall his best general, Francis, Duke of Guise, brother of Mary of Guise, and uncle of Mary Queen of Scots. Guise was made Lieutenant General of France, tasked with raising a new army in Picardy. Calais had been well out of the way of warfare for about eight years. There had therefore been no urgency to maintain its defences nor, for that matter, had there been any money for this. With Guise forming an army on Calais' doorstep the whole situation changed. Wentworth, the Lord Deputy, was well aware of the danger and sent urgent requests to the government for additional manpower and money to prepare Calais and the Pale to withstand attack. This fell on deaf ears. The Council did not have the funds to commit the fleet, army reinforcements, or still less, money, for the defence of Calais.

The English revelled in the fact that their occupation of Calais had been a long-standing affront to French pride. Above the entrance to the town was the following motto, thoughtfully written in French for the convenience of French visitors:

Les Français à Calais planter la siege
Quand le feu at le plomb nagerant comme liège.[1]

(Roughly translated as 'Never shall the Frenchmen Calais win / Until iron and stone like cork can swim.')

The Duke of Guise was about to test the buoyancy of iron and stone.

It was normal practice not to engage in military activity outside the spring, summer and early autumn campaigning season. Armies usually went into winter quarters until the weather was good enough for the dreadful roads to be passable, and soldiers slept in the open or in makeshift tents. The Duke of Guise decided to discard military convention and exploit the fact that cold winter weather froze the mash surrounding Calais and made it accessible to an attacking army. He launched a surprise attack on the Pale of Calais with a 30,000-strong army on New Year's Day in 1558. His vanguard surrounded the fortresses of Sangatte and then captured the fort of Nieulay, which had been built in 1525 to guard the vital defensive sluice gates on the River Hammes. The captured sluice gates were closed and the river was diverted to flood the area south of Calais, quickly freezing over. Within a few hours Calais had lost its vital means of protecting the town from attack by land.

The next day Guise's main force captured Fort Risban, the stronghold defending the entrance to the Calais harbour. On 3 January Guise moved his 70 pieces of artillery within range and began to bombard the Calais castle day and night for two days of deafening gunfire that could be heard in Antwerp. The massive bombardment resulted in a breach being made in the wall near the castle's water gate. Wentworth had a garrison of only 500 men and realized that the castle could not be held against Guise's nearly 30,000 attacking force. He ordered the garrison to pull back after first preparing explosives that could be detonated once a large body of French soldiers had occupied the castle. Guise saw that no garrison was manning the breach, so at the ebb tide that evening he arranged for large bundles of hurdles to be thrown into the ditch opposite the breach. Guise then led his men in fording the ditch, which was now no more than waist height, and entered the castle unopposed. The castle then filled with Guise's troops, unaware that they had entered Wentworth's trap. This afforded Wentworth the opportunity of blowing up not only a large section of the French army, but Guise himself, which would cause panic among the French troops and ensure they were ripe for counterattack by the Calais garrison. That evening Wentworth waited expectantly for the fuse to be lit. And waited; and waited. But the fuse was wet, so no explosion took place.

The next morning Guise sent troops from the castle to assault the town. They were met by Sir Anthony Agar and a handful of men who beat the French back into the castle. This minor triumph was not to last. Soon Sir Anthony, his son and seventy followers were cut down by the far superior French numbers. Wentworth knew that his position was untenable. That night he demanded a parley and surrendered to Guise on 7 January. Although Guise occupied the town, he was not yet master of the entire Calais Pale. Having ensured the town was able to defend itself, on 13 January Guise marched out to attack the town and castle of Guînes, five miles away.

Guînes was commanded by the professional soldier, Lord Grey de Wilton, who had previously served with distinction in Scotland and France. Guînes had been a small English-manned garrison, but Grey had received about 400 Spanish and Burgundian soldiers as reinforcements from King Philip. On 4 January he had sent an urgent message to England begging for more reinforcements. Mary's Council distributed a countrywide proclamation, to muster a force to go to the aid of Calais and Guînes. As a result, some 30,000 men had been assembled and were ready to embark, by which time the news that Calais had fallen had reached England, but there was still hope of relieving Guînes. On 10 January the force was ordered to cross to Dunkirk and join the Duke of Savoy's army, to relieve Guînes. It looked as though Guînes was about to be saved, but exceptionally bad weather in the Channel destroyed or dispersed much of the English fleet and forced it to limp back to port.

Grey had a total of just 1,100 men; realizing that this was insufficient to defend the town he abandoned it and withdrew into the moated castle. The Duke of Guise occupied the town and set up his artillery which began pounding the castle's badly maintained walls for three days, eventually achieving a breach. On 19 January Guise began to storm the castle and took control of its outer walls. Grey's Spanish contingent received the main onslaught of the French attack and most were killed or wounded. That left the Burgundian troops; having seen the bloodshed they refused to continue fighting and Grey was forced to surrender. The great castle of Guînes, which had guarded the southern Pale and had been the backdrop for the Field of the Cloth of Gold, had fallen. It was later recognized that Grey had done his best to defend the town and he was made a Knight of the Garter. This was some compensation for him because, like the rest of the garrison, he had been taken prisoner. In Grey's case he was held to ransom for the enormous sum of 20,000 crowns which would force him to sell his Wilton estate.

With the loss of Guînes, the little castle of Hames with its four strong towers was left as the only fortified position still in English hands. Hames was surrounded by marshes and could be approached only by a narrow causeway defended at intervals by wooden drawbridges. It therefore had the potential to hold out for some time. The castle's governor, Lord Edward Dudley, thought otherwise, and as soon as he heard of the loss of Guînes fled to Flanders with a few of the garrison. English resistance to Guise's invasion was over. Calais and the Pale were firmly in French hands. Some of the English settlers and soldiers of Calais and the Pale fled across the dunes to the safety of Gravelines which was held by the Spanish. The remaining troops were rounded up and escorted to the port. They, and the Lord Deputy, Wentworth, clutching a few personal belongings, were loaded on to boats and given safe passage back to England.

The French were overjoyed at reconquering the last territory it had lost in the Hundred Years' War. King Henry II marked the triumph by formally entering Calais on 23 January 1558. He ordered the fortifications to be much improved and as a result the mediaeval castle was pulled down and replaced by a new modern fortress, and nearly all the old buildings in the town were razed, including the church of St Nicholas. Within a short space of time there was little physical evidence of England's two-hundred-year presence in Calais.

The capture of Calais was an enormous propaganda victory for France, and quite the reverse for England. Calais and the Pale amounted to 120 square miles only, but its significance to national pride far exceeded its small territory. Not only had it been England's only colony it had been an integral part of England with its own two members of parliament sitting at Westminster. It had been the home of The Staple and a major trading centre that enriched not only its investors but England's treasury. It was the entrance to France and its port had helped the English fleet to command the Channel. Suddenly, within a matter of days, all this had been lost. Queen Mary was devastated to hear of the capture of Calais and described the town as 'The chief jewel of her realm'.[2] The entire country felt that the French attack had come out of the blue and the loss of Calais was greeted with stunned horror and disbelief, as expressed by the diarist Henry Mackyn: 'Heavy news came to England, and London that the French had won Calais, the which was the heaviest tidings to London and England that was ever heard of.'[3]

The immediate aim of Mary and her Council was to regain Calais. The treasury might be empty but somehow money had to be found to send an expedition to join Philip in his war against France. During the spring preparations were made for the invasion of France. Seven thousand troops were raised and drilled, and a hundred and forty ships were hired and assembled at Portsmouth. Meanwhile, Philip II and the Duke of Savoy were gathering an army to invade France from Flanders. The English naval and military force then sailed to link with a Spanish fleet carrying Flemish infantry, ready to ravage the coast of France. It might have been thought that their prime concern was to recover Calais, but rather surprisingly, the objective of the combined force was to attack Brest. This was not a success. The Anglo-Spanish force made no impression on Brest's strong defences and attacked the small nearby port of Le Conquet instead, burning and pillaging several miles inland. Any immediate satisfaction gained from this small revenge for the loss of Calais soon evaporated. Some 400 of the Flemish soldiers advanced too far, became surrounded and surrendered, so the remaining force returned to the ships and sailed for home ports.

Henry II also was active in the spring. Emboldened by his success at Calais, he proceeded to mount a two-pronged attack against Philip at Flanders. Guise advanced south and during the summer took both Thionville and Arlion in preparation for invading Luxembourg. Meanwhile another army under Marshal Paul de Thermes, with 12,000 infantry and 2,000 cavalry and considerable artillery, crossed the River Aa to a few miles east of Calais, with the objective of taking Dunkirk and then Nieuwpoort, and after that, threatening Brussels. The French force was met at Gravelines by the invasion army of Philip II and the Duke of Savoy. This consisted of 15,000 infantry and 3,000 cavalry under the command of Count Egmont. By this time the combined English and Spanish fleet had gathered off Calais in support of Philip's army. A battle took place on the dunes of Gravelines on 13 July which began with rather chaotic cavalry and artillery action, followed by Egmont leading a decisive cavalry charge against the French centre, while at the same time the English and Spanish fleets bombarded the French rear causing heavy casualties. The end result was a major victory for Philip II. Throngs of French troops, about 1,500 in number, fled back to the French border, but the rest of their army was either killed or taken prisoner, including de Thermes.

This resounding victory provided the ideal opportunity to retake Calais, just a few miles from the battlefield of Gravelines. However, Philip chose to follow up his victory by marching south in the hope of defeating the army of the Duke of Guise, that was threatening Luxembourg. Philip and the Duke of Savoy, with an army that had grown to 45,000 men, reached Doullens. Henry II joined his general, the Duke of Guise, near Amiens, which raised the French army to a strength similar in size to Philip's army. All Europe awaited a bloody but decisive battle, but it did not happen. Henry II indicated his willingness to negotiate, which was encouraged by Philip. Henry was concerned about unrest from the growing support for Protestantism in France. Philip was tired of bloodshed, and the endless war that had crippled both countries financially. Indeed, both Spain and France had defaulted on their debts the previous year. Henry and Philip agreed to put their armies into winter quarters while peace negotiations took place.

Their negotiations did not result in an immediate breakthrough. There were a number of sticking points. Greatest of these was that Philip demanded the restoration of Calais and Henry demanded the return of Navarre to France. While diplomats on both sides were engaged in what were difficult and lengthy discussions, Queen Mary died on 17 November 1558, aged 42. She had been seriously unwell since May, probably suffering from ovarian cancer, but it was an influenza epidemic that finally caused her death, and that of Cardinal Pole on the same day. As death approached Mary is reported to have said to her ladies, 'When I am dead and cut open, they will find Philip and Calais inscribed on my heart.'

Mary had died in mental and physical agony. Calais had been lost on her watch and she had been unable to bear a child to succeed her and ensure that England continued in the Catholic faith. In Catholic eyes her heir should have been the great-granddaughter of Henry VII, Mary Queen of Scots, but that was out of the question. Mary was married to the Dauphin, so for Queen Mary to have made Mary Queen of Scots her heir, would have been to give England to France. Queen Mary had no option but to name her protestant stepsister, Elizabeth, as her heir. Immediately after the announcement of the death of Queen Mary the smooth transfer of the crown to Elizabeth was initiated. Elizabeth was proclaimed Queen by Parliament and her coronation was held two months later, on 15 January 1559, when she became Elizabeth I, Queen of England and Ireland.

While these great events were taking place in England in the winter of 1558–9, negotiations continued between Philip and Henry II. The death of his wife meant that Philip was no longer King of England and, having lost the English crown, it might have been assumed that it was no longer in Philip's interests to keep pressing for the return of Calais to England. In fact, Philip continued to demand the return of Calais because he hoped to continue as the King of England. It was well known that no woman could shoulder the burden of monarchy by herself, and so a husband for Elizabeth was an immediate requirement. Indeed, Elizabeth's first parliament had made it plain that it expected her to find a suitable husband at her earliest convenience. Queen Mary had barely drawn her last breath before Philip instructed, Feria, his ambassador in England, to request Elizabeth's hand in marriage. Elizabeth politely declined the offer on the grounds that she and Philip did not share the same religious affiliations. Feria was so affronted by this that he failed to attend Elizabeth's coronation. But Philp was undeterred and kept sending letters to Elizabeth expressing his love for her. This went on for some months until Philip at last realized that no meant no.

In January 1559 an armistice was agreed between Spain and France while the peace negotiations continued. Elizabeth's accession to the throne had brought a new dynamic into the manoeuvring by each side to gain the advantage in the talks. Henry II decided to exploit the situation of Lord Grey who had been captured after his brave attempt to defend Guînes. Grey was granted parole to go to England and negotiate a separate peace. This initiative bore no more fruit than Philip's offer of marriage. The negotiations entered a new phase in which France and Spain would try to establish a lasting peace based on goodwill. When it became clear to Philip that Elizabeth would not marry him, he decided to use his marriage to another as an element of the negotiations. Soon it was agreed that peace between France and Spain would be fostered by the marriage of Philip to Elisabeth of Valois, the eldest daughter of Henry II, and that

Philip's general, the Duke of Savoy, would marry Margaret, the sister of Henry II, by which means Philip would regain the duchy of Savoy which had been occupied by France.

On 2 and 3 April 1559 two treaties were signed at Cateau-Cambrésis. The Peace of Cateau-Cambrésis brought an end to the Hapsburg-Valois Italian Wars that had begun in 1494. The terms were largely a recognition of the actual situation on the ground. France recognized Spain's control of Naples, Milan and the Hapsburg Netherlands. In return Spain recognized France's control of the three strategic bishoprics of Metz, Toul and Verdun, as well as the Pale of Calais. The first treaty, on 2 April, was between England and France, while the second, on 3 April, was between France and Spain. Naturally the contents of both treaties had been agreed between Philip and Henry. Philip's impending French marriage had ended any hope of him becoming king of England so he had lost interest in demanding the return of Calais to England; he could now use Calais as a mere bargaining counter to gain concessions from Henry.

Although Philip agreed to France's possession of Calais, neither he nor Henry II had any wish to seriously alienate the new queen of England. A formula was found which might make the French occupation of Calais more palatable, and it became part of the 2 April Cateau-Cambrésis agreement between France and England. The agreement recognized Calais as an English possession, but one that was temporarily in French custody. France would hold Calais and the Pale for eight years or pay Elizabeth 500,000 crowns; and four French noblemen and the bonds of eight foreign merchants would be the guarantors for this sum. Appended to this was an article which gave France an appropriate escape clause from the agreement. This article stipulated that if, during the aforementioned eight years, Henry II or Mary Queen of Scots, should make any attempt against the realm or the subjects of Elizabeth I, France would forfeit all claim to the town. Likewise, if Elizabeth should infringe the peace with either Henry or Mary, she would forfeit all claims to the return of Calais.

The people of England were still smarting from the national humiliation caused by the loss of Calais and there had been some hope that it would be returned to England through the negotiations at Cateau-Cambrésis. When the implications of the treaty were understood, there was outrage. It was very clear that despite the flimsy pretence of restoration, France would never relinquish its hold on Calais. The government decided to divert public attention from the unfortunate treaty and transfer the indignation to a scapegoat. Lord Wentworth, the Lord Deputy who had surrendered Calais, was an obvious choice for this role. He was arrested and charged with cowardice and treason, together with the governors of Fort Risban and the castle at Calais, the Chateau de Calais. A jury found Wentworth not guilty but condemned the two governors.

However, the sentences on the two governors were never carried out, as the objective of the show trials had been achieved. This did not mean that the people of England had begun to accept the loss of Calais, or that their ardour to achieve its return had decreased. It meant merely that there was no longer the urge to exact punishment for the loss, except of course from the French. But what of all those others who had been forced to leave Calais and the Pale? Most of the soldiers from the Calais garrisons had been discharged and were occupied mainly with highway robbery while waiting for the government to raise a future army. The Merchants of The Staple and their employees had moved to the City of London while they reorganized and made arrangements to re-establish The Staple in Bruges in the safety of the Spanish Netherlands where, it had been agreed, they could continue their monopoly of the wool export. As for the other English citizens of the Pale, little is known of what became of them. No doubt those with a trade would have sought work where they could find it, but all would have lost what wealth they had enjoyed and were forced to make a new start.

Clearly the future of Calais as agreed at Cateau-Cambrésis depended upon cordial relations between England and France. This did not get off to a good start. Henry II persuaded his daughter–in-law, Mary Queen of Scots, (who had married his son, Francis, Dauphin of France, on 24 April 1558), to include the lions of England on her coat of arms, thus displaying her claim to the English throne. Queen Elizabeth was furious, although the irony involved in her own display of the fleur-de-lis of France on her own coat of arms seems to have escaped her. However, mischief-making by Henry II came to an end in July 1559 when he died following a jousting accident during a tournament to celebrate the marriage of his daughter, Elisabeth of Valois to Philip II. Henry was only 40 years old when he died and was succeeded by his son, Francis, who was just 15 years of age. Francis became King Francis II with Mary Queen of Scots as his queen, but the young king was in poor health and immature for his age. His mother, Catherine de Medici, agreed that the Duke of Guise should act as his regent.

The Duke of Guise was an ardent Catholic, determined to put down Protestantism by persecution. He was also uncle to Mary Queen of Scots and the brother of Mary of Guise, regent of Scotland. At that time Scotland was undergoing the Protestant reformation and many of the Protestant peers banded together against Mary of Guise, who managed to cling to power thanks to the support of Guise and his French troops. The rebelling Protestant peers called themselves 'The Lords of the Congregation' and in early 1560 appealed to Queen Elizabeth for help to eject the French force from Scotland. Elizabeth's attitude to the young French king and his wife was decidedly negative, given that both of them were displaying the English coat of arms. This, together with her dislike of Guise and Catholicism, motivated her agreement to assist the Protestant rebel Scottish lords in driving out the French. In March of 1560 the navy and a 6,000-strong army was sent to Scotland and joined forces with the Protestant lords. The English army was commanded by Lord Grey de Wilton who had been rewarded for his gallant, but unsuccessful defence of Guînes, by being made governor of Berwick. Some might say that Elizabeth's attack on Scotland was a blatant breach of the Treaty of Cateau-Cambrésis, and therefore forfeited her right to Calais. However, Elizabeth portrayed it merely as coming to the aid of Mary Queen of Scots against French forces in Scotland.

The main French garrison was at Leith, which the Protestant lords had begun to besiege, and were joined by the English land and sea contingents. The joint siege was not a success as the French garrison managed to repel all attacks on the town. Lord Grey contented himself with attacking Edinburgh and forcing Mary of Guise to seek safety in Edinburgh Castle. In June that year Mary of Guise died of dropsy. This meant that the Protestant lords became the dominant force in the country, and a month after Mary's death they and the French came to terms and made a treaty with the English. The treaty agreed that all French and English forces would leave Scotland and that no Frenchman should hold any office in that kingdom. There was a purely Anglo-French element to the treaty which confirmed that King Francis II and Queen Mary should remove the arms of England from their coats of arms and that Calais should be returned to England.

The agreement was called the Treaty of Edinburgh and had been negotiated between commissioners representing England, France and the Protestant Lords. When the French commissioners returned to France Mary Queen of Scots refused to ratify the treaty, on the grounds that it had been made with rebels against her mother and it undermined her claim to the English throne. This impasse was largely ignored as both the French and English withdrew their forces from Scotland and the Protestant Lords demonstrated their dominance when the Scottish Parliament declared Scotland to be a protestant country. Disputes over the non-ratification of the Treaty of Edinburgh were overtaken by the death of King Francis II on 5 December 1560.

Francis had probably died of meningitis, but whatever it was, it changed the life of Mary Queen of Scots forever. The French crown passed to Francis' 10-year-old brother, who became King Charles IX. Mary was no longer Queen of France, having become, suddenly, the Dowager Queen of France, as was her mother-in-law, Catherine de Medici, which made one dowager too many. Catherine de Medici regained the regency from the Duke of Guise and assumed the position herself. She heartily disliked Mary Queen of Scots who was obliged to depart the French court and take up residence with her Guise relations. Then came the decision that Mary should leave France, where she was no longer welcome, and assume her position as Queen of Scotland.

In August 1561 Mary arrived in Calais ready to cross the Channel and travel to Scotland. However, Elizabeth refused to grant her safe passage through England, and she had to sail to Leith. So it was that 18-year-old Mary Queen of Scots left the opulent life of a senior member of the French Royal family and its cultured court, to don the crown of cold, divided and backward Scotland, which she had not seen since she had been a child of 5 years old. The Mary who disembarked at Leith was a strong Catholic in an increasingly Protestant country, but one who would try to establish religious tolerance and be guided by her Protestant bastard brother, the Earl of Moray. Fate was against her. The next 26 years of her turbulent life would involve a disastrous marriage, rebellion by Moray, being blamed for her husband's murder, then abducted and raped, another disastrous marriage, being forced by rebels to abdicate, escaping but being defeated in battle, and flight to England which resulted in nineteen years of imprisonment leading to her final execution.

While Mary Queen of Scots was beginning her tragic reign, Queen Elizabeth would have been pleased that Scotland posed no threat. The country was divided by religion with protestant peers in the ascendancy, many of whom were in Elizabeth's pay. French forces had been removed and the Auld Alliance with Catholic France had died when the Treaty of Edinburgh was signed. Elizabeth could safely turn her attention to France and attempt to regain Calais. France was in a weak state with a minority government and the country was split between Catholic and Huguenot, each led by powerful and ambitious families, and, to complicate matters, the Duke of Guise had taken custody of the young King Charles IX. An uneasy peace between Catholics and Protestants fell apart in March 1562 when the Duke of Guise attacked a crowd of Huguenots at worship in a barn at Wassy in north-east France, killing about fifty people and leaving many more wounded. Within a month the Huguenot leaders, Prince Louis of Condé and Admiral Coligny, had raised an army against Guise and the crown. This launched the French Wars of Religion which were to last, with intermittent ceasefires, for thirty-six years. It was a conflict which would lead to some three million deaths through violence, famine or disease.

France's wretched turmoil was Elizabeth's opportunity to regain Calais. The Duke of Guise was facing stubborn resistance from Condé's Huguenot forces, so he invited Philip II of Spain to provide assistance. Philip saw the possible advantage of meddling in France's civil war and at the same time supporting the Catholic faith, so he provided Guise with 6,000 men and some financial backing. Condé's response to this was to seek help from Elizabeth against the common enemy of their religion. Elizabeth sent Sir Henry Sidney to France, ostensibly to offer her mediation between the two French factions, but in reality, to make an alliance with Condé. Agreement was reached whereby Elizabeth would give Condé 100,000 crowns and 6,000 men; in return Condé would place the ports of Le Have and Dieppe in English hands. It was also agreed, in exchange for Elizabeth's help, that Calais would be restored to England. In early October 1562 a fleet landed an army of 6,000 men, led by Sir Adrian Poynings, and took possession of the two ports; overall command of the English forces in France had been given to the Earl of Warwick. England was once again in the happy position of holding French territory.

This unannounced English invasion prompted the French ambassador in London to draw Queen Elizabeth's attention to the Treaty of Cateau-Cambrésis. In particular, that by proceeding with hostilities she would forfeit all claim to Calais at the end of the prescribed time. Elizabeth replied that she was 'in arms', in fact, on behalf of the King of France who was a prisoner of the Duke of Guise. When the ambassador requested her, in the name of his sovereign, to withdraw her troops, Elizabeth said she refused to believe that the demand came from Charles IX, as he was not a free agent. She added that it was the duty of Charles IX to protect his oppressed subjects and to thank a friendly country for its efforts to assist him in that task. At this point the French ambassador gave up in despair and his audience with the Queen was terminated.

It would be pleasing to report that Elizabeth's diplomatically defiant words heralded English conquests in France, but that was not the case. England's entry into the war backfired on Condé. Recruits flocked to the standard of Guise, the man who had captured Calais, and away from Condé, who had given two French ports to the English. The King of Navarre also joined Guise, accompanied by Catherine de Medici and Charles IX, to attack the Huguenots who were in control of Rouen. Sir Adrian Poynings, the English commander at Le Havre, sent reinforcements to Rouen to strengthen the besieged garrison. Guise's force breached the city walls which were stoutly defended by the English contingent, until all 200 of them had been killed. The Catholic French surged in and massacred the remaining troops in an orgy of pillage and destruction.

When courtiers eventually summoned the courage to tell Elizabeth of the fall of Rouen, she immediately attempted to raise a new army by procuring 12,000 mercenaries from Germany. The only problem was that the English treasury was empty, so the mercenaries were never recruited. Meanwhile, Condé and his army were advancing from Orléans towards Paris but were intercepted by the Duke of Guise and his army at Dreux. A battle took place in which Condé was defeated and taken prisoner. Admiral Coligny became the main Huguenot general, fell back to Orléans, and sent urgent entreaties to Elizabeth for help. Elizabeth called on Parliament to vote money for the war but the situation in France was deteriorating, as were Anglo-French Protestant relations.

Coligny had captured the main towns of Normandy but took all the plunder for his own army, without sharing it with the Earl of Warwick's force. Coligny blamed the English for their lack of support. Guise was preparing to besiege Orléans when he was assassinated in February 1563, which changed the political landscape. Coligny decided that he had failed at his military interventions and that it was time to come to an accommodation with Catherine de Medici. He hoped to replace Guise as the dominant person in the government of Charles IX. Catherine was more than happy to restore peace to France and negotiations began, without any reference to Elizabeth. The Treaty of Amboise was signed on 19 March 1563. It confirmed that Huguenots were allowed to practice their religion in any part of France other than Paris, and in return, Huguenots would support the government of France.

Not surprisingly, Elizabeth was furious when she learned about the Treaty. The French ambassador was authorized to appease her by offering to renew the Treaty of Cateau-Cambrésis, guarantee the return of Calais, and repay all the money Elizabeth had advanced to the Huguenots. Elizabeth rejected this with scorn and declared that she would hold on to Le Havre and would defend it against the whole realm of France, which, unfortunately, is exactly what Elizabeth was required to do. In response to this, Condé and his troops joined the government forces in the siege of Le Havre. Elizabeth sent Sir Nicholas Throgmorton to France to negotiate an agreement, but he was arrested on arrival, on the pretence that his credentials were not in order. Meanwhile, the siege continued. Warwick expelled nearly all the unreliable French from Le Havre, putting his faith in defending the town with his own English garrison of 5,000 men, and 800 reinforcements under Sir Hugh Paulet.

As might be expected, Warwick's English garrison fought bravely in defence of Le Havre until the town walls were breached and their number had been reduced to less than 1,500. At this point the French made proposals for capitulation which Warwick was obliged to accept, and an agreement was concluded on 1 August 1563. Warwick and the remnants of his force were allowed to leave within six days, with all their weapons and effects. As if this defeat was not bad enough, when Warwick's men returned to England they brought with them the plague, which was to spread throughout England. The plague was particularly severe in London, where it caused the closure of the Inns of Court. Those who could fled from the city to the country. Elizabeth was livid at the loss of Le Havre and with it the prospect of regaining Calais, but she was powerless. In response to the arrest of Throgmorton she arrested the French envoy; to which the French responded by arresting the English ambassador. Diplomacy was not going well.

Elizabeth still held the bonds for 500,000 crowns, and the hostages, from the Treaty of Cateau-Cambrésis. She offered to surrender the hostages for the return of Throgmorton and reduced her claim to the 500,000 gold crowns. Following protracted wrangling the parties agreed that France would pay Elizabeth 120,000 crowns to give up her claim to Le Havre, and trade would be re-established between the two countries. The treaty known as the Peace of Troyes was signed in April 1564, but it made no mention of Calais. As far as the French were concerned the English had given up all claim to Calais by their occupation of Le Havre. Although Elizabeth did not see it that way she was in no position to do anything about it. Two years later, in 1566, the date agreed for Calais' return came and went, without comment. Elizabeth always harboured the strong desire to regain Calais but must have realized in her heart of hearts that it was no longer possible.

England's withdrawal from Le Havre ended any direct intervention by Elizabeth in the French Wars of Religion. Sadly, the Treaty of Amboise was not to last and in 1568 a full-scale war broke out between the Catholics and Huguenots. The English made no attempt to provide support for their co-religionists.

Elizabeth's reign so far had enjoyed relatively cordial relations with Spain but when Dutch Protestants in the Spanish Netherlands rejected the rule of Philip II, in 1585, Elizabeth agreed to support the Dutch rebels. This marked the beginning of a war with Spain which would last nineteen years. Although Elizabeth sent an army to join the Dutch, it was starved of funds and achieved little. Of more importance to Anglo-Spanish relations was England's state-sponsored piracy against Spain. Sir Francis Drake had attacked Spanish ships and ports in the Caribbean in 1585, and again in 1586. The following year, 1587, he destroyed much of the Spanish fleet in a raid on Cadiz, and the Spanish king, Philip II, decided to retaliate by invading England. Elizabeth's execution of Mary Queen of Scots, the previous year, made this a just cause from the Catholic point of view.

Philip's plan was to send a great fleet into the Channel and ferry an invasion force from the Spanish Netherlands to land on the south-east coast of England. On 28 May 1588 the Spanish Armada, comprising 130 ships, 8,000 sailors and 19,000 soldiers, set sail from Lisbon. It was due to rendezvous with the Duke of Parma, the Governor of the Spanish Netherlands, join his force of 30,000 men and 70 ships, and the combined force would invade England.[4] The Spanish fleet was delayed by bad weather and some ships turned back, leaving 124 to enter the Channel. On 20 July the English fleet off Plymouth engaged with the Armada. Over the next few days, a number of inconclusive engagements took place and on 27 July the Armada anchored off Calais, close to Dunkirk, where Parma's army was thought to be waiting. In fact, Parma's force had been ravaged by disease and was down to about 21,000 men, and in any case was partially blockaded by the Dutch fleet. Unknown to both sides, a Spanish invasion of England was no longer feasible.

At midnight on 28 July the English fleet sent eight fire ships, filled with pitch and gunpowder, into the closely packed Spanish fleet. None of the ships in the Armada were damaged, but the fear of fire prompted most of the fleet to cut their anchor cables and scatter in confusion – which allowed the English fleet to close for battle. Using greater manoeuvrability and broadside cannon fire it destroyed five ships and caused the Spanish flagship to run aground off Calais. Fear of running into other sandbanks, coupled with a southerly wind, forced the Armada to sail north and attempt to return home by sailing round Scotland. This voyage cost the Armada major losses through storms, shipwreck, disease, starvation and slaughter by local inhabitants when driven ashore. Sixty-seven ships and 10,000 men, only, returned safely to Lisbon.[5] England had defeated the great Spanish Armada by a combination of bad weather and the bravery and seamanship of its navy off Calais.

English history has highlighted the defeat of the Spanish Armada to such an extent that some might believe it marked England's final victory in the war with Spain. In fact, a year later (1589) England launched a Counter Armada against Spain. Sir Francis Drake commanded the fleet of 150 ships and 23,000 men, and conducted raids on Corunna, Lisbon and Madeira. Following gale damage and engagements with the Spanish, the fleet lost forty ships and thousands of men. In 1596 and 1597 Spain was able to mount two more armadas, but both were scattered by storms.

Nevertheless, Spain retained the upper hand in the war at sea until The Treaty of London was signed by Elizabeth's successor, James I, in August 1604, although England continued to control the Channel and was able to conduct piratical attacks on Spanish shipping.

While the sea battle off Calais had not won the war against Spain, it had helped to destroy the 1588 Armada and acted as a major boost to English morale. The victory over the Armada went a long way to restore English national pride, which had suffered such a terrible blow by the loss of Calais thirty years previously. As we have seen, the English success was partial and fleeting, but it did not deter Elizabeth from exploiting its propaganda value for all it was worth. The famous Armada portrait of Elizabeth was painted, and Armada medals were struck in gold and silver. The medals depicted different images of the Spanish defeat with various inscriptions, the most famous of which was *Flavit Jehovah et Dissipati Sunt* ('He blew his wind and they were scattered'). This dedication could be seen as a declaration that God Himself had supported the brave Protestant English fleet, by scattering the Papist Spanish Armada in a storm. Elizabeth's rousing speech at Tilbury and her victory over the Spanish Armada were defining events that helped to build the legendary Elizabethan Age and banish the lingering guilt over the loss of Calais.

Chapter 11

Acceptance of Loss and Role Reversal, 1588–1804

A few years after the defeat of the 1588 Spanish Armada off Calais, the town itself would feature in the Anglo-Spanish war and provide a possible opportunity for a return to English rule. Queen Elizabeth I had continued to meddle in the French Wars of Religion, but without significant military involvement. In 1589 the Huguenot leader, Henry of Navarre, inherited the French throne as Henry IV. The Wars of Religion continued, with Philip II supporting the French Catholic League against Henry. Elizabeth feared that Philip II and his forces from the Spanish Netherlands would capture the French Channel ports and use them to invade England, so she agreed to provide Henry with both financial and military aid.

English troops were once again deployed to France. None of this went well. At first, Lord Willoughby and 4,000 men roamed around northern France, achieved little, and withdrew to England in December 1589, having lost half the army. Two years later a force of 3,000 men under John Norreys was sent to Brittany but was severely defeated by the Catholic League at Craon in May 1591. Two months later the Earl of Essex was sent to help Henry IV besiege Rouen, but Rouen held out and Essex returned to England in January 1592. All these deployments had expended English lives and consumed government money but had done little to help Henry defeat Philip's forces and those of the Catholic League.

In 1593, much to the annoyance of Elizabeth, Henry IV publicly declared himself a Catholic, in order to get Paris to open its gates to him. By way of response Philip II launched a two-pronged attack on Henry's France and invaded Champagne and Picardy. Henry urgently requested financial aid and more troops from Elizabeth, but far from providing help, Elizabeth pulled her few remaining troops out of Brittany. Later, in March 1596, the Governor of the Spanish Netherlands, Archduke Albert and a force of 15,000 men advanced on Calais, took the outlying forts and began to bombard the town. Elizabeth was at church on a Sunday, in Greenwich, and the distant sound of the Archduke's cannonade plainly could be heard. Elizabeth sprang to her feet during the service and vowed that she would rescue England's former possession. She sent an order post-haste to the Lord Mayor of London, instructing him immediately to raise a thousand men and send them to Calais. But this fit of enthusiasm soon wore off and the next morning Elizabeth countermanded the order. She had devised a less expensive plan for returning Calais to English possession.

At the time, Henry IV's emissaries in London were pleading with Elizabeth for her urgent support. Elizabeth said she would provide support on condition that Calais was garrisoned by an English army. This was relayed to King Henry by Elizabeth's ambassador, Sir Robert Sidney. Henry was already extremely irritated with Elizabeth for having promised much in the past but having provided little real assistance when it was needed. He had immediately seen through Elizabeth's attempt to regain possession of Calais and was so annoyed that he turned his back on Sir Robert and muttered some unchivalrous remarks about dealing with a difficult woman. This brought the negotiations to an abrupt end without any help being sent from England to the besieged French garrison in Calais.

On 14 April 1596 Elizabeth's worst fears came to pass – Archduke Albert took Calais by storm. Under different circumstances, Calais being taken by the forces of Philip II would have been a matter for rejoicing. If Mary Tudor had lived to the age of eighty while still married to Philip, Calais would have reverted to English rule. If Elizabeth had agreed to Philip's proposal of marriage at the start of her reign, Calais would have reverted to English rule. As it was, then, Philip was at war with Elizabeth and possession of Calais gave him an ideal port from which to launch an invasion of England.

Despite the poor Anglo-French relations at the time, Henry IV needed Elizabeth's help to prevent further Spanish incursions into France; and Elizabeth needed Henry's help to prevent a Spanish invasion of England. It was agreed that England would send 2,000 men to reinforce the Boulogne garrison against any Spanish attack and, also, enable the port to harass any Spanish invasion fleet. Elizabeth's Council thought also that the war should be taken to Spain, in order to deflect Philip's attention from a possible invasion. In June 1596 an English fleet of 130 ships was joined by a Dutch fleet of 22 ships; together they carried 14,000 troops; and together they set sail to attack Cadiz.[1]

The attack on Cadiz came as a complete surprise to the Spanish and resulted in the destruction of many of their ships, followed by the emergence of English troops in the town itself. The commander of this force was the Earl of Essex who beat back the Spanish garrison and forced the town to capitulate. Essex was eager to press on into Spain, but the other commanders were more cautious; they wanted to withdraw with the booty they had collected while they had the chance. Essex was obliged to accept that the expedition had been no more than a successful raid, and sailed home to England. Soon after his return Elizabeth authorized Essex to take troops, with a naval force, to attack Spanish possessions in the Azores. This resulted in some useful plunder, but the islands were so well defended it was impossible to capture any territory.

Meanwhile, Henry IV had grown tired of the seemingly endless Wars of Religion but there was little chance of these coming to an end while Spain was supporting the Catholic League. In early 1598 Henry informed Elizabeth that he intended to negotiate peace with Philip. As may be expected, Elizabeth was less than pleased, but there was little she could do other than protest. In May that year Henry IV and Philip II agreed the Treaty of Vervins. Philip acknowledged Henry as the King of France, agreed to withdraw his Spanish Netherland troops from France, and returned Calais and the fortress of Risban to France. Philip offered to make peace with Elizabeth, but his offer was declined. Philip II died in September 1598 but his successor, Philip III, continued the war by landing a force in Ireland to support Irish rebels against the English. The rebels were defeated at the Battle of Kinsale in 1601 and the Spanish forces withdrew. The Spanish war with England gradually fizzled out and eventually, after the death of Queen Elizabeth I in 1603 and his succession to the throne, King James I of England agreed a formal peace, the Treaty of London, in August 1604.

The Treaty of Vervins had returned Calais to French hands, where it was to remain for the next three hundred and forty-two years and had brought an end to the futile attempts of various English monarchs to repossess Calais. But despite the passage of time, the loss of Calais was viewed by most Englishmen as a blot on the country's honour, which continued for many years to come. Fortunately, as England was by then largely Protestant, there was some comfort to be had by assigning blame for the loss to Catholicism. After all, it had been Catholic Queen Mary's marriage to a papist Spaniard that had led to the loss. Nowadays we are able to consider the loss of Calais with the perspective of history. It does not seem to have been the disaster it was perceived to be, at the time. Indeed, it could be said that it helped to launch England into eventually becoming a world power.

Calais was important to the English economy and crown revenue because it was the base for the Wool Staple, but by 1558 The Staple was in serious decline. It still had the monopoly for the sale of English wool, but the far greater trade in English finished cloth had overtaken it in importance. The Staple survived and the Merchant Staplers moved to Bruges in 1558, where unfinished wool remained in demand by the Dutch, who dyed and dressed it for subsequent sale. In 1614 King James I banned the sale of raw wool abroad because he wanted to promote a scheme for dyeing and dressing cloth in England, so that it could be sold at a higher price abroad. The Dutch were furious at this attempt to capture their cloth production business and in 1617 banned the import of cloth from England. This was not just a manoeuvre in a trade war, but a permanent ban and resulted in the Merchant Staplers leaving Bruges and returning to England. The company continued to function in England, supplying wool to the clothing industry until the Industrial Revolution, when it gradually changed from being a commercial organisation to the charitable body it is today.

Calais was also important to English monarchs as a secure foothold in France from which expeditions could be launched with the ultimate objective of winning back the Plantagenet territory. Much of England's military success in France was due to its powerful alliance with the Dukes of Burgundy against the French crown. Once Burgundy was once again under the control of French monarchs, that option no longer existed. France became more united and regional loyalties began to be replaced by a sense of nationalism. English monarchs became regarded as foreigners, rather than merely another overlord. As we have seen, even when France was divided by its Wars of Religion, England failed to regain Calais, let alone larger areas of France. In short, English monarchs might have styled themselves 'Kings of France', but there was no substance to the claim nor any possibility of making it a reality.

By 1558, Calais was costing a great deal in terms of payment for the garrisons and maintenance of the fortifications. The Merchants of The Staple became responsible for covering these costs but were unable to foot the bill. If the crown wanted to ensure the garrisons were paid and the defences maintained, it had to take money from its treasury to do so. This seldom happened, and the defences in particular fell into serious disrepair. Calais had been a significant source of crown revenue from the taxes on The Staple but had developed into a drain on crown funds. The loss of Calais was similar to the theft of a prized heirloom, but one whose insurance premium exceeded its current value.

The above factors all show that the loss of Calais was not as negative as it appeared at the time, and there was another factor which made it a positive outcome. It helped England turn away from its obsession with Europe and begin to look overseas for trade and commercial exploitation. England had been a slow starter in this respect. As long ago as 1415, while Henry V was winning Agincourt, King John of Portugal had captured Ceuta on the Moroccan coast and turned it into a Portuguese colony. His son, Henry the Navigator, sponsored explorations of Africa and the Atlantic and established a settlement in Madeira. In 1492 Spain sponsored Columbus to sail to the Americas, which led to the colony of Hispaniola (now Cuba and the Dominican Republic) and settlement in the Canaries in 1496. Meanwhile the Portuguese were sailing into the Indian Ocean, reaching China in 1513, Japan in 1543 and India in 1590, and developing trade with the East. Spain colonized Cuba and from there overcame the Aztec and Inca Empires to conquer Mexico and Peru, while Portugal colonized the coast of Brazil. In a hundred or so years Europe's world had expanded to offer the prospect of trade and settlement throughout much of the globe. These new opportunities for wealth and power became far more relevant than trying to regain the 120 square miles of the Calais Pale.

England was a maritime nation and had taken some interest in new discoveries. Henry VII had financed an Italian called Giovanni Cabotto to explore the Newfoundland area, as a result of which English fishermen began sailing there for the rich catches of cod. Henry VIII had done much to improve the navy and during Edward VI's short reign an expedition was made to the Guinea coast. Hugh Willoughby explored the North-East passage but died with his crew off the coast of the Kola Peninsula. Elizabeth's reign saw adventurers such as Drake and Hawkins pursuing piracy against Spanish ships to capture the cargos of gold, silver, sugar, tobacco, and other high value items from Spanish territories in the Americas. Drake's voyage into the Pacific on his circumnavigation of the world, and the capture of Portuguese and Spanish ships laden with expensive spices from the East, inspired English merchants to establish their own trade in the Pacific and Indian Oceans. This was formalized when Elizabeth granted a charter to the East India Company in 1600. By 1619 it had established trading posts in Java and India. Over the next two hundred years, despite Portuguese, Dutch, and French competition, the East India Company came to dominate trade in the east.

England's expanded maritime involvement, whether in exploration, buccaneering or trade, began to follow the Spanish and Portuguese example by attempting to establish settlements. These initiatives had little initial success. Spain and Portugal had come to dominate the rich fishing grounds off Newfoundland. Queen Elizabeth gave Sir Humphrey Gilbert letters of patent to take possession of Newfoundland, which he did in 1583, but after concluding the formalities he sailed back to England. It was not until two years later, when an English naval expedition destroyed most of the Spanish and Portuguese fishing vessels, that England established a degree of primacy, which was shared with the French. However, settlements of both English and French Basque fishermen were seasonal only. It was not until 1610 that the London and Bristol Company established a permanent colony in Newfoundland, with a governor and thirty-nine colonists. For the next hundred years there were sparse English and French settlements in different parts of the island until the whole country was seceded by France to England at the Treaty of Utrecht in 1713.

Newfoundland was England's first 'new' colony but there were other attempts to establish colonies on America's north-east coast during Elizabeth's reign. These were all failures. One of the most notable was the 1584 colony on the Roanoke Island (just south of modern Wilmington) which had disappeared without trace when it was visited six years later. A colony of 150 settlers was established in Virginia in 1587, but similarly had vanished when visited by a supply ship three years later. It was not until the reign of James I that enduring English colonies were founded.

The first was the Virginia Company's settlement in Jamestown in 1607, which only just managed to survive starvation and Indian massacres, but numbered 3,400 people in 1624, and become a crown colony which eventually thrived.

The second was in 1609 when ships from Jamestown were wrecked in Bermuda and the 150 survivors claimed the island for England. After a shaky start during which the island was abandoned, it was properly colonized in 1612 when St George's Town was founded and became the oldest continually inhabited English town in the New World.

In 1620 the Pilgrim Fathers established a small town they called Plymouth in what was to become Massachusetts. The first colonists just managed to survive their first winter and were followed later by other Puritan settlers. The settlement developed into the chartered Massachusetts Bay Colony and later into the Dominion of New England.

The first English colony in the Caribbean was settled in Barbados in 1627. By 1650 there were 44,000 English settlers in the West Indies, 12,000 on the Chesapeake estuary, and 23,000 in New England.

Almost exactly a hundred years after the loss of Calais, England had established fledgling colonies in the New World which were to increase and prosper. Together with trade in the east, these colonies eventually developed into an empire. The loss of Calais helped English merchants and seamen to look beyond Europe to the commercial opportunities of an expanding world. England had limited involvement only with mainland Europe for the majority of the first half of the seventeenth century. This was as well, as the Continent was tearing itself apart during the horrors of the Thirty Years War. England was also fully occupied by the chaos of its own Civil War. During this period England's colonies were left alone – and generally they blossomed. It was only after the 1648 Peace of Westphalia had ended the Thirty Years War, and the execution of Charles I in 1649, that England resumed an active foreign policy. The policy of the new Commonwealth regime was to enhance English trade and support Protestantism.

These two objectives came into immediate conflict when England declared war against the Protestant United Provinces to prevent the Dutch from carrying out trade with English colonies in the Americas. The war lasted two years and ended with an English victory, thanks to a much-expanded navy and the leadership of Admiral Blake. In 1654

Oliver Cromwell decided to confront Catholic Spain and, with his increasingly powerful navy, attacked the Spanish West Indies. Although the English force was repulsed from landing in Hispaniola, it managed to capture Jamaica and add it to England's list of colonies. The next year Cromwell made an alliance with France against Spain on condition that the young Louis XIV would stop sheltering the exiled Charles II. It was agreed that an English force of 6,000 men, supported by the navy, would combine with a French army of 20,000 troops, to attack the ports of the Spanish Netherlands. In 1657 England found itself deploying troops to mainland Europe after an absence of over half a century.

Not only were English troops deployed to mainland Europe, they were deployed also to England's traditional battle ground, just outside Calais. The Anglo-French objectives were to capture the ports of Gravelines, Dunkirk and Mardyck in the Spanish Netherlands. It was agreed, if the operation was successful, that Gravelines would be ceded to France and Dunkirk and Mardyck to England. This suited Cromwell as Dunkirk had long been a base for Flemish privateers who were causing considerable damage to England's mercantile fleet. The English contingent for the joint operation comprised 18 ships to blockade the ports, and an army under John Reynolds, together with troops from Cromwell's highly professional New Model Army.

In May 1657 Reynolds landed in France and the new scarlet uniforms of the English infantry were seen for the first time on the Continent. Unfortunately, Marshall Turenne, the agreed commander of the Anglo-French force, was still involved in campaigning against the Spanish in Luxembourg, so combined operations were delayed. Reynolds and his troops participated in the siege of Saint-Venant, about thirty miles south-west of Calais. He and his men had acquitted themselves well, but disease and other hardships related to siege warfare had reduced the force to 4,000 men. In September Turenne turned his attention to Flanders and captured Fort Mardyck on the western outskirts of Dunkirk. As agreed, Turenne handed Mardyck over to Reynolds, as governor. Small though it was, Fort Mardyck was England's first possession of a Channel port since Elizabeth had returned Le Havre to France, in 1564.

By this time the campaigning season was over, so no attempt was made to attack Dunkirk. Reynolds took the opportunity to return to England to plead for more troops but was drowned when his ship was wrecked on

Goodwin Sands. Cromwell directed the Commonwealth ambassador in Paris, Sir William Lockhart, to assume command of the English force at Mardyck. Only when the campaigning season re-opened in May 1658 did Turenne begin to besiege Dunkirk, and the English fleet of 18 ships resumed its station offshore.

The Spanish Army in Flanders was commanded by Don Juan-José, an illegitimate son of King Philip IV. Don Juan-José thought Turenne was using Dunkirk as a diversion and really intended to attack Cambrai. When he realized this was not the case, Don Juan-José advanced to relieve Dunkirk's 3,000-strong garrison. Don Juan-José's army consisted of the 15,000-strong Spanish Army of Flanders which included German and Walloon troops, together with a group of French rebels under the Prince de Condé, and 2,000 English Royalists commanded by James Duke of York, the brother of Charles II. On 13 June the Spanish army arrived near Dunkirk and camped on a line of dunes north-west of the town. The following day Turenne and his army advanced to meet the Spanish, his infantrymen were in the centre and the cavalry was on either wing. Turenne placed the left wing of his cavalry on the beach while the tide was in, hoping to attack the Spanish flank when the tide turned. The Spanish army took opposing positions, but in their haste, they left their artillery behind. The battle began with the Spanish right wing taking losses from Turenne's artillery and the English naval squadron. Turenne's army advanced and Lockhart's Commonwealth force, on the left wing, attacked a strongly held position on a sand dune 150 ft high, occupied by the elite Tercios Spanish infantry. With a bravery and professionalism that won admiration from Turenne and all who saw it, the redcoats took the hill and resisted two brave charges by the Duke of York and his royalist cavalry. As the tide went out, there was enough space for Turenne to send the cavalry on his left wing to envelop the Spanish right. He then advanced his infantry against the Spanish centre which broke and rushed into the Spanish cavalry behind. Soon the Spanish army was in flight, except for a force of English royalists who surrendered only when it was agreed they could return to Charles II at Ypres.

The entire battle lasted only two hours but resulted in the routed Spanish losing 1,200 killed, 800 wounded and 4,000 captured, while Turenne lost only 400 dead, the majority of whom were the redcoats who had borne the brunt of the fighting.[2] Dunkirk surrendered to Turenne soon after the battle and, as agreed, the town was passed to England, with Lockhart as governor. Exactly a hundred years after the loss of Calais, England once again was in possession of a French port just a few miles from Calais itself. Lockhart's new garrison cleared the pirates from Dunkirk but allowed the citizens freedom with which to continue their Catholic worship. Not all Lockhart's men were needed for the garrison and some men continued to serve with Turenne's army as it captured Gravelines and other Flemish territory.

The loss of Calais still registered as a humiliation for England in the national consciousness, so the victory of what became known as the Battle of the Dunes, and the occupation of Dunkirk, was met with great rejoicing.

However, it was perhaps as well that Dunkirk remained an English possession for four years only. Cromwell died later that year and the following year, 1659, France and Spain signed the Peace of the Pyrenees. The land surrounding Dunkirk, which belonged to Flanders, was ceded to France, and a year later, in 1660, Charles II returned to the English throne. Charles had sided with Spain out of necessity but by nature favoured France, the country of his mother, ruled by his cousin, Louis XIV. Charles discovered that his treasury had inherited considerable debt from the Commonwealth, which was exacerbated by the cost of maintaining the Dunkirk garrison. In 1662 he agreed to sell the town to Louis for the price of 5 million livres (£400,000). This was a considerable sum and the sale made a lot of sense. News of the sale of England's one and only continental possession to her old enemy, the French, raised an outcry; delegations of merchants protested its loss. Despite this, Charles went ahead with the sale and sent his goldsmith, Edward Blackwell, across the Channel to Calais in a fast royal yacht, to collect the first instalment of England's money.[3]

If the English public was dismayed about the sale of Dunkirk, they would have been furious had they known of another treaty between Charles II and Louis XIV, to be agreed eight years later. Fortunately for Charles this was kept secret for some years. Henrietta, sister to Charles, was married to the Duke of Orléans, the brother of Louis XIV. She and Louis travelled to Dunkirk and Henrietta sailed to Dover, where she was met by Charles. The Secret Treaty of Dover was agreed and signed on 1 June 1670. Charles undertook to join France in a war against the Dutch

Republic, and publicly to convert to Catholicism at a time of his choosing. In return Louis would give Charles an annual pension, so he would not have to rely on an interfering parliament for funding. Charles kept his side of the bargain by declaring war on the Dutch but, knowing how unpopular Catholicism was in England, he did not convert until he was on his deathbed, fifteen years later, in February 1685. During his reign, Charles received a total of £746,000 from his secret French pension.[4]

Charles II was succeeded by his brother, who became King James II in England and Ireland, and King James VII in Scotland. When James II attempted to encourage Catholicism in England, Protestant lords invited William of Orange, the Dutch leader, to replace him. Accordingly, on 22 January 1689, William of Orange became King William III of England and Ireland, and King William II in Scotland. James fled for Calais but his ship was blown off course and he landed at an anchorage a few miles south, at Ambleteuse. Louis welcomed his cousin to France and gave him full support while he tried to regain the English throne. French troops accompanied James when he landed in Ireland in March 1689, but after being defeated by William at the Battle of the Boyne in July 1690, he returned to France, followed by his French allies and Catholic Irish regiments. William, as King of England, used England's navy and army in his war with France. Once again British soldiers were deployed to the Continent, particularly in Spanish Flanders, but the fighting was far from Calais and consisted largely of sieges of towns such as Namur and Mons.

English redcoats were indeed in Flanders, but the situation had become a reversal of the past. Even during the reign of Henry VIII, England had hoped to use Calais as a base to invade France and win territory. From now on, it would be the French who would plan to invade England, and the area around Calais was used frequently as a suitable mounting base for crossing the Channel. In 1692 Louis agreed to support the exiled King James in an invasion of England. James had wanted Ambleteuse to be his point of embarkation, having arrived there after fleeing England. But although Ambleteuse or neighbouring Calais provided a short passage to England, Louis decided the invasion should be launched from the Cherbourg peninsula. An 8,000-strong French army and James' Jacobite Irish Brigade assembled near La Havre and La Hougue, to board their troop transport vessels. Louis ordered Admiral de Tourville to gather his fleet and attack the English and Dutch fleets separately, before they had time to combine, and then escort James II and his Franco-Jacobite army across the Channel, to invade England. But the invasion was not to be. The English and Spanish fleets had already combined under Admiral Russell and far outnumbered de Tourville's fleet when they met off Cape Barfleur. Fighting took place over several days, off Barfleur, and then at La Hougue, during which the French lost twelve ships of the line. Not only was the invasion impossible, but much of the French navy had been destroyed.

As the French navy was unable to take any direct action against the British and Dutch navies, the French minister of war decided that the best naval tactic would be to attack enemy merchant shipping by licenced privateers. The sailors of Dunkirk needed little encouragement to resume their traditional attacks on British and Dutch merchantmen and new privateer bases were established at Calais, Saint-Malo, Le Havre and Dieppe. The French privateers were most successful in their attacks and began causing serious economic loss to England, particularly by capturing the ships and valuable cargo of the East India Company. In 1694 a squadron of English ships bombarded Dunkirk, but little damage was caused, thanks to Louis XIV's great military engineer, Marquis de Vauban, who earlier had built strong defences. The squadron abandoned its attack on Dunkirk and sailed up the coast to Calais, where it fired over a hundred rounds into the town and damaged some of the ships and bases of the privateers. Unfortunately, this was not enough to stamp out French piracy. It was necessary to carry out further naval bombardment of Calais, and also Saint Malo, Le Havre and Dieppe, and an attempted amphibious landing at Brest, which failed. None of these efforts managed to remove the privateer threat completely, and their piracy continued until the war came to an end when the Peace of Ryswick was concluded in 1697.

William III had dragged England into the Nine Years War against France in order to prevent attempts by Louis XIV of France to annex Holland. William III died in 1702 and was succeeded by Queen Anne, the estranged daughter of James II. By this time, it had become clear that the Peace of Ryswick had not ended Louis' insatiable ambition to expand his empire, and this became manifest when Louis placed his grandson on the throne of Spain in 1701, as Philip V of Spain. England's response was to join a coalition with Holland, Austria and Savoy against Louis, in what became known as the War of the Spanish Succession. The war was wide ranging, and was fought in the Low Countries, Italy, Hungary, Spain, Portugal, North America, India and West Africa. Although the English navy sailed far and wide, the army was deployed mainly in the Low Countries. In support of Austria, Queen Anne's great general, the Duke of Marlborough, took his army to the Rhine and Moselle and won the battle of Blenheim. Aside from this, Marlborough and his redcoats fought mainly in the Netherlands. His great battles were at Ramillies (near Maastricht), Oudenarde and Malplaquet (outside Mons). Although not far from Calais the war did not take him into the immediate area of Calais, not least because north-west France was defended by Vauban's line of forts called *Le Ceinture de Fer* (The Iron Belt).

Although England made no attack by land on Calais during the war, the town was bombarded by the Royal Navy. Louis became concerned that England might circumvent *Le Ceinture de Fer* by capturing the town as a bridgehead for invasion. In 1706 Vauban was instructed to fortify the port. His first thoughts were to defend it in the way that had been used by the English, to flood the whole area, and Fort Nieulay was modified for this purpose. He then surrounded the town with ditches and thick walls with arrow shaped bastions from which artillery could cover approaches to the walls. Once these massive fortifications were complete, Calais' defences were far too strong to make any English attack feasible.

In 1708 Louis XIV decided he would support the Jacobite uprising in Scotland, in order to divert English forces from Marlborough's army in Flanders. James II had died in 1701 and Louis had recognized his son, Prince James Francis Edward (the Old Pretender) as King James III of England (and King James VIII of Scotland), in opposition to Queen Anne. Louis assembled a fleet of five ships of the line and twenty frigates at Dunkirk, under Admiral Forbin. In March this French fleet was ready to take the 19-year-old King James III, and a Franco-Jacobite force of 6,000 troops, to Scotland to launch an uprising against Queen Anne. English intelligence became aware of the plan and Admiral Byng was sent to Dunkirk with a fleet to blockade the port. However, a storm drove the English fleet off station, and Forbin was able to slip out to sea, with the prince and the invasion troops, and reach the coast of Scotland.

Byng had foreseen this possibility and had deployed some of his fleet as far north as the Firth of Forth where it intercepted Forbin's fleet and captured one ship. Forbin managed to disengage from the English fleet but as the weather was so bad it was impossible to carry out a landing elsewhere along the coast. With the wind against them, the French fleet was obliged to sail round the north of Scotland, past Ireland and return a rather sea-sick James Francis Edward to Dunkirk. All plans of a French sponsored Jacobite invasion of Scotland were abandoned.

The war came to a close with the Peace of Utrecht, a series of treaties signed between 1713 and 1715. As a result of these treaties Spain lost Flanders, Naples, Sardinia and Milan to Austria, and Sicily to Savoy; but Louis' grandson was recognized as King Charles V of Spain, on condition he did not also inherit the throne of France.

Despite Marlborough's major successes in Flanders during the war there was no question of England trying to negotiate the return of Calais. Indeed, there was no longer any desire to take possession of the former colony. Queen Anne's government knew the country's interests were based on commerce and the protection of its trade routes, and the Treaties of Utrecht served England well in this respect. England had gained Gibraltar and Minorca from Spain, which made it dominant in the eastern Mediterranean. England's colonies in North America expanded, with France ceding to England the Hudson Bay area, Nova Scotia, claims to Newfoundland, as well as Saint Kits in the West Indies. Although Calais did not feature in the treaties, Dunkirk did. England remained concerned about attack from French privateers and so a clause was included in the treaty to demolish the fortifications of Dunkirk and block up the port. Unfortunately, Louis did not comply with the agreement and privateering continued.

Queen Anne died in 1714 and the throne was left to her Protestant cousin George, the Elector of Hanover. However, having a German on the English throne was not welcomed by many English Tories and, of course, Jacobites. Louis decided this was an opportunity for mischief. Louis supported the Old Pretender in another uprising in Scotland where the Earl of Mar had raised the prince's standard for the Jacobite cause in August 1715. Louis sent two ships carrying arms, ammunition and supplies to Mar, but it was not until December that Prince James Francis Edward sailed from Dunkirk and arrived with a small group in Scotland. Mar's uprising was successful, initially, and even advanced to Preston. But it was beaten back and Mar's force was very much depleted when he was joined by the prince in Dundee. James Francis Edward was disheartened to see that his Jacobite army was so small and with news of superior government forces approaching he decided to retreat from Dundee. By February the prince had become ill with a fever and had realized that his cause was hopeless, so he took a boat back to France, leaving his followers to fend for themselves.

Louis XIV died in 1715 and was succeeded by his 5-year-old grandson, as King Louis XV of France, with the Duke of Orléans as regent. This began a period of reasonable Anglo-French relations until they came to an end, in 1740, with the start of the War of the Austrian Succession. By then George II had inherited the throne of England, but he was also Elector of Hanover and so decided to support Maria Theresa's claim to the Austrian throne, which was being challenged by France and Frederick the Great of Prussia. The War of the Austrian Succession saw British troops fighting in Germany, and the Royal Navy conducting engagements in the Atlantic, Pacific and North Sea. The war included a French scheme to invade Britain and restore the Old Pretender, James Edward Stuart, to the throne and also draw British troops away from operations against France on the Continent. It was decided that the young and accomplished Prince Charles Edward Stuart (also known as the Young Pretender or Bonnie Prince Charlie) would be a more charismatic leader for the expedition than his father, the Old Pretender.

A transport fleet and 12,000 men were assembled at Dunkirk in early 1744 but a storm the night before the Young Pretender was about to board completely destroyed the fleet. Louis cancelled the invasion but after appeals from Charles Edward he agreed to provide two vessels and 100 volunteers from the French Irish Brigade, to make a landing in Scotland. The point of embarkation was moved to Saint-Nazaire in the Loire estuary. The 25-year-old Charles and his two ships left France in July 1745 and, after losing one ship in an engagement with the Royal Naval squadron, managed to land with his small force in the Western Isles. He raised his standard at Glenfinnan and assembled 700 Highland supporters. After defeating the only government army in Scotland, he was welcomed into Edinburgh. In November Charles and his Jacobite Scottish army advanced into England and reached as far as Derby, but without gaining any English support, and the clan chiefs demanded to return to Scotland. Charles grudgingly agreed to retreat but was pursued by a government army under the Duke of Cumberland, and then suffered a complete defeat at the Battle of Culloden in the Scottish Highlands, in April the next year. Charles became a fugitive until he was picked up by a French ship in September and returned to France. He was never to see Scotland again.

In 1756 the French invaded British-held Minorca in the opening engagement of the Seven Years' War. In 1759 Louis XV's foreign minister, the Duke de Choiseul, decided to resurrect a plan to invade England and invited Charles to a meeting to discuss his participation. But when Charles arrived de Choiseul found him both drunk and argumentative. He dropped the idea of collaborating with Charles and decided to make it a purely French invasion. His plan was to land a 100,000-strong army on the south coast of England and take London while the main English army was away in Germany. With this in mind, 325 troop transport ships were assembled; the majority were at Le Havre with a smaller number at Dunkirk, for a diversionary attack. An army of 48,000 troops had already been concentrated for the invasion when the scheme was thwarted by a Royal Naval attack on Le Havre, which destroyed many of the French transports. This was followed by the defeat of the Toulon Fleet by a small British convoy at the Battle of Lagos, off Portugal in August 1759, and, finally, the destruction of the Brest Fleet at the Battle of Quiberon Bay, off Saint-Nazaire, in November the same year.

Quiberon Bay had blocked any realistic chance of France mounting an invasion of England for some time. Three years later, in 1763, the war between Britain, France and their respective allies was brought to an end by the Treaty of Paris. The Seven Years' War may have been the first ever global conflict, with Spain, Austria, Russia and Sweden allied to France, while Prussia and Portugal had supported Great Britain and Hanover. It had spread beyond Europe to the Americas and Southern Asia, and Britain's maritime and land success beyond Europe was reflected in the treaty documents. France had allied with the Mughal Empire in India against The East India Company, but after Robert Clive's victory at Plassey (1757), Britain took Bengal and became the principal trading nation on the subcontinent. The capture of Quebec by General James Wolf in 1759 resulted in Britain dominating Canada. The Seven Years' War had left the government of Britain virtually bankrupt, but Britain had avoided French invasion, had added to the number of its colonies, and had become a world power.

George II had died in 1760, before the end of the war, and was succeeded by his grandson who became King George III of Great Britain and Ireland. During the reign of George III, the colonies in America rebelled, largely because the English Parliament had raised their taxes to help cover debts incurred during the Seven Years' War. The American Revolutionary War began in 1775 when the British garrison in Boston was attacked by the Massachusetts Militia. This led to all thirteen American colonies taking up arms against Britain, eventually forcing Lord Cornwallis to surrender at Yorktown in 1781. The English Parliament recognized the independence of the United States in 1782 which was formalized two years later, in 1783, when the Peace of Paris was signed by Great Britain, the United States, France and Spain. This tragic civil war should have been a purely British concern, but the French foreign minister, Count de Vergennes, saw it as an opportunity for France to supplant Britain in America. Vergennes began sending arms, ammunition and volunteers to the colonists and then joined them in war against Britain. In 1779 Spain secretly joined France against Britain making their combined navy larger than the Royal Navy. Vergennes decided to use this naval superiority to launch an invasion of England.

In June 1779 the French fleet comprising 30 ships of the line and a number of smaller vessels, under the command of Admiral d'Orvilliers, left Brest, evaded a Royal Naval blockade and sailed to join a Spanish fleet off Corunna. When d'Orvilliers arrived at the rendezvous the Spanish fleet was nowhere to be seen. For several weeks the French fleet waited for the Spanish to arrive, during which time typhus and smallpox broke out. On 22 July the Spanish at last arrived, with 36 ships of the line. The combined fleet came under the overall command of d'Orvilliers. In the meantime, 400 troop transport ships and a 40,000-strong invasion force were being assembled at Saint Marlow and Le Havre. The plan was for the combined Franco-Spanish fleet to defeat any Royal Naval fleet in the Channel, escort the invasion force to the Isle of Wight, and from there capture Portsmouth.

The English Channel fleet of forty ships of the line commanded by Sir Charles Hardy was patrolling off the Scilly Isles. On 16 August d'Orvilliers entered the Channel and arrived off the English coast, having missed the English fleet. At this point he received orders from France to change the landing site from the Isle of Wight to Falmouth. D'Orvilliers sent a message questioning this order to France, and while waiting for a reply, he heard that the English fleet was at the Scilly Isles, so he sailed off there to engage it. Hardy managed to elude the advancing Franco-Spanish fleet and take his ships safely back to the Solent, arriving there on 3 September. It was late in the campaigning season, the English fleet was still intact, the French fleet had lost 8,000 men to disease, so it was decided to abandon the invasion. The great invasion armada, a minimum of sixty-six ships in total, dispersed and returned to their respective ports.

Ten years after the planned invasion France suffered the turmoil of Revolution. The execution of Louis XVI by guillotine in January 1793 prompted the horrified monarchs of Europe to prepare to invade France. The French Revolutionary leaders decided to conduct a pre-emptive attack on Holland and Prussia, thus triggering another period of war which lasted until 1802. During this conflict France mobilized the nation under the leadership of Napoleon Bonaparte and became masters of Italy, Netherlands and the Rhine Lands. Until then Napoleon's ambitions regarding Great Britain had been to capture its trade and colonies, but not to invade England. His ambitions changed when war was resumed in 1804 and he began to plan an invasion of England from the area of Calais.

Chapter 12

Road to Entente Cordiale, 1804–2022

The French Revolutionary Wars were brought to an end by the Treaty of Amiens in 1802. As part of the treaty George III gave up his claim to the French throne, removed the fleur-de-lis from the royal coat of arms, and acknowledged the French Republic; and France ceded Ceylon and Trinidad to Britain. The Act of Union in 1801 had united Great Britain (England and Scotland) with Ireland, to become a single state, known as the United Kingdom of Great Britain and Ireland. It might have been hoped that the Treaty heralded an amicable relationship between the United Kingdom and France, but the peace was to last just over a year. Napoleon's control of Switzerland and his disruption of trade resulted in the United Kingdom declaring war against France in May 1804. Austria and Prussia soon joined the war and what was to be called the 'Napoleonic Wars' began.

Napoleon had attempted to invade Ireland in 1796, and two years later had assembled an army on the Channel coast in preparation for invading Southern England. He abandoned this plan when he decided that these troops were needed for his new campaigns in Egypt and against Austria. When war was resumed in 1804 Napoleon had already returned to his previous plan for an invasion of England. By the following year Napoleon had assembled a 150,000-strong army, the Armée d'Angleterre, in the area of Boulogne and Montreuil and invasion barges were being built in Calais and most Channel ports.

England rightly took this threat very seriously. The militia were called out, additional defences were added to Dover Castle, and Martello towers were erected along the coast. The Royal Navy established blockades and launched a major fire-ship attack on the French vessels in Boulogne, but the raid produced little result. The one thing holding Napoleon back from launching his invasion was the ability to transport his force across the Channel without it being attacked by the Royal Navy. Napoleon is reported as having said, 'Let us be masters of the Channel for six hours and we are masters of the world.' He planned to achieve this by directing his two fleets, based at Brest and Toulon, to break through the British blockades and sail off as though they were going to attack the West Indies. The two fleets were intended to rendezvous at Martinique, then rush back to the Channel while evading the British fleet, and land a diversionary force in Ireland. The fleet would then defeat any Royal Naval ships still in the Channel and escort the main invasion force across the Channel before the main British fleet had caught up with them.

This was a bold plan by one of history's great military geniuses. Had it succeeded it would have had a good chance of overcoming the much smaller army defending Southern England, and conquering Britain. Although the Brest fleet was kept blockaded, the Toulon fleet under Admiral Villeneuve managed to break out in March 1805 and link with nineteen Spanish ships, but they were intercepted by a British fleet off Cape Finisterre where an inconclusive battle took place, and the Franco-Spanish fleet sailed for the security of Cadiz. The French invasion was no longer possible, and France was being threatened by Russia and Austria, so in August Napoleon re-named his invasion force the Grande Armée and marched it off to the Danube and eventual victory over the Austrians at Ulm. In October Villeneuve's Franco-Spanish fleet of thirty-three ships of the line left Cadiz and were met by Nelson's twenty-seven ships at the Battle of Trafalgar. The whole of Villeneuve's great fleet was either captured or destroyed. There was no question of Napoleon ever again being able to contemplate an invasion of Britain.

The year 1805 was the last time France would plan to invade England, but the Napoleonic Wars were to endure for another nine years. In 1814 Napoleon abdicated after the disaster of his Russian campaign, followed by his defeat at Leipzig and the invasion of France by Austria, Russia and Prussia. As the guillotined Louis XVI's only son had died, the claim to the French throne passed to his brother, the Count of Provence, who had been living in Hartwell House in Buckinghamshire. The French Senate invited the Count to return as King Louis XVIII and as soon as his gout allowed him to travel, he crossed the Channel to Calais, en route to Paris as the restored monarch. His restoration was short-lived – Napoleon escaped from Elbe in February 1815, the French army defected to Napoleon, and Louis fled to the Netherlands.

Napoleon rapidly raised an army of 300,000 men and decided to attack his enemies before Austria, Russia, Prussia and Great Britain had time to mobilize, but his ambitions were brought to a final halt by the Battle of Waterloo. After his defeat Napoleon abdicated a second time and Louis XVIII was again restored to the throne. The British troops who survived the battle returned to England, most of them embarking at Calais. Louis XVIII was a less than inspiring personality, but his reign initiated a period of good Anglo-French relations, helped by the friendship shown to him by the Prince Regent while Louis had been an exile in England. These cordial relations continued after Louis died, nine years later, and was succeeded by his brother, Charles X.

While relations between Charles X and the United Kingdom were good, this was not the case with his French subjects. His belief in the Divine Right of Kings, although no doubt fully justified in his own eyes, was not shared by many. He dismissed the Chamber of Deputies, suspended the free press, and excluded the middle class from elections, which led directly to the July Revolution in 1830. Charles was forced to abdicate and flee to the United Kingdom, where he took up residence in Holyrood House, later moving to Austria where he died in 1836. The Chamber of Deputies invited Charles X's cousin, the liberal minded Duke of Orléans, to succeed as King Louis-Philippe.

The new king was an anglophile. He had been a close friend of the Duke of Kent, Queen Victoria's father, and had spent fifteen years in England. In 1843 he hosted Queen Victoria and Prince Albert on a visit to Normandy and his welcoming speech used the term *entente cordiale* for the first time.[1] The next year Louis-Philippe made a return visit to London and was greeted by cheering crowds. Unfortunately, Louis-Philippe was becoming less popular in France. In 1848, economic depression, followed by demonstrations, then the banning of public gatherings, led to the February Revolution. Louis-Philippe abdicated and followed the family tradition of fleeing to England, to spend his remaining two years at Claremont in Surrey. A Second Republic was declared and Napoleon's nephew, Louis Napoleon Bonaparte, was elected President. Four years later he declared himself Emperor Napoleon III.

Napoleon III had been welcomed into London Society during his exile in Louis-Philippe's reign and wanted his good relations with Great Britain to continue. He had come to know Disraeli, but it was his good relations with the British Foreign Secretary, Viscount Palmerston, which enabled France and Great Britain to become allies against Russia in the Crimean War. This was the first time that France and England had been military allies for almost two hundred years; they had last fought side by side against Spain at the Battle of the Dunes in 1658. Cordial Anglo-French relations continued, but Napoleon's period as emperor came to an abrupt end with the Franco-Prussian War of 1870. The French army capitulated, having lost the Battle of Sedan, and Napoleon was taken prisoner. When the news of this humiliating defeat reached Paris a Third Republic was declared. Napoleon was later released and banished from France. He lived the remainder of his life as an exile at Chislehurst in Kent.

But what of Calais, during this fifty-year period of convivial Anglo-French relations? Instead of enjoying its traditional military role, Calais was becoming an increasingly important port for those travelling between the two countries. The old Cinque Ports of Sandwich, Hythe, New Romney, Hastings, Winchelsea and Rye had all silted up by the seventeenth century, making Dover the main port from Kent to France. Calais was the shortest crossing from Dover to France and became the main port for English travellers. The journey from London to France return could be achieved in a day, as was shown by Bernard Calvert in 1619. He established a record when he left Southwark on horseback at 3 am on 17 July, arrived at Dover at 7 am, took a ship to Calais, returned on the same ship, returned to London, again on horseback, and arrived at 8 pm, having covered 142 miles riding and 44 miles sailing.

A few English visitors stayed in Calais long enough to explore the town. The diarist, John Evelyn, visited in 1643 and was shown round by a French guide who pointed out one of the last traces of Calais having been an English settlement. Evelyn records: 'I remember there was engraved in stone, upon the front of an ancient dwelling which was showed us, these words in English – God save the King.'[2] Most English visitors merely passed through Calais on their way to Paris or other parts of France. English diplomats and merchants travelled to and from Calais when the two countries were at peace, but there was also an increasing number of what might be called tourists. When James II set up court at Saint-Germain many members of the gentry came to visit, not so much because they had Jacobite sympathies but just to see the exiled monarch. Admittedly, this did not last long as William III banned such visits. In much the same way there was a rush of English visitors to see Revolutionary France for themselves, during the short period of peace in 1790.

The eighteenth century also saw the beginning of young members of the aristocracy and wealthy gentry going on the Grand Tour. This tour began at Dover with a crossing to Calais, or sometimes Ostend or Le Havre, and then moved through France to Italy. In 1820 the crossing became easier when *Rob Roy*, the British-built paddle steamer, began ferrying passengers to Calais. By the mid-nineteenth century this exploration of western culture had become an educational rite of passage for the wealthy. When the rail link was made from London to Dover in 1844 travel became easier and less expensive, especially as at much the same time the Port of Dover was expanded by the construction of Admiralty Pier and Western Docks and Calais' harbour was modernized. In the 1860s Thomas Cook began organising tours and started what eventually became mass travel.

Although the great majority of British visitors merely transited through Calais, there were a few who settled there as a refuge. The most prominent were two celebrated people of their day who came to tragic ends. The first was Emma Hart, the great beauty who, as Lady Hamilton (wife of Sir William Hamilton, the Ambassador in Naples) became famous as the lover of the admiral, Lord Horatio Nelson. She was the muse of the artist George Romney, who painted her numerous times, had a magnetic personality and was a talented singer and dancer. She became a close friend of Queen Maria Carolina of Naples (the sister of Queen Marie Antoinette) and was much admired by the Prince Regent. As the companion of England's national hero, the two of them were the great celebrities of their day, entertaining and being entertained by the highest in the land. All this came to an end with Nelson's death in 1805 during the Battle of Trafalgar.

Sir William had already died leaving Emma a small annuity, but she inherited very little from Nelson, as the majority of his estate passed to his wife's family. Emma was unable to curtail the extravagant lifestyle to which she had become accustomed and fell into debt. Her debt became worse and in 1814 she slipped away to Calais where she took up residence at the expensive Dessein's Hotel. She continued to live beyond her means until her debt forced her to move to a small flat at 27 Rue Française.[3] There she lived in poverty, reliant on alcohol and laudanum to relieve painful dysentery, until her death in 1815. She was buried in Calais, but nothing remains of her grave as a result of World War II bombing.

The second notable English resident in Calais was George 'Beau' Brummell. He was the centre of London society, a close friend of the Prince Regent and a trend-setter in terms of gentlemen's fashion. This witty, larger than life figure lost the favour of the Prince Regent, amassed huge gambling debts and fled from England in 1816 to escape his creditors. He landed in Calais and there he stayed for ten years, trying to keep up appearances and surviving on occasional hand-outs from his society friends. His contacts later arranged for him to be appointed as the consul in Caen, in 1830. He received a small income from the consulate but after two years the post was abolished. His life went steadily downhill, with failing health and a period of four months in prison, for debt.[4] In 1840 this iconic figure of the Regency period died penniless and insane, in Caen's Bon Sauveur Asylum.

Calais received greater numbers of English travellers after the defeat of Napoleon and peace brought with it increased commercial activity. Although mutually beneficial for both countries, an aspect of this prosperity was distinctly bad for Britain. About the time that Beau Brummell had fled to Calais, France had conducted a major piece of industrial espionage against England. Years before, in 1589, the Reverend William Lee had invented a handloom with which his brother established a business in Nottingham, manufacturing hose and employing families who worked from their homes. When trousers replaced hose as items of fashion many of the loom frames were adapted to make lace. There was an increasing demand for lace, not only to adorn women's clothing but also for curtains and tablecloths, and Nottingham became the centre of English lacemaking, utilising 1,800 looms. So valuable was this source of income and the design of the loom on which lace was made, that the penalty for exporting the design to other countries was death. This did not deter the French. In 1816 they managed to smuggle one of the lacemaking looms from Nottingham to Calais, and this formed the basis of the Calais lacemaking industry. Later, with the advent of steam power, lacemaking in Calais expanded to the extent that Calais became one of the world's finest producers of lace. Even today the modern industry in Calais employs 3,000 people.

Despite this, as we have seen, good relations between England and France continued right up to the overthrow of Napoleon III. However, 1870 was a time when the world was changing and uniting. The USA became a united country, following its civil war; Italy had become a single country; and, most importantly, Prussia's victory in the Franco-Prussian War enabled Bismarck to proclaim Wilhelm I of Prussia the German emperor, at the Versailles Hall of Mirrors in January 1871. Tensions arose as newly united countries and old established states looked on with envy at the UK, with its control of India and other colonies stretching as far away as Australia and New Zealand. These tensions came to the fore with the Scramble for Africa, during which several European powers grabbed whatever portions of the continent they could. France already had taken control of Algeria, and now assumed control of Tunisia and Morocco, and partial control of Egypt, as well as French West Africa (which included present-day Niger, Mali, Togo, Benin, Mauritania and Senegal) and French Equatorial Africa (which included Chad, the Republic of Congo and the Central African Republic), not forgetting Madagascar. Germany took control of Namibia, Cameroon and Togo; and so it went; with Belgium, Portugal and Italy all taking their slices of Africa, until, by 1914, 90 per cent of the African continent was under European control.

The UK had been particularly successful in the grab for Africa and dominated the Sudan, West Africa (Nigeria and Ghana,) and East Africa (Kenya, Uganda, Zimbabwe and Zambia). But in South Africa, in 1880, problems arose when the Dutch Boer settlers resisted British colonial expansion. This led to two Boer Wars during which much of Europe sympathized with the Boers. When the recently crowned King Edward VII visited Paris in 1903, a year after the end of the second Boer War, he drove down the Champs-Élysées and was greeted by crowds shouting 'Vivent les Boers'. As it happened Edward was a Francophile who spoke fluent French, and was able to launch a very successful charm offensive. This was so well received by the Third Republic that it led to the Entente Cordiale the next year.

The Entente Cordiale was a series of agreements between the UK and France. It resolved disputes over Africa and elsewhere, such as agreeing that the UK should control Egypt, and France should control Morocco. The government of the Third Republic had always wanted good relations with the UK, driven by their fear of the united Germany, which had occupied France in 1870 and annexed Alsace and Lorraine during the peace. As Edward VII was the cousin of Kaiser Wilhelm II there had been concern that UK sympathies would always be with Germany. It was therefore highly satisfactory to have concluded the Entente Cordiale which, although not a treaty, bound the two countries in an historic friendship which has continued, despite numerous altercations, to this day. The outbreak of the First World War was the first real test of the entente. Germany encouraged Austria to shell Belgrade; Russia mobilized; Germany declared war on Russia; France supported Russia; Germany invaded neutral Belgium and declared war on France; at which point the UK declared war on Germany.

For the first time since the Waterloo campaign soldiers from the UK would be fighting in Europe. Once again Calais was of military significance. In August 1914 the 100,000-strong British Expeditionary Force (BEF) arrived in France under the command of Sir John French. Having advanced to meet the German army at Mons the BEF was forced back, and General French began planning the evacuation of the Force through Calais and other Channel ports. However, a successful Anglo-French counterattack on the Germans, at the Battle of the Marne in September, eventually led to a static war of attrition along the trenches of the Western Front. The important Battles of Arras and Vimy Ridge took place in the Pas-de-Calais (the French Department in which Calais is situated), but apart from receiving aerial bombing and machine gun fire, there was no fighting in Calais itself. The German advance was held a few miles south of Ostend.

The major role played by Calais in the First World War was as one of the three main ports for British and Commonwealth forces. The other two were Dunkirk and Boulogne, the latter city being the principal port. The port of Calais was used for the transport of troops to the Western Front, evacuation of the wounded and, finally, for the repatriation of the army after the Armistice. Calais provided vital logistic support for the BEF for everything, from rations to ordnance (weapons and military equipment). Not only did the port work flat out on logistics related to the troops and their movements, the area around the town also became a site for depots and field hospitals. Etaples was the main supply depot for the British forces but the importance of Calais was emphasized by the fact that more than 2,000 British officers and 70,000 other ranks were stationed there by the end of the war.

The shared experience of the horrors of the four-year long war brought the UK and France even closer together. In August 1918 their troops fought side by side in an offensive which started with the Battle of Amiens. This was a resounding success for the Allied forces and led to the German retreat, the collapse of their morale, the abdication of the Kaiser in November and the final surrender by Germany later the same month. This result by no means had been a foregone conclusion. Despite the efforts of Britain and France, victory on the Western Front would not have been possible without the support of one million troops from the British Empire – the armies of India, Canada, South Africa, Australia and New Zealand – and over two million men from Britain's former colony, the USA.

Following the Armistice, signed on 11 November 1918, British troops expected soon to return home. However, the government wanted a number of troops to remain in France, to provide security against a possible German attack, and to assure delivery of the reparations agreed with Germany. By early January 1919 there was widespread discontent among conscripted soldiers across the whole army, nowhere more so than among the soldiers in Calais. These troops were angered by poor rations, bad working conditions, harsh discipline, and began demanding their demobilization. A certain Private Panting addressed an assembly of disgruntled soldiers and was arrested and jailed. This further inflamed the troops who broke into the military prison, released Panting, then went on strike and refused to obey orders from their officers.

This mutiny in Calais spread swiftly until some 20,000 British soldiers in that area of France had joined the strike. Senior army staff realized that they had no option but to negotiate with the mutineers and agreed to improve conditions, take no action against the strike leaders, and hasten demobilization. The dissident troops were satisfied with these concessions and the mutiny ended on 30 January. Churchill became Secretary for War at this time and began demobilization on a massive scale with a popular policy which agreed that the men who had served the longest should be the first to be discharged. Had it not been for the extensive disaffection throughout the army, manifested by the mutiny of troops in Calais, there would have been a very long delay before soldiers on the Western Front returned to their loved ones.

After British forces had finally sailed home at the end of the Great War, Calais returned to its normal peacetime existence as a port. Steam turbine ships were replaced with oil-powered propeller driven vessels which carried passengers and cargo across the Channel, and the far-reaching railway networks of the UK and the Continent enabled people and goods to move rapidly across Europe. In 1928 the first car ferry came into service, but it was able to carry only 15 cars at a time. Two years later the British built *MS Forde* which carried 30 cars and provided comfortable seating and recreation zones for 168 passengers and transported 4,000 cars a year.

The Roaring Twenties brought fun back into British life after the horrors of war and the Spanish Flu. As a result, more middle-class people wanted to cross to Calais to holiday in places like Biarritz, which had been made popular by Edward VII. In the 1930s the upper middle class began sending their daughters via Calais to finishing schools in France and Switzerland. There were, of course, ways of crossing the Channel other than by boat. In 1895 Captain Matthew Webb had been the first person to swim from Dover to Calais, having first fortified himself with a breakfast of bacon and eggs and a jug of claret. In 1926 the American, Gertrude Ederle, became the first woman to swim the Channel. As early as 1785 a Frenchman, Jean-Pierrre Blanchard, had crossed from Dover to Calais by hot air balloon, and in 1909 another Frenchman, Louis Blériot, flew a monoplane from Calais to Dover in the first ever aeroplane crossing of the Channel. Passenger flights from England to France began after the First World War but these were not to Calais and the main route to France remained by sea to Calais.

The Second World War brought to an end to the growing commercial passenger and cargo traffic in Calais. On 3 September 1939 the UK and France jointly declared war on Germany after its invasion of Poland. The BEF sailed to France and Calais prepared to revert to the wartime role it had played twenty-six years earlier. In May 1940 Germany attacked France through the Ardennes with three panzer corps; their main objective was the capture of Calais and the Channel ports. The rapid German advance trapped the BEF and three French armies along the northern coast of France. There was no option but to evacuate the BEF to England, from the nearest French port of Dunkirk and Operation Dynamo was launched. Thanks to the Royal Navy, supported by a flotilla of hundreds of private boats, about 330,000 British and allied troops were ferried back to England from the beaches of Dunkirk, between 26 May and 4 June 1940.

The success of Operation Dynamo was due to good planning and of course the courage of those taking part in the sea rescue under heavy enemy fire. Two other factors aided its success. The German commander, Field Marshal von Rundstedt, decide to pause the panzer attack on 23 May because of supply problems and concerns about advancing over the marshy ground surrounding Dunkirk. This was endorsed by Hitler, who ordered the Luftwaffe to finish off the BEF. On 26 May Hitler changed his mind and ordered the panzer advance to continue, but the delay had given precious time to the BEF, to prepare defences, and for Vice-Admiral Bertram Ramsay, to activate Operation Dynamo.

A third factor contributed to the success of the evacuation – the Battle of Calais. By 21 May the Germans had captured Boulogne and the 1st and 10th Panzer Divisions had surrounded Calais. The town was defended by some French coastal artillery of the naval reservists under Captain Lambertye, a small garrison under Major Le Teller, and a lot of stragglers who had arrived in bad shape as part of the Allied retreat, making about 800 French and Belgium troops in all. British reinforcements were hastily despatched across the Channel and began disembarking in Calais on 22 May. The reinforcements comprised the 30th Infantry Brigade commanded by Brigadier Nicholson and comprised 3 Royal Tank Regiment (3 RTR), 1 Queen Victoria's Rifles (1QVR), 1 Rifle Brigade (1RB), 2 King's Rifle Corps (2 KRC), together with artillery. They had been despatched with such haste that some of their weapons had been left behind, but they immediately established roadblocks around the town. Royal Naval destroyers remained offshore to provide bombardment, supplies and evacuation of the wounded. Bomber and Fighter commands gave what support they could from the UK.

On 24 May the 10th Panzer Division launched a full attack on Calais with Luftwaffe support. The French garrison at Fort Nieulay surrendered and the Germans entered the south part of the town, forcing British troops to withdraw to the old town and citadel. The French naval gunners spiked their guns which rendered them useless and left for the docks to embark on French ships. About fifty men agreed to stay behind with Lambertye who refused to leave, and they manned the defences of the western bastion. The next day there was very heavy bombardment by the Germans. All the British anti-tank guns were destroyed and only three tanks remained operational, the water supply had been cut and rations were low. A message was sent to Brigadier Nicholson inviting him to surrender, to which he replied: 'The answer is no, as it is the British Army's duty to fight as well as it is the Germans'.[5]

Not only did the British force continue to hold out but Nicholson launched a defiant counterattack with the last tanks and 1 RB. Unfortunately, their Bren carriers became bogged down in the sand and the sortie had to make a fighting withdrawal and suffered severe casualties. During this time the remaining tanks were destroyed, and Nicholson rejected two further demands to surrender.

On the morning of 26 May German troops entered the north of the town and the defenders were subjected to massive bombardment. This was amplified by additional German artillery deployed from Boulogne, attacks by Stukas, and infantry attacks. Despite this, 2 KRC managed to hold the bridges to the old town. At lunchtime the Germans broke through, Lambertye was dead and the bastion surrendered, its French volunteers having run out of ammunition. The remnants of 1 RB made a last stand at another bastion before being overwhelmed at 3.30 pm. Soon after news arrived that the citadel was surrounded and le Tellier, the Garrison Commander, had surrendered. Brigadier Nicholson was obliged to surrender at 4.45 pm but still managed to get 400 of his men out of Calais using small boats to deliver them to the Royal Navy destroyers.

Between 3,000 and 4,000 British troops were taken prisoner, including Brigadier Nicholson who later died in captivity. Almost four hundred years after the loss of Calais in 1558, English forces had again lost the town. However, the brave defence of Calais by British and French troops had kept the 10th Panzer Division occupied for sufficient time to allow the Dunkirk evacuation to begin.

Calais had been almost completely flattened by artillery and air attack, but the Germans quickly began building fortifications and established it as the command post for the Pas-de-Calais region. After the fall of France in June 1940 Hitler hoped to reach a negotiated settlement with

Britain. When this was not forthcoming, he began planning for an invasion to take place in September 1940. The code word for the invasion was *Unternehmen Seelöwe* (Operation Sea Lion) and transport ships began assembling along the Channel coast. Three German armies were assigned to the invasion. The 6th Army was to be launched from Cherbourg, the 9th Army from Le Havre, and the 16th Army from Boulogne, Dunkirk, Ostend and Calais. The objective of the Calais force was first to take Folkestone and then attack London. Over and above these German troops for the beach landings in England, 3,000 airborne parachutists would land in advance of the invading forces. However, for an invasion to be possible it was necessary for Germany to gain sea and air superiority in the Channel. In July 1940 the Luftwaffe began to launch major attacks against RAF aircraft and airfields, at the start of what became known as the Battle of Britain. By mid-September it was clear to Hitler that the Luftwaffe had failed to overcome the RAF and there was also no likelihood of naval supremacy, so *Unternehmen Seelöwe* was called off. Then, just as Napoleon had done before him, Hitler turned his attention to the invasion of Russia.

The invasion force moved out of Calais ready to be deployed against Russia, but German occupied Calais remained a threat to Britain. The Calais area became the site of five gun batteries, including three massive 16 inch railway guns, based at the old English fortress of Sangatte, all of which were able to fire across the Channel and inflict considerable damage on Dover. An even greater threat from the Calais area was the V-1 flying bomb, known as the buzz bomb or doodlebug. Attacks by V-1 rockets started in London and the south-east of England in June 1944. Between then and the end of the war, 10,492 V-1 rockets were launched, causing massive destruction to property, 6,000 deaths and 18,000 serious injuries.[6] These consequences could have been considerably worse had it not been for the Royal Artillery's anti-aircraft gunners, and the RAF interceptors nudging V-1 wing tips off course, and Bomber Command destroying V-1 sites, having located them through photographic interpretation of air reconnaissance imagery.

Planning began in 1943 for the D-Day landings in Normandy, the next year. It was essential that the location of the landings be kept secret and that the German High Command deployed their defensive forces as far away from Normandy as possible. Accordingly, a major military deception called Operation Fortitude was fabricated. The ruse required two elements: Fortitude North, to suggest there would be an invasion of Norway from Scotland; and the more realistic Fortitude South, to indicate that the invasion would utilise the shortest route across the Channel and into Germany, by landing in the Pas-de-Calais. It was hoped that even when the Normandy landings had taken place the Germans would assume it was just a diversion and send only a few troops to counter them, keeping their largest forces in place to repulse the main allied invasion near Calais.

All sorts of means were used to convince the Germans that the allied landings would be in the Calais area. The most important was the creation of a fictitious invasion force named the First United States Army Group (FUSAG) under General Patton. This imaginary force of six divisions had a skeleton headquarters and some real troops, but otherwise was completely simulated. This was done by creating dummy camps, equipment, airfields, decoy lighting, and invented wireless traffic. King George VI himself took part in the deception operation by making a visit to a large fake oil storage complex near Dover, built by Shepperton Film studios. This was reported in the English press, and of course got back to Germany. MI5 added to the disinformation by using double agents to feed reports to their German handlers of the build-up of an Allied invasion force in Kent.

Hitler and the German High Command became convinced that there would be diversionary attacks on the French coast, but that the main Allied invasion force would land in the Calais area. The German commander, Field Marshall Rommel, ordered extra defences to be built along the Pas-de-Calais coast. British Bomber Command instigated heavy attacks on Calais providing further indication of the intent to land in that area. Unfortunately for the French citizens of Calais it meant that much of those parts of the town that had not been destroyed during the German siege of 1940 were turned to rubble by British bombing. The success of Operation Fortitude led to the Normandy landings on 6 June 1945, without the massive German counterattack that otherwise would have occurred. It was the largest sea invasion in history – 160,000 men landed on D Day and a further 875,000 landed by the end of June. This was a huge force, but Germany had some fifty divisions in France and the

Low Countries. If even a fraction of those German divisions had been concentrated in Normandy the allied invasion would have been defeated.

As it was the German army in Normandy put up a strong defence and the Allied advance was much slower than anticipated. Depletion of the Luftwaffe enabled the Allies to win air superiority, which helped the land forces break through the German defence and continue their advance to Paris, which was liberated on 5 August. General Montgomery, Commander of the Allied Ground Forces, ordered the First Canadian Army to clear the heavily fortified Channel ports. By 17 September the 3rd Canadian Infantry Division had reached Boulogne which was surrendered by the Germans after a ten-day siege. The 7th and 8th Infantry Brigades of the 3rd Division advanced to reach Calais on 25 September. The town was then bombarded from land, sea and air. An infantry assault followed, supported by armour and artillery, including flame thrower tanks, which cleared the outer defences. On 29 September a 24-hour truce was agreed with the German commander, Oberstleutnant Schroeder, to allow the evacuation of 20,000 civilians. The next day the Canadians resumed the attack and Schroeder surrendered. The Calais German artillery attacks on Dover which had continued until 26 September were finally silenced. The liberation of Calais should have brought safety to its inhabitants, but the war was by no means over. Just a few miles away Dunkirk remained held by determined German troops.

At much the same time as the siege of Calais, the 5th Infantry Brigade, part of the 2nd Canadian Division, began the siege of Dunkirk. The town was very heavily fortified and held by 10,000 German troops, so there was little prospect of a swift surrender. Montgomery wanted a port suitable for supporting allied troops once they advanced into Germany, but war damage had rendered Boulogne and Dunkirk barely operable, and the port of Calais completely inoperable. Montgomery decided that Antwerp would be the best Allied *entrepôt* and ordered the 2nd Canadian Division to waste no more time on Dunkirk but to advance with all speed to capture Antwerp. The 1st Czechoslovak Independent Armoured Brigade was given the task of containing Dunkirk, to ensure that the German troops did not break out, and in the meantime the town continued to suffer bombing raids. The siege of Dunkirk continued even after the Russians had taken Berlin and Hitler had committed suicide.

Only on the unconditional surrender of Germany on 8 May 1945 did the German vice-admiral in command of Dunkirk surrender.

With hostilities still raging along the coast around Dunkirk, Calais did not experience real peace until the very end of the war in Europe. Indeed, the town continued to experience occasional bombing attacks from the Luftwaffe, the last of which took place on 27 February 1945. Sadly, and ironically, this was a raid by RAF bombers who had mistaken the town for Dunkirk. When peace eventually came Calais faced the enormous challenge of bringing the devastated town back to normal. It took years to rebuild the bombed-out houses and town infrastructure; the port was in ruins and most of the warehouses had been destroyed. Slowly the town rose again, and reconstruction of the port meant that it was once more open to trade and passengers from Britain.

Of course, the return of Calais to its pre-war state was achieved hand in hand with that of its sister port of Dover. Dover and its port had suffered severe damage, much of it inflicted by the German guns in Calais, and over 10,000 premises had been destroyed. It was not until 1950 that both towns returned to something resembling normality. In 1953 the first roll-on, roll-off (Ro-Ro) ferries were launched, operating between the two ports from newly constructed terminals. In 1965 two lane, double-deck berths were introduced and enabled the simultaneous loading and discharge of vehicles. The population of both countries had become more prosperous and car ownership had greatly expanded, as had the desire to holiday overseas.

Charter flights and package holidays meant that many British citizens began flying abroad for holidays and therefore bypassed Calais. Nevertheless, the Ro-Ro ferries became very popular for tourists in cars or coaches, and 10,000 vehicles per year utilised the service. Today the P&O ferries, the *Spirit of France* and the *Spirit of Britain* can both accommodate 2,000 passengers. As well as passengers, there was a major expansion in the flow of cargo between Dover and Calais, greatly facilitated by the use of containers. For many years Calais has been the principal trade link between the UK and the Continent. Over 42 million tons of traffic now passes through every year, and the ports of Dover and Calais are repeatedly enlarged to further increase the flow of cargo and passengers.

Another route was opened between the UK and France in 1994 when the Channel Tunnel between Folkestone and Calais was completed. A tunnel had first been considered in 1802 by Napoleon when he was planning to invade England. His mining engineer, Albert Mathieu, had drawn plans for a tunnel illuminated by oil lamps and large enough to allow horse drawn carriages to pass through. Since then, there have been numerous proposals for tunnels, such as those made by Napoleon III, Gladstone, Lloyd George and Churchill, but it was not until 1986 that the UK and France formally agreed to build a railway tunnel. Today the Eurostar passenger service and the Eurotunnel Shuttle for vehicles together carry 20 million passengers and 23 million tons of freight each year.

The end of World War II brought an end to hostilities against Germany but the start of the Cold War with the Soviet Union. In March 1947 the Treaty of Dunkirk was signed between the United Kingdom and France, as an alliance of mutual assistance in the event of an attack by Germany or the USSR. This association was expanded and developed to include other West European countries, and the USA, and resulted in the formation of the North Atlantic Treaty Organization (NATO) in 1949. When West Germany joined NATO in May 1955 the Soviet Union reacted by forming the Warsaw Pact with seven other socialist countries of Eastern Europe. In 1945 the British Army in Germany controlled the British Zone of occupied Germany, but after the return of government to German civilians it became the British Army of the Rhine (BAOR). At its peak BAOR totalled 80,000 troops and, together with the Royal Air Force Germany (RAFG), formed British Forces Germany.

Antwerp continued as the main sea supply base for British Forces Germany, but Calais was the main port used by English service personnel and their families who travelled by car to and from Germany. Ground forces in NATO were allocated areas to be defended against possible Warsaw pack attacks on West Germany. The sector allocated to Britain's 1st British Corps faced the Soviet Union's 3rd Shock Army. The war plan of the 3rd Shock Army was to use its mass of T64 tanks to break through British defences and reach Calais and the Channel ports in five days. The only way to withstand such an overwhelming assault would have been for NATO to use tactical nuclear weapons, which almost certainly would have led to a tactical nuclear response and the strong possibility of a full nuclear war. Fortunately, Mikhail Gorbachev's policies of *glasnost* and *perestroika* in the mid-1980s led to the end of confrontation and the dissolution of both the Soviet Union and the Warsaw Pact, in 1991.

British Forces Germany was disbanded, and the UK is now free from the threat of invasion from Calais and the Channel ports.

The Second World War had laid the foundations not only for the Cold War but also for the European Union. The bloodshed and destruction of war had motivated Western European countries to integrate with one another, to counter any future extreme nationalism. The Council of Europe was established in 1949, followed by the creation of the European Coal and Steel Community in 1951, and the formation of the European Economic Community (EEC), in 1957. The EEC established a customs union between six countries: Belgium, France, Italy, Luxembourg, the Netherlands, and West Germany. The United Kingdom joined in 1973 and the European Union (EU) was established in 1993. By 2002 the original seven member countries had been joined by a further eight and a single currency – the Euro – was introduced for those members who wished to adopt it. The Lisbon Treaty of 2007 further extended the power of the EU but there was growing concern in the UK about the erosion of national sovereignty. This disquiet culminated in the referendum of 2016 and, ultimately, in February 2020 the UK voted to leave the EU.

Migration and control of the UK's own borders were major issues in the EU referendum. The EU policy of free movement between countries and its enlargement in 2004 to include poorer East European states meant that the UK was experiencing an influx of economic migrants who arrived in their thousands. Social services were being strained and there was the perhaps unreasonable perception among some British citizens that migrants were taking jobs away from them. The situation intensified in 2014 when the European migrant crisis began in earnest. There was a mass movement of people from Syria, Afghanistan, Iraq and Africa who were attempting to escape persecution, poverty or natural disaster. They reached Europe mainly via Italy and Greece and many of them made their way to France and tried to travel to the UK.

In 2015 many asylum seekers, or economic migrants, began to concentrate outside Calais near the old English fortress of Sangatte, in what became known as the 'Calais Jungle'. The situation came to a head when more than 8,000 refugees were living in the Jungle and making numerous attempts to enter the UK illegally, by stowing away in trucks or being taken across the Channel by human traffickers, in overcrowded and unsafe boats. The Jungle was cleared in 2016 but within a year 1,000 migrants had returned and their attempts at illegal entry continued, but at a reduced rate because of cooperation between the English and French authorities. Media coverage of illegal immigrants crossing the Channel from Calais gave graphic emphasis to immigration concerns and played a major part in the result of the EU referendum and 'Brexit' – the withdrawal of the UK from the EU.

Ironically, Brexit did not enable the UK to take control of its own borders and put an end to illegal immigration. Human traffickers based in France ferried migrants in increasing numbers, on flimsy inflatables across the dangerous waters of the Channel, at a rate that sometimes reached over a thousand a week in 2022. Since Brexit, Anglo-French political relations have deteriorated, with mutual recriminations over illegal immigration and the disputed rights of the fishermen of Calais and neighbouring ports to have access to British waters. This present bad feeling is yet another phase in the many ups and downs in Anglo-French relations over the centuries.

Today the UK has long since shed its empire and colonies, but despite being a small country it remains the seventh-largest world economy. Since Brexit the UK has sought to establish strong trading relations around the world. Currently, Europe is the UK's most important trading partner, and Calais is its main port of entry. It is now over 460 years since England lost Calais, its first colony and an integral part of the nation with its MPs sitting in Westminster. Although Calais has not been an important part of Britain for a very long time, it is certainly an important part of British history. It is a shared history which will continue to bind the two rival nations across twenty-one miles of sea.

Appendix 1

Outline Family Tree of English and French Sovereigns 1150–1350

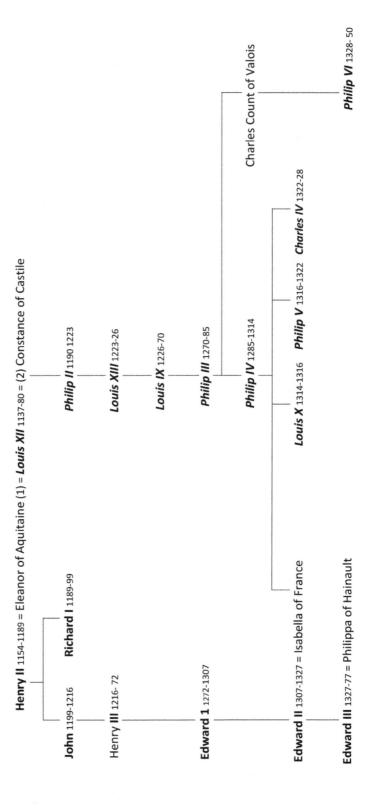

Appendix 2

Outline Family Tree of English and French Sovereigns 1327–1559

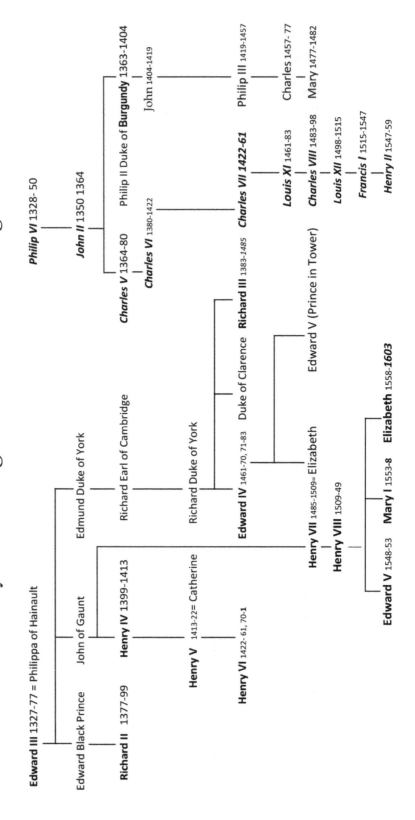

Appendix 3

Outline Family Tree of English and French Sovereigns 1558–1760

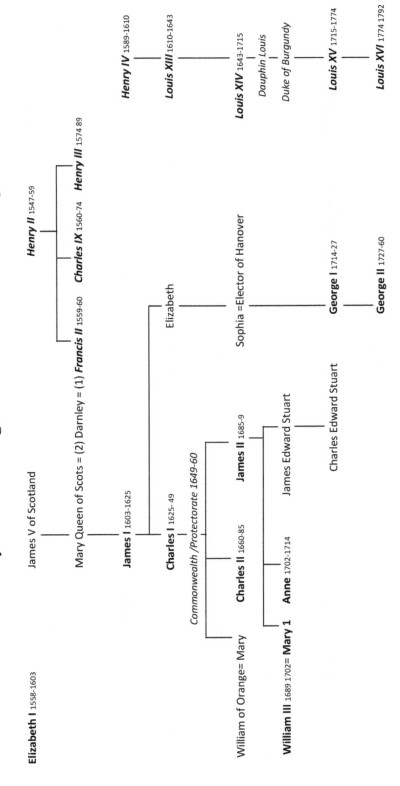

Appendix 4

Outline Family Tree of English and French Sovereigns 1727–1901

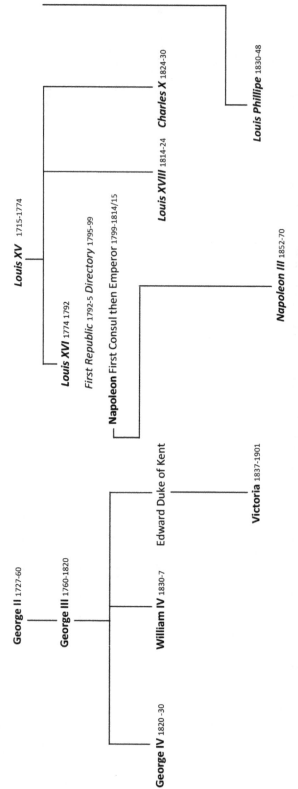

George II 1727-60

George III 1760-1820

William IV 1830-7

Edward Duke of Kent

George IV 1820-30

Victoria 1837-1901

Louis XV 1715-1774

Louis XVI 1774 1792

First Republic 1792-5 Directory 1795-99

Napoleon First Consul then Emperor 1799-1814/15

Louis XVIII 1814-24   Charles X 1824-30

Louis Phillipe 1830-48

Napoleon III 1852-70

Presidents of the 3rd Republic 1870 -1940

Notes

Chapter 1: Claim to the French Throne, 1327–47

1. John H. A. Munro, *Medieval Woollens: The Western European Woollen Industries and their Struggles for International Markets, c. 1000–1500,* ed. David Jenkins, The Cambridge History of Western Textiles, vol 1, (Cambridge University Press, 2003), pp. 228–324 & 304–5
2. Rodger Nicholas A. M. *The Safeguard of the Sea: A Naval History of Britain. 660–1649.* (New York: W. W. Norton & Company, 1999), p. 99
3. Norman Davies, *The Isles: A History* (London: Macmillan, 1999), p. 413
4. Andrew Ayton, *The Battle of Crécy: Context and Significance* (Woodbridge: Boydell Press, 2007), pp. 19–20
5. Susan Rose, *Calais: An English Town in France* (Woodbridge: Boydell & Brewer, 2008), p. 8

Chapter 2: Becoming an English Colony, 1347–57

1. Jean Froissart, ed. John Jolliffe, *Froissart's Chronicles* (London: Faber & Faber, 2012), p. 156
2. W. M. Ormrod, *The Reign of Edward III* (Stroud: Tempus, 2000), p. 323
3. Jeremy Goldberg, *The Black Death in England* (London: Stamford, 1996), pp. 1–15
4. Richard Barber, *Edward III and the Triumph of England,* (London: Penguin Books, 2014) p. 415

Chapter 3: A Commercial Centre, 1357–1400

1. Jonathan Sumption, *Trial by Fire: The Hundred Years' War Vol II,* (London: Faber & Faber 2011), p. 425
2. May McKisack, *The Fourteenth Century 1307–1399* (Oxford: The Clarendon Press, 1985), p. 247
3. John H. A. Munro, *Medieval Woollens: The Western European Woollen Industries and their Struggles for International Markets, c.1000–1500,* ed. David Jenkins, The Cambridge History of Western Textiles, Vol 1, (Cambridge University Press, 2003), pp. 228–324 & 304–5
4. Jonathan Sumption, *Trial by Fire: The Hundred Years' War Vol II* (London: Faber & Faber 2011), p. 425
5. John H. A. Munro, *Medieval Woollens: The Western European Woollen Industries and their Struggles for International Markets, c.1000–1500,* ed. David Jenkins, The Cambridge History of Western Textiles, Vol 1, (Cambridge University Press, 2003), pp. 228–324 & 304–5
6. Duncan Cameron, *Invasion: The Forgotten French Bid to Conquer England* (Stroud: Amberley Publishing, 2019), p. 194
7. Jean Froissart, ed. John Jolliffe, *Froissart's Chronicles,* Book III 174, London: Faber & Faber, 2012), p. 276

8. Jonathan Sumption, *Cursed Kings: The Hundred Years' War Vol IV* (London: Faber & Faber, 2015), p. 831

Chapter 4: The Burgundian Factor, 1400–26
1. John H. A. Munro, *Medieval Woollens: The Western European Woollen Industries and their Struggles for International Markets, c.1000–1500*, ed. David Jenkins, The Cambridge History of Western Textiles, Vol 1, (Cambridge University Press, 2003), pp. 228–324 & 304–5
2. Jonathan Sumption, *Cursed Kings: The Hundred Years' War Vol IV* (London: Faber & Faber, 2012), p. 299
3. Anne Curry, *The Battle of Agincourt: Sources and Interpretation* (Woodridge: Boydell Press, 2000), pp. 38, 53, 93
4. John H. A. Munro, *Medieval Woollens: The Western European Woollen Industries and their Struggles for International Markets, c.1000–1500*, ed. David Jenkins, The Cambridge History of Western Textiles, Vol 1, (Cambridge University Press, 2003), pp. 228–324 & 304–5

Chapter 5: The Loss of France, 1426–64
1. Jonathan Sumption, *Cursed Kings: The Hundred Years' War Vol IV* (London: Faber & Faber, 2015), p. 215
2. Michael Prestwich, *A Short History of the Hundred Years' War* (London: I. B. Tauris, 2018), p. 176. For more information on Henry VI's dire finances see Ralph Griffiths, *Reign of Henry VI, the Exercise of Royal Authority* (Berkley California: University of California Press, 1981), pp 376–91
3. A. J. Pollard, *Warwick the Kingmaker: Politics, Power and Fame* (London: Hambledon Continuum, 2007), p. 133
4. A. J. Pollard, *Warwick the Kingmaker: Politics, Power and Fame* (London: Hambledon Continuum, 2007), p. 128
5. A. J. Pollard, *Warwick the Kingmaker: Politics, Power and Fame* (London: Hambledon Continuum, 2007), p. 129

Chapter 6: The King Maker's Calais, 1464–85
1. A. J. Pollard, *Warwick the Kingmaker: Politics, Power and Fame* (London: Hambledon Continuum, 2007), p. 130
2. *Cassell's History of England Vol II* (London: Cassell & Company,1897), p. 38

Chapter 7: Tudor Bling, 1485–1520
1. Philip Edwards, *The Making of the Modern English State 1460–1660* (Basingstoke: Palgrave, 2001), p. 93
2. John H. A. Munro, *Medieval Woollens: The Western European Woollen Industries and their Struggles for International Markets, c.1000–1500*, ed. David Jenkins, The Cambridge History of Western Textiles, Vol 1, (Cambridge University Press, 2003), pp. 228–324 & 304–5
3. William Samuel Lilly, *The Claims of Christianity* (Chapman & Hall, London, 1894), p. 191
4. Glenn Richardson, 'Field of the Cloth of Gold', *BBC History Magazine*, (Northampton, July 2020), p. 26

Chapter 8: Religious Strife, 1520–42

1. Frieda Leonie, *Francis I: The Maker of Modern France* (London: Weidenfeld & Nicholson, 2018), p. 186
2. Tracy Borman, 'Anne Boleyn's Final Battle', *BBC History Magazine*, (Northampton Oct 2020), p 22–25.
3. John H. A. Munro, *Medieval Woollens: The Western European Woollen Industries and their Struggles for International Markets, c. 1000–1500*, ed. David Jenkins, The Cambridge History of Western Textiles, Vol 1, (Cambridge University Press, 2003), pp. 228–324 & 304–5
4. Chris Given-Wilson & Alice Curteis, *The Royal Bastards of Medieval England* (London: Routledge, 1988), pp. 162–173

Chapter 9: The Last Hurrah, 1542–57

1. *Calendar State Papers Spanish*, Vol. 9 (1912), p. 274
2. David Loades, *Henry VIII: Court, Church and Conflict*, (Kew: National Archives, 2009), pp 79–80
3. David Loades, *John Dudley, Duke of Northumberland 1504–1553*, (Oxford University Press, 1996), p. 170
4. George Sandeman, *Calais under English Rule* (Oxford: B. H. Blackwell, 1908), p. 102

Chapter 10: Loss and Aftermath, 1557–88

1. George Sandeman, *Calais under English Rule* (Oxford: B. H. Blackwell, 1908), p. 51
2. George Sandeman, *Calais under English Rule* (Oxford: B. H. Blackwell, 1908), p. 137
3. Anna Whitelock, *Mary Tudor: England's First Queen* (London: Bloomsbury, 2010), p. 291
4. Robert Hutchinson, *The Spanish Armada*, (Weidenfeld & Nicholson, Croydon 2013), p. 89
5. Robert Hutchinson, *The Spanish Armada*, (Weidenfeld & Nicholson, Croydon 2013), p. 89, p. 202

Chapter 11: Acceptance of Loss and Role Reversal, 1588–1804

1. William Camden, *Annales 1596* in Ben Dew's, Commerce, Finance and Statecraft: Histories of England (1600–1780) (Manchester University Press 2018), p. 12
2. Sir Frederick William Hamilton, *The Origin and History of the First Or Grenadier Guards* (London: John Murray, 1874), p. 27.
3. Jenny Uglow, *A Gambling Man: Charles II and the Restoration* (Faber & Faber, London 2009), p. 204
4. Antonia Fraser, *King Charles II* (Weidenfeld & Nicholson, London, 1979), p. 276

Chapter 12: Road to Entente Cordiale, 1804–2022

1. Stephen Clarke, *1000 Years of Annoying the French* (London: Black Swan Books, 2011), p. 473
2. John Evelyn, *The Diary of John Evelyn* (London: Everyman's Library, Temple Press, 1950), entry for 11 November 1643, p. 42
3. Tom Pocock, 'Emma Hamilton', *Oxford Dictionary of National Biography* (Oxford University Press, 2004), Vol 24, p. 793

4. Philip Carter, 'George Brummell', *Oxford Dictionary of National Biography* Vol 8 (Oxford University Press, 2004), Vol 8, p. 352

5. H. Sebag-Montefiore, *Dunkirk: Fight to the Last Man* (London: Penguin Books, 2006), p. 230

6. Rick Atkinson, *The Guns at Last Light: The War in Western Europe, 1944–1945* (Henry Holt, New York 2013), pp.110–1

Selected Bibliography and Sources

Ashley, Maurice, *England in the Seventeenth Century (1603–1714)*, (London: Jonathan Cape, 1947)

Atkinson, Rick, *The Guns at Last Light: The War in Western Europe, 1944–1945* (New York: Henry Holt, 2013)

Barber, Richard, *Edward III and the Triumph of England*, (London: Penguin Books, 2014)

Barker, Juliet, *Conquest: The English Kingdom of France, 1417–1450* (Cambridge MA: Harvard University Press, 2012)

Borman, Tracy, Anne Boleyn's Final Battle' *BBC History Magazine* (Northampton: October 2020)

Cooksley, Peter G, *Flying Bomb* (London: Robert Hale, 2006)

Calendar of State Papers Domestic Series of the Reigns of Edward VI, Mary, Elizabeth 1547–1580

Callow, John, *King in Exile, James II: Warrior, King and Saint*, 1689–1701 (Stroud: Sutton Publishing, 2004)

Cameron, Duncan, *Invasion: The Forgotten French Bid to Conquer England* (Stroud: Amberley Publishing, 2019)

Carter, Philip, 'George Brummell', *Oxford Dictionary of National Biography* Vol 8 (Oxford University Press, 2004)

Cassell's History of England (London: Cassell & Company, 1897)

Castor, Helen, *Blood and Roses: The Paston Family in the Fifteenth Century* (London: Faber & Faber, 2004)

Clarke, Stephen, *1000 Years of Annoying the French* (London: Transworld Publishers, 2011)

Curry, Anne, *The Battle of Agincourt: Sources and Interpretation* (Woodridge: Boydell Press, 2000)

Curry, P, *Arms, Armour and Fortifications in the Hundred Years' War* (Woodbridge: Boydell & Brewer, 1994

Davies, Norman, *The Isles: A History* (London: Macmillan, 1999)

Dockerty, Keith, *Henry VI, Margaret of Anjou and the Wars of the Roses* (Croyden: Fonthill 2016)

Edwards, Philip, *The Making of the Modern English State 1460–1660* (Basingstoke: Palgrave, 2001)

Evelyn, John, *The Diary of John Evelyn* (London: Everyman's Library, Temple Press, 1950)

Froissart, Jean, ed. John Jolliffe, *Froissart's Chronicles* (London: Faber & Faber, 2012)

Fraser, Antonia, *King Charles II*, (London: Weidenfeld & Nicholson, 1979)

Fletcher, Christopher, *Richard II: Manhood, Youth and Politics* (Oxford University Press, 2008)

Given-Wilson, Chris & Alice Curteis, *The Royal Bastards of Medieval England* (London: Routledge, 1988)

Goldberg, Jeremy, *The Black Death in England* (London: Stamford, 1996)

Griffiths, Ralph A, *Reign of Henry VI, the Exercise of Royal Authority 1427–1461* (Berkley California: University of California Press, 1981)

Gummitt, David ed, *The English Experience in France c1450–1558, War, Diplomacy and Cultural Exchange* (Aldershott: Ashgate, 2020)

Hamilton, Sir Frederick William, *The Origin and History of the First Or Grenadier Guards* (London: John Murray, 1874)

Hutchinson, Robert, *The Spanish Armada* (London: Weidenfeld & Nicolson, 2013)

Lilly, William Samuel, *The Claims of Christianity* (London: Chapman & Hall, 1894)

Lander, J. R., *The Wars of the Roses* (Stroud: Sutton Publishing, 2007)

Frieda, Leonie, *Francis I: The Maker of Modern France* (London: Weidenfeld & Nicholson, 2018)

Loades, David, *Elizabeth I* (London: Hambledon & London, 2003)

Loades, David, *Henry VIII, Court, Church and Conflict* (Kew: National Archives, 2009)

Loades, David, *John Dudley, Duke of Northumberland 1504–1553* (Oxford University Press, 1996)

Matusiak, John, *Henry V* (London: Routledge Historical Biographies, 2013)

McKisack, May, *The Fourteenth Century 1307–1399* (Oxford: The Clarendon Press, 1985)

Meyer, GJ, *The Tudors, Henry VII to Henry VIII* (Stroud: Amberley, 2010)

Mortimer, Ian, *The Fears of Henry IV: The Life of England's Self-Made King* (London: Jonathan Cape, 2007)

Munro, John H. A., *Medieval Woollens: Textiles, Textile Technology, and Industrial Organization c.1000 –1500*, ed. David Jenkins, The Cambridge History of Western Textiles (Cambridge University Press, 2003)

Munro, John H. A., *Medieval Woollens: The Western European Woollen Industries and their Struggles for International Markets c.1000 –1500*, ed. David Jenkins, The Cambridge History of Western Textiles (Cambridge University Press, 2003)

Nicholas, Rodger, *The Safeguard of the Sea: A Naval History of Britain 660–1649* (New York: W. W. Norton & Company, 1999)

Ormrod, W. M, *The Reign of Edward III* (Stroud: Tempus, 2000)

Oxford Dictionary of National Biography (Oxford University Press, 2004)

Pocock, Tom, Emma Hamilton, *Oxford Dictionary of National Biography* Vol 24 (Oxford University Press, 2004)

Pollard, A. J., *Warwick the Kingmaker: Politics, Power and Fame* (London: Hambledon Continuum, 2007)

Prestwich, Michael, *Plantagenet England 1225–1360* (Oxford: The Clarendon Press, 2005)

Prestwich, Michael, *A Short History of the Hundred Years' War* (London: I. B. Tauris 2018)

Richardson, Glenn, 'Field of the Cloth of Gold', *BBC History Magazine* (Northampton: July 2020)

Rose, Susan, *Calais: An English Town in France 1347–1558* (Woodbridge: Boydell & Brewer, 2008)

Sandeman, George, *Calais under English Rule* (Oxford: B. H. Blackwell, 1908)

Sebag-Montefiore, H., *Dunkirk: Fight to the Last Man* (London: Penguin Books, 2006)

Sumption, Jonathan, *The Hundred Years' War*, Vols I–IV (London: Faber & Faber, 2015)

Uglow, Jenny, *A Gambling Man: Charles II and the Restoration* (London: Faber & Faber, 2009)

Whitelock, Anna, *Mary Tudor: England's First Queen* (London: Bloomsbury, 2010)

Index